D1548589

moving writing

Cultural Critique

Norman K. Denzin
General Editor

Vol. 2

PETER LANG
New York • Washington, D.C./Baltimore • Bern
Frankfurt am Main • Berlin • Brussels • Vienna • Oxford

moving writing

crafting movement
in sport research

EDITED BY
jim denison
& pirkko markula

PETER LANG
New York • Washington, D.C./Baltimore • Bern
Frankfurt am Main • Berlin • Brussels • Vienna • Oxford

Library of Congress Cataloging-in-Publication Data

Moving writing: crafting movement in sport research /
Jim Denison and Pirkko Markula, editors.
p. cm. — (Cultural critique; 2)
Includes bibliographical references.
1. Sports—Anthropological aspects. 2. Sports—Research—
Methodology. 3. Movement education. 4. Literature and anthropology.
5. Qualitative research. I. Denison, Jim. II. Markula, Pirkko.
III. Cultural critique; vol. 2.
GV706.2 .M68   796'.07'2—dc21   2001038447
2003   ISBN 0-8204-5541-5
ISSN 1530-9568

Bibliographic information published by **Die Deutsche Bibliothek.**
Die Deutsche Bibliothek lists this publication in the "Deutsche
Nationalbibliografie"; detailed bibliographic data is available
on the Internet at http://dnb.ddb.de/.
ISBN 0-8204-5541-5

Cover design by Lisa Barfield

The paper in this book meets the guidelines for permanence and durability
of the Committee on Production Guidelines for Book Longevity
of the Council of Library Resources.

© 2003 Peter Lang Publishing, Inc., New York
275 Seventh Avenue, 28th Floor, New York, NY 10001
www.peterlangusa.com

Printed in the United States of America

To Bevan Charles Grant, whose support and friendship enabled us to succeed.

CONTENTS

FOREWORD

Jacques Derrida reminds us that nothing stands outside representation, and Laurel Richardson asserts that "writing is never innocent" (Richardson, 2001, p. 879). We create the worlds we inhabit
through the words we use. The craft of writing is the most theoretical of all our interpretive practices. It is an honor and a privilege, accordingly, as series editor to introduce this wonderfully
bold collection of essays from around the world about how we
write.

Jim Denison and Pirkko Markula and their co-contributors are
international leaders in the "new writing" school of interpretive
ethnography. Working outward from kinesiology, cultural studies,
and sport sociology these scholars creatively subvert traditional
modes of social science writing. Drawing on personal experience,
and prior writing selves, each author charts the central features of
a new set of interpretive, evocative writing practices for the human disciplines.

It is fitting that *"Moving Writing": Crafting Movement in Sport
Research* appear in Peter Lang's 'Cultural Critique' series. The
works in this interdisciplinary series are premised on a critical,
performance-based cultural studies agenda. The series privileges
experimental, risk-taking projects that are at the intersection of
interpretive theory, critical methodology, culture, media, history,
biography, and social structure. This is exactly what this volume
does.

"Moving Writing" is about writing the sporting body and writing about embodied movement from a personal or autoethnographic perspective. Accordingly, I want to briefly discuss the
practices of autoethnography (see Denzin, 2002). As the chapters
in this book indicate, reflexive, interpretive autoethnographies

"range along a continuum" (Ellis & Bochner, 2000, p. 740), start-ing with texts that focus solely on the writer's experiences to eth-nographies "where the researcher's experiences are actually stud-ied along with other participants, to confessional tales where the researcher's experiences of doing the study become the focus of investigation" (p. 740). In each of these forms the writer-as-performer is self-consciously present, morally and politically self-aware, using her own experiences in a culture "reflexively to bend back on self and look more deeply at self-other interactions" (p. 740). The task of autoethnography is now apparent, it helps the writer "make sense of the autobiographic past" (Alexander, 1999, p. 309). Autoethnography becomes a way of "recreating and re-writing the biographic past, a way of making the past a part of the biographic present" (Pinar, 1994, p. 22).

Performance autoethnographers anchor their narratives and performances in an on-going moral dialogue with the members of a local community. Troubling the usual distinctions between self and other, they fold their own life histories and testimonies into the self-stories of others. These are dialogic performance events. In them "different voices, worlds views, value systems and beliefs. . . have a conversation with one another" (Conquergood, 1985, p. 9).

This performance framework imagines and works with the mutiple ways in which performance and movement can be under-stood, including: as imitation, or *mimesis*; as *poiesis*, or construc-tion; as *kinesis*, motion, or movement (Conquergood, 1998). The autoethnographer moves from a view of performance as imitation, mimesis, or dramaturgical staging (Goffman, 1959), to an empha-sis on performance as poiesis, liminality, and construction (Turner, 1986), to a view of performance as struggle, as an inter-vention, as breaking and remaking, as kinesis, as a socio-political act (Conquergood, 1998). Viewed as struggles and interventions, performances and performance events become transgressive achievements, political accomplishments that break through "sedimented meanings and normative traditions" (Conquergood, 1998, p. 32).

The gendered sporting, dancing body moves through space and time. The dancing body is a performing body, a body stitched into cultural narrative, into local history. This body is an original, every one of its performances is new and different, even as each performance is measured against an ideal, mimesis. The transgressive body boldly breaks out of routines, struggles against convention, seeks out the in-between performative spaces of liminality.

This performative, reflexive ethnographic project relentlessly interrogates the relationship between text, context, performance and praxis (see Conquergood, 1998; Pollock, 1998a). Text and context first. Following Conquergood (1998) and Pollock (1998b), performance is used as a lever for decentering an earlier generation's ethnographic textualism, a textualism that produces books with titles such as "writing culture". Textual models turn ethnography and hence culture into sets of material practices. Using the methods of inscription and thick description, the ethnographer produces interpretations and representations of culture. In this way, culture becomes an ensemble of texts. The traditional ethnographer recovers the meanings embedded in these texts, reading culture as if it were an open book. Textualism operates within an ocular, visual epistemology. It privileges distance, detachment, the said, and not the said, the done, or the doing.

In contrast, the performance autoethnographer struggles to put culture into motion (Rosaldo, 1989), to perform culture by putting "mobility, action, and agency back into play" (Conquergood, 1998, p. 31). The performance paradigm privileges an "experiential, participatory epistemology" (p. 27). It values intimacy and involvement as forms of understanding. The autoethnographer meets others on the ground of their experience, "exposing oneself to their expressive performances" (p. 27). The emphasis is on the hermeneutics of experience, on making the self vulnerable to its own experiences and the experiences of the other as well (Behar, 1996).

In this epistemology context replaces text, verbs replace nouns, structures become processes, the emphasis is on change, contingency, locality, motion, improvisation, struggle, situationally specific practices and articulations, and the performance of con/texts (Pollock, 1998b, p. 38). By privileging struggle, the performance ethnographer takes a stand (Conquergood, 1998; Kirshenblatt-Gimblett, 1998). The dividing line between text and context falls away. Texts are inseparable from "the processes by which they are made, understood, and deployed" (Pollock, 1998b, p. 38).

Fitted to the topics of movement and sport, these arguments suggest that personal performance narratives are best suited to explore athletes', dancers', and everyday movers' complex experiences. The writers in this volume are drawn to the beauty of sport and physical activity, to kinesis, to movement, to liminality, to transgression. They marvel at the grace, elegance, and power of the sporting body and its material practices. They tell performance stories about movement, writing that moves, writing crafted to movement in sports research. At the beginning of the twenty-first century, there is a pressing demand to show how the practices of critical, interpretive qualitative research can help change the world in positive ways. This bold, innovative book is a model for the rest of us. We owe these writers a great debt.

Norman K. Denzin,
Series Editor

REFERENCES

Alexander, B. K. (1999). Performing culture in the classroom: An instructional (auto)ethnography. *Text and Performance Quarterly, 19*, 307–331.

Behar, R. (1996). *The vulnerable observer: Anthropology that breaks your heart.* Boston: Beacon.

Conquergood, D. (1998). Beyond the text: Toward a performative cultural politics. In S. J. Dailey (Ed.), *The future of performance studies: Visions and revisions* (pp. 25–36). Annadale, VA: National Communication Association.

Conquergood, D. (1985). Performing as a moral act: Ethical dimensions of the ethnography of performance. *Literature in Performance, 5*, 1–13.

Denzin, N. K. (2002). *Performing ethnography: Critical pedagogy and the politics of culture.* London: Sage

Ellis, C. & Bochner, A. P. (2000). Autoethnography, personal narrative, reflexivity: Researcher as subject. In N. K. Denzin and Y. S. Lincoln (Eds.), *Handbook of qualitative research* (Second edition) (pp. 733–768). Thousand Oaks, CA: Sage.

Goffman, E. (1959). *The presentation of self in everyday life.* New York: Doubleday.

Kirshenblatt-Gimblett, B. (1998). *Destination culture: Tourism, museums, and heritage.* Berkeley: University of California Press.

Pinar, W. (1994). *Autobiography, politics and sexuality.* New York: Peter Lang.

Pollock, D. (1998a). Performing writing. In P. Phelan and J. Lane (Eds.), *The ends of performance* (pp. 73–103). New York: New York University Press.

Pollock, D. (1998b). A response to Dwight Conquergood's essay: "Beyond the text: Toward a performative cultural politics." In S. J. Dailey (Ed.), *The future of performance studies: Visions and revisions* (pp. 37–46). Annadale, VA: National Communication Association.

Richardson, L. (2001). Poetic representation of interviews. In J. F. Gubrium and J. A. Holstein (Eds.), *Handbook of interview research* (pp. 877–892). Thousand Oaks, CA: Sage.

Rosaldo, R. (1989). *Culture and the truth*. Boston: Beacon.

Turner, V. (1986). *The anthropology of performance*. New York: Performing Arts Journal Publications.

PREFACE

Moving. When aren't we? To counter the gunman's idiom, One move and you're dead, the truth is, *Stop* moving and you're dead. And not just moving through space, covering ground, getting somewhere, and being up and about. Because in some way we're always moving: blood pumps, synapses fire, oxygen circulates, cells regenerate. In fact, when are we ever still? Even at rest there's rapid eye movement, swallowing, breathing, tossing and turning. So then, is living moving? Is movement life?

In a sense, movement *is* life. But to move means more than just being alive, that is, a functioning organism with a pulse and brain waves. Communication involves movement. We gesture, open our mouths, and bend an ear. We scratch our head, pace, nod, jump up, sit back down, or change direction. To feel we embrace, reach, grab, or lend a hand. And in hearing a symphony or viewing a sunset we are moved—emotionally, spiritually, aesthetically.

To experience life we chew, sniff, touch, heat up, cool down, or take a fall . . . All movement. Moving, in other words, contains and elicits meaning; it also excites, expands, and enriches every aspect of our lives. To know we have to move; to understand ourselves and others we have to move. But how much do we know about moving? What do we know about ourselves as movers?

Actually, we know a great deal about moving. Textbooks diagram how the body fits together and operates. We know how digestion works, why we grow, and how we walk. Through observation we can describe people's movements and whereabouts —immigration, emigration, settlement. We can explain how people move through their day and ask them why they move the way they do—Why do you go jogging at six every morning? But is this really knowing, really understanding? Is it enough to say we know what movement is simply because we can draw our insides or ask a question and record a response? We don't think so. For to know and understand ourselves as movers, we need ways of representing movement that articulate more closely what movement means to people—the rush of gliding, the joy of soaring, the pain of crashing—while also revealing the constructed relations that produce movement—gendered, classed, raced.

With this volume, we hope to provide a fleshed-out, embodied portrait of movement as a practice of living. Because that's what we believe evocative representational styles such as autoethnogrophy and ethnographic fiction can offer readers. Crafted well, these ways of writing appreciate life, experience, culture, and people by going beyond the upfront and obvious. The researchers in this collection all bring with them a certain postmodern sensibility that enables them to consider movement not with an eye toward producing the truth with a capital T, but with writing stories that are open-ended, critical, visceral, and captivating. And it's this honesty, courage, and dedication to writing about themselves and others in such an artful manner that we would like to thank our co-contributors for. We would also like to thank Norman Denzin for his assistance in initiating this project, as well as Chris Myers and Jackie Pavlovic from Peter Lang, Inc. for their encouragement, patience, and enthusiasim. Further thanks in seeing this project reach its final form must also go to our typesetter, Erin Staples. And finally, to our colleagues over the years in our own movements to, from, and between campuses in New York, Jyväskylä, Finland, Toledo, Ohio, Champaign-Urbana, Illinois, and Hamilton, New Zealand, thank you for your support and kindness. We feel your presence every day and everlastingly.

JD & PM
Hamilton,
New Zealand

INTRODUCTION

Moving Writing

Jim Denison and Pirkko Markula

Reading Sport

To read the leading journals in sports studies often means reading articles that adhere to traditional notions of reporting and analyzing people's experiences. In these studies, writing as a way of knowing is often left unproblematized, as language is regarded as innocent, not a constitutive force that creates a particular view of reality. Here the researcher remains concealed; he or she deploys a neutral voice; he or she is outside of history and separate from the influence of society and culture. For example, in the numerous studies concerning young people and sport, one almost never sees the author reflecting on his or her own childhood experiences in sport. Even apparent qualitative studies around topics such as pain and injury, burnout, winning and losing, and body image tend to be characterized by a dominant scientific narrator. Thus, how the author's biography has influenced the text we are reading and the conclusions drawn remains a secret. Similarly, in all the gender studies done in sport, or the numerous investigations into issues of race and social class in sport, seldom do we come across a position statement from the author in which he or she openly discusses the social categories that he or she belongs to. It's these criticisms that bring to our attention key questions that we believe all sports studies scholars must ask themselves with regard to who speaks in a text, whose story is being told, and how.

Of course we are not the first ones to critique the rhetorical strategies employed in traditional writing projects, what are commonly referred to as realist tales. Nor are we the first to consider how scholars can and should become more open-ended or self-reflexive in their "scientific" renderings. Rather, our book is the result of a trend that we can trace back to the late 1970s, and the connections made by philosophers between practices of writing and practices of power. In this introduction we would like to discuss this history in an attempt to situate our recommendations for new ways of writing sport research within a broader social science perspective.

Writing Exposed

The epistemological awakening, where writing lost its authority as a means of directly capturing the lived experiences of others, was largely due to French post-structuralism and its influence on the social sciences. Prominent philosophers such as Michel Foucault, Jacques Derrida, and Michel de Certeau turned to investigate the ways that philosophical texts had been written. They found that these texts emulated a language of science that favored transparent signification above rhetoric, facts ahead of fiction, and objectivity over subjectivity. Together they questioned the many taken-for-granted practices of scientific writing. However, each of these men approached and analyzed the "problem" of writing and language differently.

Foucault (1979), for example, focused on the role of the author in scientific writing. He argued that in this type of writing the individual author is seen as a figure outside the objective, scientific text and, therefore, as someone who precedes the text. However, he or she, is also the writing subject who constantly disappears into the objective accounts rendered, thus, becoming "reduced to nothing more than the singularity of his [sic] absence" (p. 142). The absent author, Foucault argued, is replaced with an "author-function," which then enables discourse to construct the author instead of the other way around. As the writing subject turns into an author-function created through scientific discourse, the meanings expressed through writing become seriously limited.

Derrida (1976), on the other hand, studied the position of writing itself within Western society, as he believed that writing philosophy was more than "just writing." Writing as an activity, he argued, unveils the structure of philosophy as "logocentric." Logocentrism, according to Derrida, is based on the privileged position of "logos," or writing that requires a rational subject, and language that refers directly to the "real," observable world. Logocentrism also assumes a privileged singular voice, which in most cases is a male voice. Therefore, for Derrida, logocentrism is a phallic, oppressive posture that needs to be dismantled. The logocentric voice, however, is not immediately recognizable, meaning that researchers should approach "texts" with the idea that there is more to the text than what the author claims. As a tactic to expose the logocentric voice, Derrida advocated several deconstructive strategies which he thought would unveil these "unintended meanings." Derrida based his deconstructive strategies around the notion that meanings only become comprehensible in relation to other, different meanings. Thus, meanings produced through signifieds (concepts) and signifiers (sounds or written images) only acquire meaning when one examines the difference between them. Establishing an exact meaning is arbitrary and always depends on the discursive context of the meaning-making. But deconstruction will reveal the arbitrariness of any so called dominant meaning by pointing to its "different," or absent binary, as well as to its specific context. For example, the dominant logocentric male voice can become obvious if a researcher connects her or himself with its absent binary opposite, female writing. Therefore, like Foucault, Derrida challenged researchers to think of writing as a field of force relations invested with dominant meanings. He also urged scholars to create texts that were not locked into a single position of dominance, but instead would perpetually perform the deconstructive game of making multiple meanings.

De Certeau (1984) assigned a broader, or more symbolic meaning to writing in Western society than both Foucault and Derrida. To de Certeau, writing has taken the place of myths that symbolically used to teach us the underlying meanings and values of our society. But through writing, de Certeau argued, we have invested our ambitions to compose our history. Unlike oral myths, however, where the fundamental values of a culture were *embedded* in the content of the stories, in what he calls our modern "scriptural economy," the practice of writing or the "transport" of meaning, has become one of *representing* core values: "The origin is no longer what is narrated, but rather the multiform and murmuring activity of producing a text and producing society as a text"

(p. 134). In this process, meaning, read "reality," has to become detached from the process of writing: "the 'meaning' . . . of scriptural play, the production of a system, a space of formalization, refers to the reality from which it has been distinguished *in order to change it*" (p. 135, italics original). This idea of change, for de Certeau (1984), symbolizes the Western idea of governing a taken-for-granted right to act on the environment and culture and transform it according to one's will. In addition, the process of writing is a metaphor for the principles of Western capitalism: we receive information that through the act of writing is appropriated until finally it comes out as an endless line of "fabricated products." De Certeau concluded:

> The scriptural enterprise transforms or retains within itself what it receives from its outside and creates internally the instruments for an appropriation of the external space. It stocks up what it sifts out and gives itself the means to expand. Combining the power of *accumulating* the past and that of making the alterity of the universe *conform* to its models, it is capitalist and conquering. (p. 135, italics original)

These three philosophers, then, all contend that writing is more than a transparent practice of storing information. Modern writing, for them, is invested with dominance; it is a power tool for the capitalist, conquering, male voice that has suffocated the subjective voice of the author and reduced multiple fields of meaning to a singular position.

Crisis of Representation: Viewing Texts Differently

It didn't take long for Foucault's, Derrida's, and de Certeau's influence to spread beyond philosophy. In fact, their concerns over the transparency of writing created what many have referred to within the social sciences as a "crisis of representation" (e.g., Denzin, 1997). In anthropology, for example, Edward Bruner, James Clifford, and George Marcus began the meta-analytic exercise of writing about writing. For them the process of writing and the act of interpretation became the center of inquiry; language was no longer treated as thin black lines etched on a white surface to describe experience. In his introduction to *Writing Culture*, Clifford (1986) characterized "doing anthropology" as a historical and linguistic process. Thus, in one bold statement he distanced himself and his discipline from the reductionistic nature of traditional empirical social science.

Clifford's (1986) anti-positivist stance raised countless scholars' awareness to the fact that anthropological texts were "man-made," and artificially constructed to reflect the authority of Western science. Clifford emphasized that ethnography always represents partial truths: "all constructed truths are made possible by powerful 'lies' of exclusion and rhetoric. Even the best ethnographic texts—serious, true fictions—are systems, or economies, of truth. Power and history work through them, in ways their authors cannot fully control" (p. 7). Clifford was not suggesting that we stop writing but that we should openly discuss the nature of writing in ethnographic research and begin to acknowledge it as a site of power: "An interest in the discursive aspects of cultural representation draws attention not to the interpretation of cultural 'texts' but to their relations of production" (p. 13).

To acknowledge the partiality, subjectivity, and contextuality of social science writing, it is, according to Clifford, best to understand research texts as fictions that are ever changing, inventive, and invested with literary qualities such as metaphor and synecdoche. From this standpoint, academic and literary writing genres can be seen as the same thing: both are reflexive accounts where the author's personal experiences together with the voices of others' are woven into a single polyvocal text. Such a reflexive account "locates cultural interpretations in many sorts of reciprocal contexts, and it obliges writers to find diverse ways of rendering negotiated realities as multisubjective, power-laden, and incongruent" (p. 15). Therefore, Clifford advocates anthropological writing that, through more literary qualities, recognizes the author's experiences, the experiences of the people studied, and the cultural context of interpreting these experiences.

The philosopher Richard Rorty (1991) spoke about similar matters when he discussed how the social sciences have a moral charge to deepen our sense of community. He said that this could only be done by carefully interpreting other people's experiences and giving life to their accounts through rich, well-plotted stories. This, he argued, will make it possible to converse with people different from us. Rorty's call, we believe, disrupts the fragmentation we normally associate between disciplines, and makes the relationship between qualitative studies and literature, for example, much more continuous. Further to Rorty's point, Harry Wolcott (1994) spoke about qualitative researchers and ethnographers as storytellers. "To be able to tell a story well," he said, "is crucial to the enterprise" (p. 17).

Norman Denzin and Laurel Richardson have also challenged social scientists to think about writing differently. Denzin (1994) argued that there can no longer be a forced scientific separation between the research experience and the resulting interpretation, or between ourselves and our research subjects. Richardson (1994) pointed to the dull and boring nature of sociological writing. Conceiving scholarly interpretation less as a method and more as an art, she argued, would enable researchers to think about creating qualitative research texts that are vital: texts that grip readers and invite them to engage in the subject matter.

At this time there were also a number of feminists whose work challenged scientific traditions of reporting experience. These writers lifted women's experiences to the center of inquiry as a deliberate strategy to show how women's everyday personal experiences reflect the historical, cultural, and political contexts of their lives. Parallel to this interest in personal experience, many feminists began to expand the possibilities of writing feminist research. They promoted ways of writing beyond the monolithic, objective, dominant male voice of traditional social science writing. One of these, Liz Stanley (1992), encouraged a style of feminist autobiographical writing that not only recorded individual women's experiences but also contextualized them to show how women are constructed "within a network of others" (p. 254).

These critiques of academic writing practices had a profound effect. To begin, they changed the accepted mode of academic writing and theorizing. One early proponent of new ways of writing was Clifford Geertz (1973, 1983), who called for "thick description" and ethnographies that blurred the boundaries between the social sciences and humanities. Following Geertz, social scientists became wary of older models of truth and meaning-making. Slowly, the "essay as art form" began to replace the standard third-person realist scientific article. Through the work of Paul

Stoller (1994) and Renato Rosaldo (1989), for example, scholarly procedures started to become more synonymous with traditions found in storytelling. As Denzin (1994) noted in commenting on this rapid period of change within qualitative research, researchers were now central characters in their research stories: their methods of analysis included accounts of their own experiences in the field portrayed through memoirs, fiction, or dramatic readings. Thus emerged the era of the personal experience narrative (Dolby-Stahl, 1985), where more and more scholars' writings were based on private but shareable experiences, which through storytelling worked to create an emotional bond between the listener and the teller in order to express part of the inner life of the storyteller and his or her experiences in the field. Denzin (1989) clarifies further this fertile moment of experimental academic writing:

> The personal experience narrative is a genre, or form, of storytelling. It is dependent on the "private" folklore of the person or the group, although it may draw on broader cultural and ideological themes. Such a narrative draws on everyday experiences, and may be a "true" story which identifies core, shared values of the teller and listener. They may be based on single-experience episodes or be multiepisodic. Their significance lies in their ability to create an intimate bond between teller and listener. They connect selves in a context of shared and shareable experience. (p. 186)

From the ontological and epistemological advances and possibilities that arose through the increased use of personal experience narratives came a burgeoning of new evocative writing practices all spearheaded by the early philosophical criticisms concerning language and writing as neutral practices and the ensuing crisis of representation. In her comprehensive review of various contemporary evocative writing practices, Richardson (2000) outlines the possibilities available to social scientists interested in moving beyond the received traditions of positivism and post-positivism. She credits movements in postmodernism and poststructuralism as enabling scholars to understand themselves "reflexively as persons writing from particular positions at specific times" (p. 9). Collectively she labels these new writing approaches Creative Analytical Practices, or CAP ethnography.

CAP ethnography, Richardson (2000) contends, is made up of a range of writing practices, including evocative representations, autoethnography, ethnographic fiction, poetic representation, and ethnographic drama. She also suggests ways to evaluate these new texts that subvert traditional scientific notions of validity and reliability and instead stress such characteristics as impactfulness, reflexivity, and aesthetics. Drawing on literary techniques such as flashback, alternative points of view, and dialogue, she argues, will allow scholars to open up the dimension of mystery that surrounds individuals' lives. Furthermore, she says, through writing "stories as research" it's possible to avoid closure, enabling the reader to see that interpretation is never finished. Moreover, stories show instead of tell, she points out, and they are less author centered; they allow the reader to interpret and make meaning, thus recognizing that the text has no universal or general claim to authority; and they can communicate in emotional as well as intellectual ways what has been understood.

In his book *Interpretive Ethnography*, Denzin (1997) advocates the same goals and objectives for narrative and performative social science writing that fiction writer James Joyce used in his highly original texts.   Denzin begins by explaining how Joyce "knew that understanding was not seeing; it was more than visual knowledge" (p. 25). Adding that, "the fully interpretive text plunges the reader (and writer) into the interior, feeling, hearing, tasting, smelling, and touching worlds of subjective human experience" (p. 25).

And in a recent special issue of *The Journal of Contemporary Ethnography* that focused on ethnographic practices for the twenty-first century, Arthur Bochner and Carolyn Ellis (1999) discuss at length the advent of a larger, expanding, more diverse and inclusive field of qualitative research that will contain poetry, short stories, memoirs, plays, conversation, dances, novels, and performances. Collectively, they say, these modes of representation will share a disdain for brute facts and instead celebrate human meanings and the practices of culture.

Writing Sport

The calls advanced above for new ways of writing ourselves and others did not go completely unnoticed by scholars within sport studies. Several sport sociologists, for example, have issued justifications for more evocative ways of writing people's movement experiences (e.g. Bain, 1995; Bruce, 1998; Cole, 1991; Nilges, 2001; Sparkes, 1995; Tomlinson, 1999). C. L. Cole argued for a new vision for the field of sport studies, a vision that would embrace writing styles beyond the normative realist writing approaches. Similarly, Alan Tomlinson (1999), in referring to C. Wright Mills (1959), argued that social science texts that experiment with form and style and include more creative ways of depicting social life can problematize the connections between reason and freedom in society and thus have lasting significance as important social documents. These creative texts are particularly effective when examining issues in sport, he claimed, because they "highlight how general social processes are lived and experienced in specific settings" (p. 57). Furthermore, those of us who research and write about sport and physical activity have usually experienced the beauty, grace, power, and exhilaration associated with movement. More than anyone, we appreciate the physical and mental subtleties that are part of moving. We remember how sport filled our lives as children; we recognize how it satisfies our present lives either as participants, fans, teachers, researchers, or coaches. And we are aware that sport and movement experiences can be elusive, bodily, intense, and contradictory. Much of the qualitative research done in kinesiology or physical education, however, is still written in a way that preserves the objective stance of the researcher, and thus fails to provide an in-depth interpretation of the meaning movement holds for people (Bain, 1995). This is why we believe that if we want to capture or portray aspects of movement through our writing, we can't be afraid to depart from traditional practices of representation and experiment more freely with form, content, and style.

One early attempt to put the call for new ways of writing sport into practice originated from Finland. A group of Finnish researchers had started to experiment with memory work back in the mid-1980s, and from these experiments they produced highly subjective "autobiographical," "narrative" accounts of their sport experiences. They presented this work in some Finnish collections (Sironen, 1988; Sironen, Tiihonen & Veijola, 1992), in the 1993 conference proceedings of International Society for the History of

Physical Education and Sport (ISHPES), and in a special issue of the *International Review for the Sociology of Sport* (1994). According to Henning Eichberg, the editor of that special issue, the distinguishing characteristic of the Finnish memory work was the inner dialogue they included that exposed their otherness in connection with how they interpreted themselves. Following these experiments with memory work, other types of personal experience writing projects began to appear within sport studies. A volume titled *Talking Bodies: Men's Narratives of the Body and Sport* (1999) examined the subjective experiences of men, their multiple senses of self, and the relationships they form with their bodies. Mark Sudwell (1999), for example, spoke to his connection to his father through changes in his own body:

> I remember finding an old picture of my father when he was nineteen or twenty, stood on top of a diving board: it could have easily been a photo of me. For months I carried it around in my pocket, showing it to everyone I knew. I was everything he was. (p. 20)

Characteristic of narratives of the self such as Sudwell's is a sweeping sense of ambiguity and transparency that would never be found in more traditional representations of sport or identity that attempt to nail down a single interpretation. These new sport texts also disrupted the dominant power relations associated with movement and the body. No longer did participating in sport have to result in the objectification of one's body. Now it was all right to be critical, or at least reflective of what sport meant or did to people as a modern everyday discursive practice.

Soon more sports studies researchers began to insert their personal experiences into their research texts. Typically, these papers consisted of vignettes or short descriptions of the researcher's sporting history accompanied by a theoretical interpretation explaining the meaning of these events. A good example of this way of writing is Andrew Sparkes's (1996) multilayered, multiepisodic essay around his personal history with back pain. Sparkes draws on medical reports, diary extracts, memories, newspaper cuttings, conversations, as well as theories of pain and identity to explore his relationship with his body. Here he puts into practice Denzin's (1989) call for research texts that connect selves in a context of shared and shareable experience. His article concerns a number of different bodies he has inhabited and how his biographical project was interrupted by pain, injury, and fear. His is an unfolding story about the fragile and vulnerable nature of the self that is made possible by his use of alternative writing practices that de-mystify the author as a figure outside the text.

Robert Rinehart (1998a) also produced an innovative social science sport text when he merged his researcher voice with his own feelings about sport to examine the highly commercialized world of global sport. Rinehart's text merges beautifully the per-sonal with the contextual, and as a result reads as much like a drama of our times as it does an ethnography. This is playful, in-tellectual writing that draws on a variety of writerly devices to allow the reader to form her or his own opinion about what sport is today and what it means. Further interpretive writing experi-ments like Rinehart's were celebrated in the collection *Sport and Postmodern Times*. Nate Kohn and Synthia Sydnor (1998), for ex-ample, perform a highly personal, yet contextual, theoretical, ironic, and critical dialogue around the explosion of sporting arti-facts into our daily cultural rituals and how this effects our rela-tionships with ourselves and others. Personal experience writing gained further public recognition when Margaret Duncan (1998), in her presidential address at the annual North American Society for the Sociology of Sport (NASSS) conference, used several self-reflective stories to increase "our sensitivity to the pain of others" (p. 95), thereby obtaining a closer approximation of people's lived experiences and the cultural contexts that surround them.

While this heightened focus on personal experience and contex-tuality certainly increased the quality and accessibility of writing within sport studies and offered new insights into the world of sport and physical activity, most of the accounts remained rather realist in their style. That is, they were still very descriptive with a strong adherence to straight memory or recall. This gave them more of documentary feel than a creative or artistic one. In addi-tion, accompanying these descriptions would often be lengthy theoretical explanations to attest to the meaning of the experi-ences described and their connection to larger social processes. Were these the "vital texts" advocated by Richardson? Did these works draw on literary techniques to further illuminate the mysteries of everyday experience? Or did literary quality take a back seat to the author's theoretical acumen?

In many ways, these texts still preserved the artificial separation between authors' experiences in the field and their analysis that Foucault, de Certeau, and Derrida critiqued. The rendering of life and culture still wasn't seen as a "fiction" the way Clifford (1986) advocated, and left to perform and inform on its own. Articles still needed to be interpreted; these research stories still required an explanation. A critical artistic essay, however, must be able to work on its own. The continued inclusion of footnotes or discussion sections will never extend readers, or get them to plunge into the interior of a text where "raw" human meanings and emotions truly lie, nor will they push or encourage social science writers to tap into more visceral or embodied aspects of being human. For researchers to produce texts that communicate and effect readers in their own right, a bolder shift into practices of fiction is necessary, where understanding, knowledge, and analysis are achieved not just through description and self-reflexivity, but by creating highly evocative, sensual, polyvocal texts.

One early example of a more fictionalized sports study came in 1996, when Jim Denison examined the retirement experiences of twelve elite New Zealand athletes (1996). He used his interview transcripts not in an effort to capture directly his subjects' experiences but instead to write three short stories that emphasized the primacy of imagination above memory and fact and the partiality of truth. However, this study still embraced a strong theoretical perspective. For example, every decision Jim made, from the specific questions he asked his subjects to his decision to use short stories as an interpretive style, was influenced and effected by his theoretical understandings of the body, identity in sport, gender in sport, and how sport retirement had been theorized previously. Therefore, in writing those stories his concern became how theory enacted and inscribed itself within a storied analytical process (Daly, 1997). The notion of converting field experiences and interview transcripts into literary pieces was also practiced by Joanne Halas (2001), who in an attempt to convey the importance of physical education in the daily lives of adolescents used her time spent at a treatment center/school to write twenty-four vignettes.

Turning to fiction, Halas said, allowed her "to create a running narrative that, like a kaleidoscopic lens, focuses in turn on the various lives lived at the school" (p. 79).

However, a turning point with regard to new ways of writing sport could be considered to have followed the special issue of the *Sociology of Sport Journal* published early in 2000 titled "Sociological Imaginings, Sociological Narratives." The work of the scholars assembled within attempted to bring a critical yet creative sensibility to issues in sport, physical activity, and body culture by writing autoethnographies and ethnographic fictions that for the most part stood on their own merits as stories. For example, Eleanor Miller's (2000) article, "Dis," explores how physical activity for children might be simultaneously daunting, disconcerting, and disempowering. Toni Bruce (2000), who depicts with her piece, "Never Let the Bastards See You Cry," the reality of the female sports reporter within the male locker room, exposes and confronts in an artful and provocative manner how sexuality, power, and misogyny are still ripe in many male-only gatherings.

Another contributor to that special issue, Tosha Tsang (2000), examined critical issues in elite level sport pertaining to identity by writing five short stories about her own career as a Canadian-Chinese Olympic rower. In the introduction to her paper, she conceptualizes identity as something "constantly in the process of being (re)created" (p. 46), and thus continually shifting and changing due to time, context, and her interaction with others. Her stories convey this theme through her refusal to follow a clear linear structure. In her writing she never gives primacy to one of her identities, but instead her identity is revealed as a series of overlapping and coexisting layers of identification.

Tsang and the other contributors to that volume help us understand that evocative writing practices such as autoethnography and ethnographic fiction can portray movement in a rounder, richer, more expressive way that both stirs the imagination and enlarges our appreciation of movement in our own and others' lives. More fictionalized writing practices, therefore, can lead us to develop an informed and sophisticated appreciation of the place of movement, sport, and physical education in contemporary society. In this way, evocative research texts must do more than explain differences, quote subjects verbatim, and point out general trends. They must also inspire, illuminate, and challenge us to think and act in critically reflexive ways. These ways of writing and doing research we have referred to previously as "Moving Writing" (Markula & Denison, 2000). And moving writing practices, we believe, through the power of language, imagery, and sensory detail have the capacity to change how we view sport and physical activity. Thus, our rationale for this book: to promote new ways of representing movement and moving—and subsequently human life—by providing those researchers interested in subverting traditional social science writing genres and experimenting with such innovative writing and research styles as autoethnography and ethnographic fiction with specific advice on how to craft effective research stories that make an impact on the lives of others.

Sport Stories: Meaning and Analysis

Naturally there will be those who might suggest that effective story writing rests on aesthetic qualities alone and avoids criticism, analysis, and theory and therefore fails to extend or deepen our understanding of social life—the hallmarks of social science research (Atkinson & Silverman, 1997). While this may be true of certain types of genre fiction (e.g. mystery, science fiction, romance), the type of writing we are promoting through this book needs to be more than just aesthetically pleasing. The criteria for success must be greater than that. As Richardson (2000) states, "the practices that produce CAP Ethnography are both creative and analytical. And any dinosaurian beliefs that 'creative' and 'analytical' are contradictory and incompatible modes are standing in the path of a meteor. They are doomed for extinction" (p. 10). Indeed, through ways of writing that are both creative and analytical, points can be made, hard and difficult issues dealt with, and important and crucial themes raised and discussed. In this way, theoretical interpretations or critical analyses never need to be eliminated from our work. Instead, as Kerry Daly (1997) states, "We need to rearticulate what theory is according to the lessons of postmodernity and narrative practices" (p. 343).

Richardson (2000) discusses further how she values writers' aesthetic touches and abilities as much as she does their contribution to our understanding of social life. She says that she expects writers to provide a fleshed-out, embodied sense of lived experience. And in his classic text *The Art of Fiction*, John Gardner (1983) speaks about good writing incorporating three landscapes: the landscape of action, where description and what people are doing is revealed; the landscape of consciousness, where characters' motives and intentions are illustrated; and the landscape of meaning, where it becomes evident to the reader that the author has a reason for writing what he or she did and that the story is not simply a collection of pretty sentences but that together every word, every phrase, every matter of punctuation and detail coheres to present a commentary on social life, on being human, and on the tensions, conflicts, and contradictions that are part of our every decision and action. It is the cumulative effect of these three landscapes, therefore, that can turn story writing into what Ivan Brady (1991) has termed, "an artful-science" (p. 10).

What Richardson (2000) and Gardner (1983) are describing as commentaries on social life can also be referred to as a story's theme. This is where prose and theory intersect and work together to enlarge a piece of writing's meaning. By "theme" we mean the analytical or interpretive framework a writer brings to her or his topic, or the central ideas he or she has in mind throughout the whole project, thus ensuring that the final write-up goes beyond a collection of clever and artful touches to include a particular vision or point of view about social life and the relationship between history and biography. Themes to take into a study could be a feminist or Marxist perspective to craft the resulting story or stories with an appreciation of how that particular framework understands power relationships and human nature.

In many ways, presenting one's theme through a story is much more difficult than through a traditional research essay. In a research paper a writer can state explicitly his or her themes (i.e. gender inequity, disempowerment, oppression), but stories convey meaning differently. A story's theme or themes must be revealed via dramatic action, not straightforward statements. Through dialogue and scene setting, for example, a reader must be persuaded to accept a particular interpretive viewpoint, therein temporarily shifting his or her focus and seeing the world through the writer's eyes. And it is the writer's hope that this temporary shift in focus will leave a lasting effect, thus changing the way the reader understands that particular issue.

This is not to say that stories are a better way to represent issues in sport than scholarly articles. By no means is it our intention to divorce theory and story, or social science and literature. Rather, our main objective with this book is to expand or enlarge the possibilities we have as researchers to write in different ways, and to become different kinds of writers. As we see it, drawing on Denzin (in Denison, 1998), ethnography and qualitative research in the twenty-first century must take on various forms. And as researchers we need to be able to move across various forms of narrative. If we develop the ability to write prose, poetry, autoethnography, and so on, this will give us multiple tools and multiple ways of representing and interpreting the world and its problems. Through this book we hope to open up these writing spaces. In some instances a traditional essay will better illuminate a significant moment in sport or body culture; in other instances a story will. Those decisions have to be made one case at a time. Therefore, we are not trying to make the point in this book that researchers must choose, for example, between standard ethnography and ethnographic fiction. Instead, we want people to realize that they have options and that these days there is no longer a default style of research.

However, one point that we are trying to make through this book is that because most of us never received any formal training in graduate school to write anything but traditional quantitative or qualitative realist tales, often when we turn to story to interpret our subjects and topics we lose our critical edge and produce studies without much impact. Now that the novelty of narrative studies has passed, no longer can brief descriptions, or a few personal recollections, or snippets of dialogue suffice as storied research. How well we write, craft, or stage our evocative tales will become increasingly important as issues around their legitimization fade into the background and issues around their quality emerge in the foreground. As readers become more accustomed to new types of narrative studies, the demands for sophistication, intelligence, and competence will only rise. Instead of writing just any old story, scholars "will be expected to write critically informed stories with the power to illustrate, illuminate, inspire, and mobilize readers to think and act critically and reflexively" (Denzin, 1998, in Denison, 1998, p. 53), what Denzin has also called the "art of interpretation" (1994, p. 500), where it is seen as increasingly important that researchers consider how they "move from the field to the text to the reader" (p. 501).

With the recent exception of Andrew Sparkes's (2002) excellent new volume, there are almost no guidelines for academics who want to make the shift into more creative analytical practices. Richardson (1994) does advise joining a writing group or enrolling in a creative writing class, and Rinehart (1998b) does suggest studying with a master writer and reading fiction with an eye toward incorporating methods that seem to work in producing certain desired effects. While these are helpful suggestions, they may also appear vague and out of reach for many academics. For many traditionally trained social scientists, concepts such as plot, tension, characterization, and point of view that writers toss around casually as the basic elements to a good story can be very intimidating (Markula, 2000).

Through this book, therefore, we hope to offer some concrete creative writing strategies and points of reference that researchers can begin experimenting with immediately in order to refine and develop their narrative voice. In this way, we also hope to demystify romantic notions we sometimes hold about imagination, creativity, and art. These are often what lead to barriers and insecurities forming in people's minds about their ability to write in new ways. For example, Pirkko recently told an apprehensive graduate student considering ethnographic fiction as an interpretive style for her research on adolescent girls' experiences in physical education, "You've been living and breathing these stories for years. They are inside you, you just need some strategies to begin accessing them." So it's strategies for crafting movement in sport and body research that we intend to provide through this book. And all the authors assembled, we believe, do an excellent job of commenting on their ways, means, and processes of producing artful research texts and evocative accounts of sport, physical activity, and the body.

However, before turning to a more specific discussion concerning the content of this book, we think it is important to clarify one final time that we do not believe that all of the answers or solutions to the limitations of producing truly embodied texts can be solved by turning to literature. In a previous paper (Markula & Denison, 2000) in fact, we asked if it's possible to produce truly embodied accounts of people's movement experiences given that the act of studying movement privileges language and writing (the intellect) and often reduces any movement experience (the physical) to an object of analysis. Because essentially that's what language and writing do and have done through the scientization of sport and physical education. They turn us and our complicated, sophisticated, intense, and personal movement patterns into a flat, one-dimensional text. This, then, results in the disappearance of the person or people studied, not to mention the author or any of the social conditions that produced that text.

While we concluded our paper by stating that at the present moment it seems unlikely that we will ever be able to produce truly embodied accounts of people's movement experiences given the current research climate and the emphasis on language and texts, we did acknowledge that more evocative ways of writing might approximate closer interpretations of people's movement experiences. However, this should not be taken to mean that we are advancing literature at the expense of social science or that are we claiming that creative exposition somehow privileges experience above language and writing. What we do think, though, is that there is much to learn from fiction and nonfiction writers about how to write more emotionally sensitive, dynamic, sociologically imaginative, visceral research texts, particularly from a craft, style, and technical standpoint.

Again, this doesn't mean that we should discard all that we know. We believe that our training in the social sciences has provided us with some valuable skills that even many fiction writers would benefit from learning and applying to their work. For one, we have a strong understanding of the connection between history, biography, and social structure, something that we think is invaluable for writing stories that are not only creative but analytical. Also, we have learned how to listen. We have developed strong empathy skills through spending time out in the field conducting lengthy interviews or running focus groups. And we are keenly aware of power relations and the importance of asking difficult "Why?" questions when it comes to understanding complex issues and problems such as oppression and discrimination. We feel it's combining this knowledge with the sensibilities of an artist that is the challenge we face as ethnographic and qualitative research practices move into the twenty-first century. Such works, we believe, will enable us to share our critical understandings with others, thus redefining knowledge within a framework that says that a text must connect to the personal experience of the reader. To produce effective stories of sport, physical activity, and the body we must learn how to artistically and critically incorporate our sentiments and sensibilities into one piece of Moving Writing.

Moving Writing: Crafting Movement in Sport Research
This book is presented via three major sections: Crafting Autoethnography in Sport Research, Crafting Ethnographic Fiction in Sport Research, and Author Interviews, Notes on Craft. In section one, we offer four examples of autoethnography, and likewise in section two we provide four examples of ethnographic fiction. Section three of this book contains interviews with two prominent sport fiction writers. These interviews focus on various practical issues involved in developing one's narrative voice (e.g. getting started, making revisions, creating characters) in what we see as an effort to offer readers guidance and inspiration from two master writers.

In addition to compelling examples of autoethnography and ethnographic fiction in sections one and two, respectively, each author has also included in his or her chapter a commentary on the act of writing. These commentaries cover a discussion around two points: 1) a relevant craft technique found in that respective chapter (e.g. dialogue, metaphor, inflection); and 2) the advantages each author gained in adopting autoethnography or ethnographic fiction, respectively, to treat a particular issue related to sport or physical activity (e.g. embodiment, timelessness, pain).

These commentaries are intended to provide readers with an introduction, or initiation if you will, into some of the conventions and traditions of fiction and nonfiction that contribute so importantly to the satisfactory crafting of autoethnography and ethnographic fiction.

To open the first section on autoethnography, Pirkko outlines her development as a researcher/writer and the factors behind her transition from a realist writer to an evocative writer. Her aim here is explicit. She hopes to inspire other social scientists who are apprehensive about the demands of these new, more creative writing practices to embark on a similar journey as she has. She presents her case through an examination of notions of subjectivity, data collection, and analysis in a critique of both the aerobicizing and dancing female body.

From Pirkko's story of a body in motion, we move to a story of a body in pain. Andrew Sparkes characterizes a failed middle-age body set against memories of a younger elite, sport-performing body. Through this highly personal rendering, we enter Sparkes's flesh, where bones, muscles, and emotions contract. But in displaying his embodied sensuality and confronting his shifting aches and interruptions Sparkes begins to understand his place in the world, and how his multiple positions as a man, a father, and a son have expanded due to injury and its lingering effects.

Arto Tiihonen picks up Sparkes's vision of hope in a strong treatise concerning the actualities and potentialities of freedom through movement. Discoveries are unearthed and revealed in this chapter involving the vicissitudes of age, discipline, illness, and health, and the multiple ways bodies are fragmented and inscribed through relations of power. Tiihonen puts his memory to good use as his phenomenological prose style enables physicality and emotionality to intertwine and intersect at various key developmental crossroads.

Also exhibiting a powerful memory is Katherine Parrot. But her story of a girl and her horse and the forces of commercialism that drove them apart is so much more than straight memory work. Parrot's sensitive and caring voice makes for an exquisite gift that carries forward one layer of sensory detail and imagery after another, which in the end offers a heart-wrenching account of childhood, love, and loss.

Section two, Crafting Ethnographic Fiction in Sport Research, marks this book's move from evocative portraits of memory and personal body experiences to acts of imagination brought to bear via various realms or settings that have been studied ethnographically. All four authors in this section rely on fiction for a purpose: to express their visions of social-scientific truths within sport.

To begin, David Rowe offers a highly charged stylization of football (soccer) fanaticism that of necessity locates women on the fringes. Rowe's rhythmic, rich prose verges on verse as he hypnotizes us with his phrasings, puns, and allusions. At the same time, he never forgets to extend his meanings so that he can expose larger issues of power and influence that exert themselves on our will and our various subjectivities.

Rowe's fast pace continues with Toni Bruce's story of sexual identity in sport. Speed is set alight through her well-developed metaphor of teamwork, banter, and quick passes that so aptly capture "the feel" of women's basketball. There is joy, exhilaration, and of course confusion in this tightly plotted account of the struggles female athletes encounter on and off the court as they try to come to terms with various relations and expectations that encompass gender, sexuality, and identity.

Remaining on the margins, we go from issues around lesbianism in Bruce's chapter to Bob Rinehart's chapter on displaced kids. Very appropriately, Rinehart locates his tale on the fringes of "real" sport—skateboarding, inline skating, BMX—where his "outsider" main character is denied institutional credibility and recognition, and therefore must seek fulfillment and satisfaction on his own. Rinehart's story is an indictment of systems and traditions of power that works evocatively to impress upon us how difference can be read as trouble.

Staying with boys, sport, and growing up, Martti Silvennoinen, in his chapter, connects movement to nature and culture. By going beyond the confines of chronology into narrative, Silvennoinen draws on various storied traditions within psychology, sociology, and literature to expound on the multiple dimensions of identity. Finally, Silvennoinen uses the unique Finnish particulars of snow and ski-jumping to offer a captivating vision of a "nationalized" body.

In the concluding section of the book, we tune in to the voices of two sport fiction writers as they reflect on their craft. This could be seen as a radical departure for a scholarly monograph, but to us the two chapters in this section highlight and encapsulate the central aims we brought with us to this project. To begin, writer and editor Joli Sandoz interviews author Jenifer Levin in an attempt to uncover and present Levin's assumptions and processes around the art of fiction, and the suitability of fiction to represent issues and critical themes in sport. Writer and teacher John Morefield covers a host of ideas and topics in his conversation with novelist Donald Hayes as together they consider the value of stories today and how they are made.

Finally, as researchers, we have been trained to notice, ask, describe, understand, and ultimately present our interpretations of embodied life experiences. We believe the time is now to create a style of representation and interpretation that can speak more directly, specifically, and wholly to these experiences. We can't be afraid to establish our own representational niche within academe; yes, to turn to story involves a philosophical and conceptual shift towards the way we approach topics, ask questions, and make sense out of sport and movement, but this is a challenge we must accept if autoethnography and ethnographic fiction are to achieve their rightful place within the academy. These research forms hold the potential to expand the public debate over the socially constructed nature of sport and physical activity; they can enhance our critical understanding of sport and movement in contemporary society, and provide us with a new vision of our bodies to carry forward into this century and beyond.

REFERENCES

Atkinson, P., & Silverman, D. (1997). Kundera's *Immortality*: The interview society and the invention of the self. *Qualitative Inquiry, 3*, 304–325.

Bain, L. L. (1995). Mindfulness and subjective knowledge. *Quest, 47*, 238–253.

Bochner, A. P., & Ellis, C. S. (1999). Which way to turn? *Journal of Contemporary Ethnography, 28*, 485–495.

Brady, I. (1991). *Anthropological poetics.* Savage, MD: Roman and Littlefield.

Bruce, T. (1998). Postmodernism and the possibilities for writing vital sports texts. In G. Rail (Ed.), *Sport and postmodern times* (pp. 3–19). Albany, NY: SUNY Press.

Bruce, T. (2000). Never let the bastards see you cry. *Sociology of Sport Journal, 17*, 69–74.

Clifford, J. (1986). Introduction: Partial truths. In J. Clifford & G. E. Marcus (Eds.), *Writing culture* (pp. 1–26). Berkeley: University of California Press.

Cole, C. L. (1991). The politics of cultural representation: Visions of fields/fields of visions. *International Review for the Sociology of Sport, 26*, 36–49.

Daly, K. (1997). Re-placing theory in ethnography: A postmodern view. *Qualitative Inquiry, 3*, 343–365.

Denison, J. (1996). Sport narratives. *Qualitative inquiry, 2*, 351–362.

Denison, J. (1998). An interview with Norman K. Denzin. *Waikato Journal of Education, 4*, 51–54.

Denzin, N. (1989). *The research act* (3rd edition). Englewood Cliffs, NJ: Prentice Hall.

Denzin, N. (1994). The art and politics of interpretation. In N. Denzin & Y. Lincoln (Eds.), *Handbook of qualitative research* (pp. 500–515). Newbury Park, CA: Sage.

Denzin, N. (1997), *Interpretive ethnography.* London: Sage.

Derrida, J. (1976). *Of grammatology.* Baltimore, MD: Johns Hopkins University Press.

de Certeau, M. (1984). *The practice of everyday life.* Berkeley: The University of California Press.

Dolby-Stahl, S. K. (1985). A literary folkloristic methodology for the study of meaning in personal narrative. *Journal of Folklore Research, 22*, 45–70.

Duncan, M. (1998). Stories we tell about ourselves. *Sociology of Sport Journal, 15*, 95–108.

Foucault, M. (1979). What is an author? In J. V. Harari (Ed.), *Textual strategies.* Ithaca, NY: Cornell University Press.

Gardner, J. (1983). *The art of fiction.* New York: Vintage.

Geertz, C. (1973). *The interpretation of culture.* New York: Basic Books.

Geertz, C. (1983). *Local knowledge: Further essays in interpretive anthropology.* New York: Basic Books.

Halas, J. (2001). Shooting hoops at the treatment center: Sports stories. *Quest, 53*, 77–96.

Kohn, N., & Sydnor, S. (1998). "How do you warm-up for a stretch class?" Sub/in/di/verting hegemonic shoves toward sport. In G. Rail (Ed.), *Sport and postmodern times* (pp. 21–32). Albany, NY: SUNY Press.

Markula, P. (2000). *Bodily dialogues.* Paper presented at the International Society for Comparative Physical Education and Sport Conference, University of the Sunshine Coast, Queensland, Australia.

Markula, P., & Denison, J. (2000). See Spot run: Movement as an object of textual analysis. *Qualitative Inquiry, 6*, 406–431.

Miller, E. M. (2000). Dis. *Sociology of Sport Journal, 17*, 75–80.

Mills, C. W. (1959). *The sociological imagination*. London: Oxford University Press.

Nilges, L. M. (2001). The twice-told tale of Alice's physical life in wonderland: Writing qualitative research in the 21st century. *Quest, 53,* 231–259.

Richardson, L. (1994). Writing: A method of inquiry. In N. Denzin & Y. Lincoln (Eds.), *Handbook of qualitative research* (pp. 516–529). Newbury Park, CA: Sage.

Richardson, L. (2000). New writing practices in qualitative research. *Sociology of Sport Journal, 17,* 5–20.

Rinehart, R. (1998a). *Players all: Performances in contemporary sport.* Bloomington, IN: Indiana University Press.

Rinehart, R. (1998b). Fictional methods in ethnography: Believability, specks of glass, and Chekhov. *Qualitative Inquiry, 4,* 200–224.

Rorty, R. (1991). *Objectivity, relativism, and truth: Philosophical papers Vol. 1.* Cambridge, England: Cambridge University Press.

Rosaldo, R. (1989). *Culture & truth.* Boston: Beacon.

Sironen, E. (1988). *Uuteen liikuntakulttuuriin.* Jyväskylä, Finland: Vastapaino.

Sironen, E., Tiihonen, A., & Veijola, S. (1992). *Urheilukirja.* Jyväskylä, Finland: Vastapaino.

Sparks, A. C. (2002). *Telling tales in sport and physical activity: A qualitative journey.* Champaign, IL: Human Kinetics.

Sparkes, A. (1995). Writing people: Reflections on the dual crises of representation and legitimization in qualitative inquiry. *Quest, 47,* 158–195.

Sparkes, A. C. (1996). The fatal flaw: Narrative of the fragile body-self. *Qualitative Inquiry, 2,* 463–494.

Stanley, L. (1992). *The auto/biographical I: The theory and practice of feminist auto/biography.* Manchester, UK: Manchester University Press.

Stoller, P. (1994). Embodying colonial memories. *American Anthropologist, 96,* 634–648.

Sudwell, M. (1999). The body bridge. In A. C. Sparkes & M. Silvennoinen (Eds.), *Talking bodies: Men's narratives of the body and sport* (pp. 13–28). Jyväskylä, Finland: SoPhi.

Tomlinson, A. (1999). *The game's up: Essays in the cultural analysis of sport, leisure and popular culture.* Aldershot, England: Ashgate.

Tsang, T. (2000). Let me tell you a story: A narrative exploration of identity in high performance sport. *Sociology of Sport Journal, 17,* 44–59.

Wolcott, H. (1994). *Transforming qualitative data.* London: Sage.

PART I

Crafting Autoethnography
in Sport Research

Writing has always been a way of knowing—a method of discovery and analysis. Autoethnography is one way for researchers to know themselves and others. As a rule, autoethnographers tell stories about their lives and how their experiences connect to larger cultural contexts—nations, institutions, identities. The author is alive and well in these tales, born to speak, feel, and reflect openly through his or her memories, self-talk, recollections, dreams, and conversations. Autoethnographies display multiple layers of consciousness; the researcher is concerned with producing an evocative text that carries with it a sense of anticipation, exuberance, and intimate detail. The contributors in this section all examine human experience and meaning from the inside, but with a view beyond themselves, too. It's in this way that autoethnographers show a concern for others and the political and social consequences associated with living life today.

CHAPTER 1

Bodily Dialogues: Writing the Self

Pirkko Markula

Introduction

Evocative writing practices have become increasingly visible within the socio-cultural analysis of people's lived experiences, including examinations into physical activity and sport. Some even argue that "the celebration of personal narratives has become a major preoccupation within the social sciences" (Sparkes, 2000, p. 42). However, the majority of scholars attempting these kinds of writing projects, including myself, are typically trained in more traditional realist writing styles. That is, writing that produces objective accounts of experience based on data such as statistics, life history, media quotations or interview quotations that are often inserted verbatim into the research text (e.g., Foley, 1992; Richardson, 1997; Stanley, 1992). Evocative writing, in turn, refers to more subjective, personal narrative writing practices such as autoethnography, ethnographic fiction, or performative writing (e.g., Bruner, 1993; Pollock, 1998; Richardson, 2000). Because of the challenges evocative writing practices present, making the transition from a realist writer to a narrative writer is not always painless. In this chapter, I recount my own path from realist writer to evocative writer. While this development has been a gradual process over a number of years, I have framed my transition within a recent visit to an international conference. The events at the conference provoke memories of my encounters with different evocative writing practices. I then conclude this chapter by discussing the contribution narrative writing can make for a greater understanding of the physically active body.

Conference

Walking

I decide to walk to the conference center. Finlandia Hall is a short walk from my hotel. I hope I find it easily, as I am relatively unfamiliar with the city of Helsinki. A map would help, but I trust my luck in spotting it—its gleaming white walls and gracious, clear lines. Perhaps taking a little detour is not wasted either—I have time—and what was it that Michel de Certeau (1980) said about walking in a city? He felt that walking is an elementary form of experiencing the city, because when walking, we can immerse ourselves into the everyday. The everyday that "has a certain strangeness that does not surface . . . outlining itself against the visible" (p. 154) but that is an important aspect of understanding culture. I walk in the morning sun, aiming to detect the "opaque and blind mobility characteristics" (p. 154) of the city as de Certeau would advise. Helsinki seems to advertise prominently its status as a "Culture City of Europe 2000." In addition to numerous billboards informing the passersby of this nomination, the city has invested heavily in planting. They certainly didn't use to have so many flowers. On my way to the conference center, I can smell the blooming lilacs. As a child growing up in Finland, purple lilacs and white nights meant summer had arrived. These clear signs of summer, I realize, are especially striking now as I have just left the cold, wet, lingering New Zealand winter.[1] Curious as to how one can switch from one season to another in only a day, I admire the broad façade of Finlandia Hall—it is designed by Alvar Aalto. Then I step inside.

Registration

A blond woman, her posture so perfectly aligned that, as it seems, she will be able to jump up immediately to greet any visitor, sits behind the registration desk in the foyer. When I ask her for a copy of the conference program, she compliments me on speaking Finnish so well for a New Zealander. Smiling in response, I take the complimentary conference bag that she, now standing up, offers me over the desk. She instructs that all the information regarding the conference, including the program, should be in the bag. I dig out the conference program. The cover displays "Congress on Women and Sport," and accompanying the title is an attractive picture of a green, shady, calm Finnish pine forest. Before I find my own session, "The Physically Active Body," I pass several colorful pages that introduce the sponsors and organizers of the conference. Finally, I find it: the last session of a very long day, and my talk is the last one and not only that—none of the other speakers are focusing on the researcher's subjective experience. My talk appears so out of place; perhaps I should just leave? Nobody will miss my presentation. While the thought of not being missed is somewhat comforting, it also saddens me to be an unknown visitor in my home country. Never mind, I have come this far, I'll just have to give my paper. Anyway, it is time for the first session.

Keynote
I open the door into a huge lecture room using both hands. The lights are dimmed and a woman stands at the speaker's podium. She is introducing the keynote speaker from America, a professor in sport sociology that I have met at previous conferences. He will be talking about children's understanding of gender–appropriate sport behavior. I walk carefully and quietly fold down a seat in the back row. I plan to be attentive to hear what the professor has to say, but I am unable to concentrate on his theoretical presentation. I reach under my seat and pull out my own paper from my bag. Perhaps my talk is not such a misfit after all? Or perhaps, I will have time to change it? Anyway, I begin reading my paper to myself.

As a lecturer in Leisure Studies, my colleagues from other departments on campus often ask what exactly do I teach. "The sociological strand within our department," is my usual reply. One friend, a scientist, persisted further.

"Sociological strand," she wanted to know, "what does that entail?"

"Basically, I study and teach the socio-cultural aspects of leisure," I attempted to clarify.

"What is that exactly? Like, what do you research?"

I tried again: "My main interest is in women's body-image and exercise."

"Body-image!" came her surprised response. "Of all the people, you, with the perfect body, study body image!"

My friend's response unsettled me. What made her say that I had a perfect body? I certainly didn't recognize any resemblance between me and Elle Macpherson. Besides, my body problems were private and personal, and I was unprepared to discuss my personal connection to women's body struggles. In addition, I never intended to become a body-image expert. Rather, my research focused on the meaning of aerobics for participating women. However, in our conversations, my subjects often brought up their struggles with their body shapes, and their relationship with their bodies turned into my major research theme. These women seemed to have been engaged in an endless struggle to achieve the ideal body, and aerobics was one method toward this bodily transformation. Because of my research on women's body experience in exercise, I have often been asked to give lectures on this topic. Recently, I was invited to the Women's Studies program at my university to talk to their students.

In my lecture, I asked the students to identify the characteristics of an ideal Western female body. First and foremost, they concluded, one has to be thin. "That's right," I confirmed, "an attractive female body is definitely thin." To verify my statement, I then quoted Sandra Bartky (1988): "The current body of fashion is taut, small-breasted, narrow hipped, and of slimness bordering emaciation" (p. 64). "Because of this image," I continued, "many women who according to the available body composition measures are considered 'normal' or underweight, diet and exercise to lose weight because they perceive themselves as being fat."

Finishing my sentence, I suddenly remembered how surprised my friend had been to hear that my main research interest was women's body image. I began to wonder what these students thought of my body as I stood in front of them dressed fashionably in black attire. The convener of the course had introduced me as Dr. Markula, a lecturer as well as a dancer, from Leisure Studies. I was quite happy to have been identified by my two public personas: an academic and a dancer. But I wondered if I looked like a dancer to these students? I certainly didn't always have a dancer's body. Dance, nevertheless, had long been my passion, although I grew up in the Finnish countryside without much of an opportunity to attend dance classes or dance performances. However, as an undergraduate student at the University of Jyväskylä, I eagerly took classes in jazz dance, ballet, and modern dance. Despite my enthusiasm, I didn't particularly excel in dance. Judged by the mirror in the dance studio, I was hopelessly too big, too heavy, and too slow to become a real dancer. Somehow, I always seemed to be the biggest person in the room. It was very painful to admit that I was fat, and once I made that confession, I was very ashamed of my body. I have only kept one photograph of myself dancing from those times, and I remember being quite upset by being caught in such an embarrassing picture. The photo showed me practicing a dance combination with the rest of the class. While the others wore leotards and tights, I was dressed in an oversized T-shirt and loose sweat pants to hide my big body. When I look at that picture now, my clothes seem much more distinctive than my body size, but then I was deeply troubled with being overweight. With my clothing, though, I marked myself visibly as an obese person. When I later read what Carol Spitzack (1990) said, "The woman who is marked, and marks herself, in the language of excess [weight] is required to both see and declare her deviance, to stand before self and others, confessing her excess" (p. 58, emphasis original), I realized that I was confessing my excess weight in front of everybody by covering my body as completely as I could. Like an alcoholic who, after confessing her excess drinking discovers the "truth" about herself and admits the need for cure, I required a rescue from my excess eating.

Back then my curative practice was a strict dieting regime. It was based partly on self-punishment, partly on my newly acquired knowledge concerning the scientific principles of proper nutrition that I had learned in my nutrition class, and partly on popular dieting lore. For example, I had read somewhere that for some women just seeing food and consequently desiring it can result in weight gain. As devastating as that information was, I concluded that I was obviously one of those women, and that weight loss for me would be particularly trying. In my diet, I avoided my favorite foods to prevent triggering an eating binge, a problem I had had since I started university. I also decided to eat only twice a day: a small breakfast of porridge followed by a proper lunch at noon. In addition, I decided to reserve one day a week for fasting. While I followed my diet diligently, I could not see much change in my body shape. I now know that this was likely caused by a lowered metabolism due to my insufficient food intake, but then I took it as a sign of my "natural" inclination towards obesity. Consequently, while I didn't lose any weight, I felt that if I didn't adhere to my diet I would only become bigger. Instead of a dancer, I was doomed to be a big woman . . .

Suddenly the room fills with clapping. I lift my head. The talk has ended, and other conference participants are trying to get past me. I stand up, clutching my papers close to my chest. Still standing, I hear that all presenters are required to report their audio-visual needs to a conference organizer downstairs. After reporting, no audio-visual needs, I search for the room where I will present. I finally find it downstairs behind the corner from the foyer. I can only peek into the room through the small windows on the locked door. It is a lot smaller than the room reserved for the keynotes. Who will ever find this room? I wonder. I sit on a wooden bench by the toilet opposite to my presentation venue and flip through the conference program again: "Women and Coaching," "Women in Sport Organizations," "Women and Successful Leadership . . ." I decide to skip the next sessions and practice the rest of my talk. I silently move my lips to rehearse clear pronunciation. I always read too fast when I get nervous, and then mispronounce words. I remind myself about regular breathing and to sustain a slow, even pace.

". . . It is not surprising," I told the students in my lecture, "that women exercise to lose weight and that our exercise practices have been transformed to maximize weight loss. For example, aerobics classes include a twenty-minute session of continuous exercise, because this type of physical activity utilizes the cardio-vascular system that burns fat for its energy."

"But can't one also be too thin," a student from the back row of the lecture theatre shouted, "the anorexics, they look starved, not beautiful."

"That's a very good point," I said, and we added a further requirement for the ideal body.

Like Susan Bordo (1993), we concluded that it was no longer enough to eliminate excess fat, but in addition to appearing thin, women's bodies must look toned. Appropriate muscle tone, we discovered, however, was not easy to define. While an essential aspect of our body ideal, too much muscle mass could be considered repulsive. I told the students that the aerobicizers I studied did not want to look like bodybuilders, but rather longed for a firm body.

In fact, I remember talking about the contrasting perceptions of muscle size in dance and aerobics with one aerobicizer I interviewed for my study. One thing she had said she liked about aerobics was that muscles were more acceptable than in her ballet class. In aerobics, she said, muscles showed that you were dedicated and worked hard, but in ballet they meant that you needed to lose weight or that you simply didn't have a suitable body for ballet. Women's exercise classes, she felt, provided an environment that was more accepting to a variety of body types than dance. I agreed with her. The requirements for a dancing body were indeed stricter than the requirements for an exercising body. When I lived in the United States I became a certified aerobics instructor to earn extra income to top up my meager graduate student stipend. In the process, my body went through a transformation. In my aerobics instructor uniform, a sleeveless leotard and short tights, I looked the part. I had well-defined deltoids, abdominals, and quadriceps as a result of a regular teaching schedule. I was strong, and without a doubt my fitness center clients could immediately identify me as an instructor. Shouldn't I be proud of my body, the body that I had earlier thought was destined to lifelong obesity? But at the same time that I was teaching aerobics, I was also attending dance classes and instead of tights and leotards, I wore T-shirts and sweat pants. Now I had to cover my muscles.

For a dancer, even for a modern dancer, my body was still hopelessly too big. I was particularly embarrassed about my arms, and I did not want to bare them during movement combinations. One of my dance teachers described my thighs as containing "lots of energy," a euphemism for thighs that were too muscular, and she recommended I do more stretching to contain that "energy." Following a recent performance I gave in New Zealand, one audience member asked me if I was a former gymnast. Thus, while I was no longer judged too fat, too uncoordinated, or too slow, I still didn't quite fit the dancer mold. In its visible muscularity, my body was too big to be a dancer's body. As much as I detested the connection to gymnastics, photographs from that performance verified my muscular image. One particular photo depicted me dancing in a leotard with a low–cut back. My muscles rippled under the harsh stage lighting and I looked like a bodybuilder posing my sweaty, striated, defined muscularity. But where had these muscles come from? After graduate school, when I moved from America to New Zealand to take up a position in Leisure Studies, I had no time *to teach aerobics. I didn't have time to go to the gym at all. At least in front of those students my body was safely hidden under layers of loose clothing. Moving on, then, I decided to disregard any further discussion about proper feminine musculature and I changed the topic . . .*

I hear the sharp, rhythmic sound of high-heel shoes crossing the tiled floor—a group of women are approaching the toilets. The sessions must be over; it must be lunchtime now. When I reach the large room where lunch is being served, most of the conference participants are already sitting down with their plates. Their chatter fills the room. I am supposed to meet the other women in my session. I know only one of them, and I cannot spot her among the numerous heads. Gazing around, I realize that this is a Finnish-style lunch. This "midday meal," as I have labeled it, consists of a full meal served in buffet style. Today it is salmon with rice and an assortment of salads. How healthy and proper! I feel like skipping lunch, I am so disappointed. After years of living abroad I have grown to love my sandwich and Diet Coke for lunch. Perhaps my dieting days ruined all the enjoyment of midday meals for me. I have, however, promised to meet the others. Somebody calls my name and I find my group. While we eat we share our research interests and approaches. For some reason, I avoid talking about writing personal experience, and throw lofty concepts like "narrativity," "postmodern writing," "representation," and "subjectivity" into the conversation until we all have to rush from our seats and hurry to the next set of sessions.

I decide to attend the session on women and coaching, as one of the presenters is a friend of mine. However, after the first talk I find myself again outside, sitting next to the toilets. I just have to get through the rest of this paper, I tell myself. After all, my session is next. I take a deep breath and begin where I left off.

". . . Many aerobicizers feel that their abdomens, their butts, their thighs, and their underarms are particularly prone to excess flab and need concentrated attention in exercise classes," I pointed out to the class, adding, "No wonder the fitness industry offers specialized classes, like 'ABT' (abs, bums and thighs) or the 'New Body' for us to attend to these troublesome spots. Notice that these parts that we hate the most and fight the hardest to shape are the very parts of our bodies that identify us as females. Logically," I continued, "we are conditioned to hate

looking like women as we unceasingly work toward the contemporary boyish body ideal."

I then prompted the students for more characteristics of the ideal body, but as they were all in their early twenties, none of them realized that the ideal woman's body was also young. "While we can actively try to become thinner and more toned," I explained to them, "age is something we cannot reverse. Moreover, the aging process exacerbates the problems we have with our bodies. You are still young," I added, "but at my age, the problem areas tend to get flabbier and even more resistant to shaping. The women's body ideal is comprised of numerous requirements and is, therefore, very difficult to achieve." As I paced across the front of the lecture theatre I continued. "Very few women are born with these eternally young, taut, and slim boyish bodies and therefore, the majority of women work continuously towards the elusive ideal. Nevertheless, despite this hard bodywork most of us will fail. This almost guaranteed failure," I finally concluded, "has resulted in great body dissatisfaction among women. Some feminist research indicates that throughout the 1980s and 1990s there has been a dramatic escalation of diagnosed cases of body image related illnesses and eating disorders, like anorexia and bulimia. As the unnatural ideal body causes so much suffering for women, we have to fight it," I proclaimed. I paused for a moment to put up an overhead from a paper I wrote:

> Instead of advising women to cope with the body ideal and accept that they will never achieve it, we should concentrate on altering the unnatural stereotype of the body beautiful. Similarly, when we advise women to exercise to reconstruct their bodies into a slimmer or tauter form, we ask them to cope with the oppressive image. Through such advice we perpetuate the cause for women's body dissatisfaction and support the oppressive body ideal. If we promote fitness in this light, we actually do a disservice for women. The path to the healthy look can be filled with pain and disappointment; in the worst case it can end with greater ill health than it started: eating disorders, overuse injuries, obsessive behaviour or low self-confidence. (Markula, 1998, p. 11)

I then followed this lengthy quote by posing another question to the students: "What is obsessive behavior?"

"It's like, when you spend all your time in the gym," one young woman with a pierced eyebrow volunteered. "Like you feel guilty if you're not constantly exercising."

"Yes, that's it. It is called an exercise obsession, and it has become so prevalent that the medical profession is starting to diagnose it as an illness, much like eating disorders. Do you know anybody who spends hours in the gym every day?"

Leaving the students to think about their friends' exercise habits, and perhaps their own, I too searched for real-life examples of exercise obsession to add to the discussion. What about my friends in graduate school? What about me? As a graduate student, I used to go to a dance class every day and afterwards run. I had created a scientifically correct running program to improve my performance through the proper application of the principles of periodization. I started by building endurance and then gradually added intensity before tapering. Only I didn't have an upcoming race to taper for, it was more like a lifelong race, this continuous competition with my body and with fat. I later agreed with Carol Spitzack (1990), who observed that, "Moving into the afterlife of thinness . . . entails a constant recollection of the body's unacceptability. In many respects, the body is supplanted with an all-seeing, all-knowing other who guarantees the need for ongoing confession through remembrance" (p. 68). Dancing and running weren't my only exercise forms at that time. I also taught aerobics five times a week and after class I went for a swim. I thought teaching a class on Saturdays and Sundays would keep me exercising over the weekends. I chose a fitness center six miles away, and for a warm–up and cool–down I biked the distance. I was terrified of becoming fat again, and even if it meant having muscles, I'd rather have those than be fat . . .

Lively chatter and a stream of conference participants gathering for a coffee break disrupts my concentration, and I put my paper down. When I line up for some tea, the woman next me to remarks that coffee seems important to the Finns, considering the frequent and numerous breaks. "Yes," I say, "did you know that Finns consume the most coffee in the world when measured in kilograms of beans per year?" She had not been aware of yet another world record held by the Finns, but agrees to the necessity of caffeine for her conference experience. She then recounts her conference day: "It is amazing," she exclaims, "how hard conferences are, although one just sits down, listens, and drinks coffee. I think I need some shopping therapy." She must deduce from my name tag that I am a native and asks me where to shop for Finnish design glass in Helsinki. I have to admit that I am familiar only with the two big department stores on the main street. But I tell her that they are fine establishments. I wish her happy shopping and wonder if the rest of the conference goers will join her, leaving no audience for the final session, my session. Suddenly, I wonder why I am so worried about the lack of an audience. A smaller audience might be more receptive to my semi-confessional paper. Anxious again, I quickly put down my teacup and hurry down the stairs, as there is still enough time to go through my paper before my session starts. Besides, I need to visit the toilet anyway.

. . . I eventually left my memories of my own obsessive exercise behavior and turned my attention back to the students in front of me, where one student had begun to tell a story about one of his friends who exercises seven hours every day . . .

This bench is so uncomfortable. My back. Okay, better posture and slow down, I remind myself. I straighten up, ignoring the flow of people going in and out of the toilet. I continue reading, remembering to breathe deeply and to articulate clearly without speeding up.

". . . What a frightening example of an exercise obsession," I remarked, and we discussed other examples and tried to decide what exact amount of exercise could be considered obsessive.

"Like, what about athletes? They certainly train a lot every day, but isn't that what they need to do to become successful competitors?" asked a tanned woman with a thin line of elaborate tattoos circling her toned upper arm.

"That is correct. Which shows that you have to consider the context before you judge anyone's behavior. For an athlete to win, she needs a demanding training program, but for someone else to engage in similar behavior for dieting purposes is an entirely different story." At this point I noticed the clock on the side wall. The end of the class was approaching. Before I could say anything further, the course convener thanked me for my talk and presented me with a final question: "It is wonderful to conclude that the ideal body is just a societal construction, just an image that we should actively reject. However, I cannot help but ask you, as you already have the ideal, slim, and fit body, how you feel about providing the rest of us with body-image advice?" There it was again. This idea that I somehow had the ideal body. "I am just like the

rest of you," I replied. "I am equally influenced by the societal body-image requirements." And there the class ended, luckily, before I had time to explain what I meant by feeling similar to everybody else in the lecture room. Not that I had any intention of dwelling on my personal body experiences in front of these people anyway. After the class, one student approached me.

"You are so right about the image, it's designed to keep us occupied with trivial body problems when we could be doing many more important things. It makes sense . . . I know that, but I still struggle. I go to the gym and do hundreds of awkward outer thigh exercises just to have smaller legs . . . I still do it, I still struggle."

"Yes," I nodded, "it is very difficult."

I hesitated a moment; should I tell her how, despite my feminist awareness, I could not disrupt my own disciplining gaze? Or that one of my feminist friends suffered from anorexia when she was a college athlete and felt that she never completely recovered despite her scholarly understanding of eating disorders. She believed instead that she had been permanently left with an "anorexic mind." Perhaps I also possessed an anorexic mind? In fact, I used to be so angry with myself for not having the discipline to become an anorexic. Through feminist research, though, I had become aware of the oppressive nature of the ideal body, yet still I constantly watched what I ate. Even now, as a lecturer, I feel guilty if I am unable to fit my weekly runs into my schedule. To battle my own obsession, I started a tai chi class that included a small meditation section. As I was a beginner, my mind tended to wander during the meditation exercises. In our first session, I found myself thinking if this could possibly count for my daily exercise bout, as I didn't seem to be burning much fat. Perhaps, I should run to and from the class? I thought.

It took me some time to convince myself that tai chi was not about weight loss, but the idea was to feel more relaxed. And being more relaxed, I realized, could help me improve my dance technique. Dance continues to be the yardstick of my body problems. If before my body had been too fat and too muscular to look like a dancing body, I now encountered the most irreversible body problem in dance: the aging body. As I was approaching the usual retirement age of a dancer, I faced the consequence of years of dance training: a battered body. But despite the numerous body struggles I had had due to dance, the thought of *giving up my highly technical level of dancing because of my aging body, hurt. It hurt even more than my knees that, like most dancers' knees, had worn out due to stressful and constant training. As a feminist researcher, I was aware of alternative types of dance suitable for mature dancers, but, I wondered, would they provide the same exhilarating dancing that I was trained for? I didn't believe so. At the same time, I was witnessing some of my feminist colleagues at the university reaching menopause and complaining about sudden, uncontrollable, and substantial weight gain. They dieted desperately, but to no avail. "That will definitely happen to me," I thought, "and then what will I do?" I didn't see an end to my body troubles. So what was I to say to this student in front of me? That she should just be prepared for an ongoing body struggle? And that it just gets worse with age? Or should I tell her that an awareness of the oppressive and constructed nature of the body image was the first step in fighting it. In the end I said, "It is all right to struggle. But you should try to disengage from exercise practices that support the oppressive image." Then I asked her, "Have you tried tai chi?"*

Well, at least the ending is all right. It does portray the contradictory nature of women's body relationships; it also raises the possibility of a positive understanding of one's body. I stand up from the bench and my knees crack. Jet lag, not age, I conclude, and I head toward the room I will present in. Inside I meet the professor whose keynote I attended. He has just finished listening to the previous session on women and coaching. I introduce myself and we politely talk about our current research.

"I heard your keynote address—children learning about gender through sport—it was very interesting. Is this your main line of research nowadays?"

"No," he says, "I'm still writing on violence and sport, but my real interest is the concept of masculinity. What about you? Are you still examining aerobics?"

"Yes," I answer quickly, wondering how much he knows about my research. Does he just remember me as a graduate student, back when I wrote in a realist way?

When I first wrote about women's body problems in the early 1990s, the social sciences, in particular anthropology, were in a crisis of representation. We had started to admit that our research texts were merely representations: researchers' interpretations of experiences created within a web of diverse social forces. In my dissertation, I too acknowledged my subjective influence on the interpretation of my field data. I asserted that I, the researcher, significantly shaped the writing and interpretive process. Nevertheless, I described my subjects' experiences in a realist manner using a blend of interview quotations and theoretical analysis. This was the kind of research I presented in conferences back then. This must be what he is referring to, and I elaborate on my earlier response.

"I'm still interested in women's exercise, but I have grown increasingly fascinated with the new ways of writing that have become more prominent in the social sciences. I'm talking about that here in my presentation."

"Oh really, what session are you in?" he asks.

"The next one. In this room," I say.

"I might come and listen," he promises, before walking away to get some coffee.

Session

I see the other presenters, all of whom I have met earlier over lunch, sitting in the front row with other delegates scattered behind them. Not everyone went shopping, I think. I say hello to the session chair and take a seat among the presenters, all of whom have copies of their neatly printed papers on their laps. I think again about my paper: Why did I decide to write about such a personal experience when I could have just analyzed the body experiences of other female aerobicizers using quotes from my dissertation? Or I could have read my latest paper, a theoretical examination of the dancing body. Perhaps this was a big mistake? But then I remember what inspired me to write this paper.

A few years ago, I was part of a conference panel on new voices in ethnography. I talked about a paper on tourism I had recently published (Markula, 1997a). This paper was based on my personal experiences as a tourist in Tahiti and its premise was a travel diary through which I, the ethnographer, reflected on my trip. In that paper, I analyzed my personal experience in a separate theoretical discussion on authenticity and nostalgia in postmodern culture. At the conference, I focused on the meaning of including the ethnographer's personal experiences within the research text. Deriving from Norman Denzin (1997), who points out that as ethnographers we have always involved ourselves within our texts because, through ethnographic research, our lives inevitably become entangled with the lives of others, I challenged the traditional professional/personal division in ethnographic writing. I further justified turning my personal experience into a professional account by quoting Edward Bruner (1993), who finds that separating the professional and personal artificially breaks the unified field experience into a process and a product. "Due to the heightened awareness of self-reflexivity," I said in my conference presentation, "many ethnographers now celebrate their subjectivity by weaving their identities and locations together with their field observations into one colorful text" (Markula, 1997b, p. 3). Such vivid writing, I continued, is best accomplished through more experimental modes of writing styles that emphasize the subject's experience. Personal experience, I cautioned, should not replace theory, but enact and embody it. My tourism paper, with its separate diary and theory sections, was exactly such a hybrid of personal narrative and scholarly analysis. I then concluded my presentation by stating that we should openly celebrate personal experiences in order to become aware of our taken-for-granted Western conceptualizations that we, no doubt, bring to our research projects . . .

Clapping signals the end of the first paper. The chair decides to move on to the next presentation and have questions collectively at the end of our session. The following presenter examines her subjects' sport experiences by reading three short stories. I enjoy her experimentation with storied writing, and again I am left feeling increasingly uncomfortable with my own paper. Instead of a personal story, why didn't I write a theoretical discussion of the possibilities provided by new ways of writing? That was what I wrote originally in my abstract. I am not sure what made me change my topic. Particularly, as that would have complemented the other presentations brilliantly. Now my highly personal account will stand embarrassingly alone. But this is not the first time I have struggled with this paper. I have always felt self-conscious about dwelling publicly on such a personal aspect of my life as my body.

At that same conference where I urged other ethnographers to embrace their personal experiences as part of their research projects, I participated in another session about body-image issues in women's exercise. Along with a group of other women presenters, we laid out new information and referred to previous studies to better understand the construction of the female body ideal in the fitness industry and the anxiety it caused women. We emphatically talked about women's attempts to negotiate a subject position within the dominant discursive construction of the feminine body without one reference to our own bodies. I knew that many of us were active exercisers and fitness instructors and looking at the nearly perfect bodies around me, I realized that our own bodies were conspicuously absent from our research. My own ethnography on aerobics depicted me as a bodiless, intellectual academic: I didn't include any references to my own body shape in my research, as if my own body-image experiences, due to my educated academic awareness, were unproblematic. After that session, I felt strongly that the absence of the researcher's embodied voice created a false dichotomy between us, the researchers with no body trouble, and them, the researched who continuously and unsuccessfully battled their body-image problems. Who would take us, I pondered, the body-image experts without a body image problem, seriously?

But how seriously will this audience take my personal story? The next speaker stands up to present her paper on the meaning of partnering in dance. It is a strong paper, theoretically sound, and she argues her case well without situating herself in her research at all. Perhaps I should have used more theory to support my paper? Perhaps, I should have focused on the problems I faced as a researcher of body-image problems? My hands are sweaty, I suddenly realize. I have held on to my paper too tightly; it is all crumpled on the sides. Smoothing it out, I revisit my initial commitment for writing my personal body story.

When I returned home from that earlier conference, where I was hit by the necessity of including the researcher's voice in body image research, I was determined to write my own body story and openly acknowledge how my research into women's body image issues derived from my personal experiences as a physically active woman. My first thought was to supplement my previous realist writing on aerobicizers' body experiences with a personal body account. Such personal confessions of "what really happened" in the field from the point of view of the researcher had begun to appear in connection with many realist ethnographic works. While these confessional tales (Bruner, 1993; Crick, 1995; Richardson, 1994; Sparkes, 1995; Van Maanen, 1988) elaborated on the accompanied realists accounts, they invariably supported their results. But despite the focus on the researcher's own experiences, the emphasis was always on the person's role as an ethnographer, as an academic. I was uninterested in yet another confessional tale of the troubles that a researcher examining other women's body-image problems faced in the field. Rather, I wished to write about my embodied experience as an exercising researcher. To capture such an experience, I had to be evocative, I had to tell a story . . .

It is time for me to present my paper. I stand up and walk slowly to the podium. I turn around and face the audience. I notice how weary they look: they have sunken deep into their chairs, some have closed their eyes, others stare emptily ahead. Once behind the podium, my leg muscles won't stop twitching. My body is safely sheltered by the high podium, however, and I decide to defy the droopy, tired conference mood and start reading my paper. I raise my voice to convey the contradictory relationship I have had with my body. After all, despite my serious body dissatisfaction, I am a Western academic committed to alleviate other women's body struggles through awareness of the social construction of the perfect body.

Questions

I finish reading and I can feel that my face is glowing red, as if I had just completed an exhausting solo dance piece. Like my dance choreography, I have also just "put my body on the line" in a public performance to promote a meaningful message. While I organize my papers, the chair opens the general discussion. The first question is for me.

"In your abstract," an audience member reminds me, "you write about providing a critical reflection on issues of narrative writing. While I know from my own experience," she continues, "that our final papers often take a different form from our abstract, I would be interested in hearing your views on different types of narrative writing as you now merely gave an example of just one."

I knew I should have opted for a theoretical paper, I think quickly to myself. I also realize that the audience has no idea about the troubled path I have led in writing this paper and gaining the confidence to read it aloud in public. Still I try my best to answer the question.

"Writing this paper has probably been one of the most difficult projects for me to complete, as it is quite embarrassing to publicly, in the first person, talk about one's body problems. I previously contemplated just about every form of narrative writing until I finally arrived at the conclusion that this form—an autoethnography—was the best way for me to write this paper. As you know, we have heard examples of other ways of writing social science research today, and all those forms have their role. The issue I struggled the hardest with was the confessional nature of writing about myself. I confronted questions such as, How does one justify including personal experience in research? How does one make personal experience a meaningful part of research writing? Perhaps my next conference presentation," I end my reply by saying, "should focus on these kinds of issues."

Epilogue

My account of the experiences leading up to my conference presentation that summer day in Helsinki should demonstrate how determined I had been to write my personal body story, but that the problem was that I was unsure how to proceed. At that time I had certainly heard of sociological narrative writing, but I had no idea how to attend to my body experiences in a storied way. I was keen to learn, however, so I immersed myself into the literature on new writing practices. This literature was certainly not devoid of possibilities. For example, Dan Rose (1990) declared that "the postmodern moment . . . calls for new forms of ethnography, polyvocal texts, multigenre narratives, impressionistic tales, cinematic reconstructions, lyrical sociology, and poetic anthropology" p. 5). Norman Denzin and Yvonna Lincoln (1994) advocated that problematic moments and meanings in individual's lives should be collected in personal experience, introspective, life story, observational, interactional, or visual texts. Laurel Richardson (2000) found autoethnography, fiction stories, poetry, drama, performative texts, mixed genres, ethnographic fiction, or plain writing stories characterizing the new "ethnographic" writing. While I supported the philosophical rationale for this kind of research writing, I was unclear how to create any of these texts or how they would suit my purpose of writing about my body. I knew how I had struggled to write about my personal tourism experiences in Tahiti. How the editor had insisted on better literary quality for my two-page "travel diary." She returned my manuscript to me three times, requesting more "tension" for the "story." What the hell is tension? I despaired, and rearranged my words yet again. That experience left me thinking that writing in a literary manner was too demanding, and I decided to avoid fictionalized accounts of my body-image troubles. That ruled out ethnographic fiction. Instead of creating characters influenced by imaginary events to illustrate my point, I was more interested in recording my own story. While I did not mind bending some facts for the sake of a more enticing story, my intended work was essentially "autobiographical." I looked into writing genres that were based on the inclusion of the author's voice and my body story started to take the shape of what Andrew Sparkes (1995) described as a narrative of the self and Laurel Richardson (2000) as autoethnography.

Richardson (2000) characterizes autoethnographies as "highly personalized, revealing texts in which authors tell stories about their own lived experiences, relating the personal to the cultural" (p. 11). These are essentially "true stories" about events that really happened to the writer. Their narrative power depends on how well the author can stage her story to evoke the reader to emotionally relive the event with the writer. "In telling the story," Richardson continues, "the writer calls upon such fiction-writing techniques as dramatic recall, strong imagery, fleshed-out characters, unusual phrasing, puns, subtexts, allusion, the flashback, the flashforward, tone shifts, synecdoche, dialogue, and interior monologue" (p. 11) to construct a "plot." Although I was unaware what these techniques might entail, and Richardson did not stop to explain, autoethnography seemed the appropriate form for my personal body story.

Through an autoethnography I hoped to write about my lived body experience in a vivid manner that would resonate with other women. I grew, however, increasingly uncomfortable with the idea of an autoethnography. My uneasiness escalated during a research project I conducted on eating disorders. I came across very revealing personal stories written by anorexics, some of whom were researchers recovering from the illness. While I found their stories very touching, and felt for the sufferers of anorexia, I was unsure what this personal writing added to the knowledge of anorexia already filling the research journals. I then grew ashamed of my passion to write my own body story. If the personal accounts on anorexia, a serious, visible, almost incurable illness, sounded like therapy for the recuperating anorexics rather than valuable research, what would my much more commonplace tale contribute to the research on women's body image? Was my enthusiasm for a personal bodily confession a disguise for therapy? Should I write a diary instead, or confess my problems to a therapist?

Partly, my discomfort derived from my understanding that an autoethnography would contain personal confessions. I was uneasy with the word "confess." In my research on exercising women's body image problems, I had found Michel Foucault's notion of disciplined control through docile bodies persuasive. Foucault believes that telling the truth about oneself and to oneself is a means to ensure control and order in culture. Therefore, confession is used by powerful societal institutions like justice, medicine, and education as a means to control, to normalize, individuals who try to transgress accepted societal boundaries. "One confesses one's sins, one's thoughts and desires, one's illnesses and troubles; one goes on telling, with the greatest precision, whatever is most difficult to tell," says Foucault (1980, p. 59). Carol Spitzack (1990) argues that confession characterizes particularly women's lives. While ultimately a tool of domination, according to Spitzack, confession is framed with promises of liberation and increased self-knowledge. At first, I concluded, my body story might increase my self-knowledge and liberate me to conduct more informed research on other people, but could telling what is most difficult for me to tell, my body-image problems, also act as a normalizing practice?

Concerned with discoursive control, I abandoned my body story project, but continued to experiment with ways of writing myself into my research texts. I wrote evocative accounts that addressed theoretical concerns regarding new ethnographic writing; I experimented with poetry; I attempted an academic presentation combining text with dance movement; and I created a dance performance where I inserted academic text into my choreography. While all of these works were about social issues surrounding the body, movement, and physical activity, my own body experiences still remained unattended. Nevertheless, my suppressed intention on writing a personal body story kept resurfacing, and I started to rethink my previous discomfort with that project.

Perhaps my uneasiness was only an excuse to avoid confronting a deeply personal, but also culturally perplexing issue. To feel comfortable about writing about my body, I obviously had to go beyond a confession. I agreed with Ben Morrison (1998) who asserted that "Confessionalism has to know when to hold back . . . it takes art. Without art, confessionalism is masturbation. Only with art does it become empathy" (p. 11). Evidently, instead of engaging in a mere self-indulgent confession my problems, my personal story had to resonate with the experiences of a larger audience. Morrison recommended that art lifted confession above personal whining, and my research writing, I definitely believed, had insufficient artistic quality. On the other hand, was pure literary artistry sufficient criteria for a worthwhile autoethnographic body story? As a social scientist, I believed that women's varied, but simultaneously strikingly similar personal body experiences stemmed from a specific cultural context. Obviously, then, my story had to depict the context of my body struggle to resonate with other women's experiences. I concluded that it was necessary, after all, to write about my body, but I resolved to emphasize the cultural boundaries of my experience instead of simply complaining about my terrible body troubles. This way, I confirmed, my story would not only function as personal body therapy, but also increase our understanding of women's cultural condition in Western society. As creative ways of writing can effectively and sensitively expose the societal construction of our experiences, I set to write my personal narrative of the body.

I began by jotting down my bodily recollections chronologically. While that was a very efficient way to record my experiences, it did not feel too evocative, neither did it articulate the social nature of my body troubles. Although a mere chronology proved uninteresting, I clearly needed to reflect on the past to make sense of my present body experiences. As I was determined to write about myself as a physically active researcher, a university context, I resolved, would be the most appropriate location for my story. But how would I open this story? How would I frame my experiences? That was when I remembered a recent guest lecture I gave on the female exercising body for the course, Gender and Body. That, I decided, would create a perfect context for my story. In the course of the story, the students' questions about the women's ideal thin, toned, and young body shape could prompt a number of my own recollections about my struggles with my body shape. These recollections could include a memory of myself as an aspiring, but hopelessly plump dancer during my undergraduate years, my time as a lean but muscular aerobics instructor obsessed with exercise, and my troublesome relationship with my aging body. Collectively, I thought, they would present a portrait of me, an educated, feminist academic, attempting to understand her own contradictory body experiences through/with/against/in social theory, as I faced the never ending battle to resist the body ideal in Western culture. My story could end, I thought, with my attempt to confront my body image troubles by engaging in exercise forms like tai chi that de-emphasize the bodily reconstruction. But regardless of this nisus for resistant practice, I would aim to show how I am still faced with my inability to disrupt my own disciplinary gaze. Therefore, I would not offer a clear solution to the ideal feminine body shape. Instead, I would create an open ending that would allow me to emphasize the postmodern cultural context of my life.

Although I still struggle to implement even the simplest evocative writing techniques into my papers, I continue to experiment with new writing forms because I believe in the power of evocative writing to acknowledge the context of the writer's experience as well as the context of the audience's reading. As Richardson (2000) assures, new writing practices "evoke new questions about the self and the subject; they remind us that our work is grounded, contextual, and rhizomatic. They can evoke deeper parts of the self, heal wounds, enhance the sense of self—or even alter one's sense of identity" (p. 11). Certainly, this has happened to me. My experiments with different ways of writing have, not only improved the quality of my writing, but also helped me to refine my sense of self as a feminist researcher and a physically active woman within the contemporary global cultural condition.

NOTE

1. When the events in this chapter took place I was living in New Zealand and working as a lecturer in sport sociology in the Department of Sport and Leisure Studies, University of Waikato.

REFERENCES

Bartky, S. L. (1988). Foucault, femininity, and the modernization of patriarchal power. In I. Diamond & L. Quinby (Eds.), *Feminism & Foucault: Reflections on resistance* (pp. 61–86). Boston, MA: Northeastern University Press.

Bordo, S. (1993). *Unbearable weight: Feminism, western culture, and the body.* Berkeley, CA: University of California Press.

Bruner, E. M. (1993). Introduction: The ethnographic self and the personal self. In P. Benson (Ed.), *Anthropology and literature* (pp. 1–26). Urbana, IL: University of Illinois Press.

Crick, M. (1995). The anthropologist as tourist: An identity in question. In M.-F. Lanfant, J. B. Allcock, & E. M. Bruner (Eds.), *International tourism: Identity and change* (pp. 205–223). London: Sage.

de Certeau, M. (1980). Walking in the city. In S. Hall (Ed.), *Culture, media and language* (pp. 151–160). London: Hutchinson.

Denzin, N. K. (1997). *Interpretive ethnography: Ethnographic practices for the 21st century.* Thousand Oaks, CA: Sage.

Denzin, N. K., & Lincoln, Y. S. (1994). Introduction: Entering the field of qualitative research. In N. K. Denzin & Y. S. Lincoln (Eds.), *Handbook for qualitative research* (pp. 1–17). London: Sage.

Foley, D. (1992). Making the familiar strange: Writing critical sport narratives. *Sociology of Sport Journal, 9,* 36–47.

Foucault, M. (1980). *History of sexuality, Vol. 1: An introduction.* New York: Vintage Books.

Markula, P. (1997a). As a tourist in Tahiti: An analysis of personal experience. *Journal of Contemporary Ethnography, 26*(2), 202–224.

Markula, P. (1997b, November). Writing ethnography, writing the self. Paper presented at the annual conference of North American Society for Sociology of Sport, Toronto, Canada.

Markula, P. (1998). Women's health, physical fitness and ideal body: A problematic relationship. *Journal of Physical Education New Zealand, 31*(1), 9–13.

Morrison, B. (1998). *Too true.* London: Granta Books.

Pollock, D. (1998). Performing writing. In P. Phelan & J. Lane (Eds.), *The ends of performance* (pp. 73–103). New York: New York University Press.

Richardson, L. (1994). Writing as a method of inquiry. In N. K. Denzin & Y. S. Lincoln (Eds.), *Handbook of qualitative research* (pp. 516–529). London: Sage.

Richardson, L. (1997). *Fields of play: Constructing an academic life.* New Brunswick, NJ: Rutgers University Press.

Richardson, L. (2000). New writing practices in qualitative research. *Sociology of Sport Journal, 17,* 5–20.

Rose, D. (1990). *Living the ethnographic life* (Qualitative Research Methods Series 23). Newbury Park, CA: Sage.

Sparkes, A. C. (1995). Writing people: Reflections on the dual crises of representation and legitimation in qualitative inquiry. *Quest, 47,* 158–195.

Sparkes, A. C. (2000). Autoethnography and narratives of self: Reflections on criteria in action. *Sociology of Sport Journal, 17,* 21–43.

Spitzack, C. (1990). *Confessing excess: women and the politics of body eduction.* Albany, NY: State University of New York Press.

Stanley, L. (1992). *The auto/biographical I: The theory and practice of feminist auto/biography.* Manchester: Manchester University Press.

Van Maanen, J. (1988). *Tales of the field: On writing ethnography.* Chicago: University of Chicago Press.

CHAPTER 2

Bodies, Identities, Selves: Autoethographic Fragments and Reflections

Andrew C. Sparkes

Jars

Three small jars. The contents are not visible unless turned upside down. The sides are surrounded by a white seal with "official" writing on it: "specimen for histology," a name—Andrew C. Sparkes, gender—M, DOB—2-7-55, dates—1988, 1994, 2000, and a note detailing the disc levels operated on—L3/L4, L4/L5 (right side), L4/L5, L5/S1 (left side).

I pick them up in turn and hold each one just above eye level so I can see the debris (disc material, bone shavings, and other gristle) in the bottom of the jar. Swishing them around, they move slowly in the formalin that preserves them, long after they should have rotted outside of my body. The bits of me from 1988 and 1994 look blanched and pale, slightly ragged, flaky. The debris from 2000, has more substance, it looks fresher, moves and sinks faster to the bottom. There is a red tinge to the formalin. I suddenly get the urge to smell these remains. The lids come off. I inhale. I inhale memories.

I'm 17. The forwards win the ball, quick ball, good. I check where my opposite number is and drop back deeper. The outside half has the ball. He hears the call, flings a long pass out in front of me. I stretch, fingertips touch, then caress the ball as I hit the line at an angle. I cut air, feeling speed oozing through my lean, sinewy body as it arcs to the right, swerving away from the flailing hands of the tackler. I hear his body crumple to the ground. The crowd roars me on. Lightning strides. Moving so fast the world turns molten, melting in wavy space around me. Detached, floating, I watch myself in slow motion. Every fiber focused on this fluid moment of being, untouchable, balanced, harmonious, running fast, running so fast. A state of grace. Touchdown.

I'm 39. I have walked down this hospital corridor many times before. The navy blue carpet is familiar as are the handrails on either side. Determined not to use these for support, I hobble slowly down an imaginary center line. It's hot and I'm sweating. I'm crying and afraid. Here, in 1988 I had surgery on my lumbar spine. I have the feeling this hospital is soon going to swallow me up again. I want it to, I want this pain to be taken away.

Stopping for a rest I turn toward Kitty, my partner, 6 months pregnant. "Déjà vu," I say to her, "It's happening again." The tears well up in her eyes. We hold each other close in the corridor. I kiss the tears on her cheeks. I kiss her eyes, I want to drown and be saved in the blueness of those eyes. As the roundness of her stomach presses against me, a wave of guilt washes over me. Kitty is pregnant, so tired, caring for Jessica, our three-year-old, now having to worry and cope with the stress of me and my body failure. My uselessness makes me angry with my body. At that moment I hate it intensely.

An elderly woman is coming out of the shop. She is limping in a similar pattern to me. We cross trajectories like some infirm ballet dancers. We do not acknowledge each other. I feel embarrassed at our similarities in gait and our differences in age. People looking at me, but as I catch their eyes they avert their gaze.

I'm 45. Feeling the ice injected into the vein of my right arm. It spreads. Time slipping, sliding, so gently away. Drifting now. Count to ten. One , two, three, four, five, six, seven . . . Is this like dying?

Shivering, shaking. Cold so cold. Teeth chatter uncontrollably. Body twitching.

In the distance. "Andrew . . . Andrew . . . Can you hear me?"

Closer now. Holding my arm. "Andrew. Can you hear me?"

"Ye-ye-ye-yeesss."

"Everything's fine. You're in the post-op room. How are you feeling?"

"C-c-cold."

"He's cold. Let's get some heat on him."

"Andrew, are you in pain?"

"Y-y-y-yes."

"On a scale of 1 to 5, where are you? Five is a lot."

"Four."

"This is morphine I'm giving you. It will help with the pain."

Cotton wool. Cocooned. Warm. Undulating. Pain slips out of my body as silently as it crept in.

Still 45. I feel the tug of the wound and the stitches in my back as I shift my knees to see him better. He sits in a chair at the end of my bed. I look at him. My gaze envelops him, holding his image in my brain. Sitting, doing nothing, just talking, does not come easy to my 76-year-old Dad. Eternally shy and self-conscious, he normally hides behind a newspaper. But now, with me lying once again in a hospital bed, he talks. He tells me stories. Stories about his own youth, growing up fatherless from the age of two, growing up working class, but most of all growing up poor. Stories of the armed forces and national service. Stories of laboring as a shoe cutter in a factory, dreaming of escape from the daily grind, the drudgery, and the brain-numbing boredom. Stories of breaking away, of his dreams and aspirations, his successes and disappointments. But mostly the stories are about sport. It's woven into the tapestry of my Dad's life. He tells me stories of performing bodies, his, mine, my brother's, sportsmen he remembers. All told in the past tense. He tells me stories because he feels my pain, my bewilderment, my confusion about my body, about who I am and who I might become. It's his way of coping, of helping. It's his way of telling me he loves me.

Maybe when I was younger he would have held me in his muscular arms, as I have held my own young son and daughter. Perhaps my childish soft cheeks would have felt the pressure of his chest. I would have smelled him, a young man, a young father, and just perhaps, I might have even heard his heartbeat, as he made the pain, the demons, and the fear go away. Will my own children, Jessica and Alexander, remember me by my smell, will they remember hearing my heart beat when I held them in troubled times and wiped away their tears?

Maybe, I held him tight to me then, hugging him, and feeling my own growing strength in relation to his. Today, I know for sure I want to hold him close and tell him just how much I love him. How, I want him to live forever, to always be there when I fall. I want to squeeze away the anxieties, depressions, and insecurities that have haunted him throughout his life. I want to tell him that whatever mistakes he made, how many things he felt he got wrong, whatever guilt he feels, he is still my *Dad and I'm proud of him. And, whatever else I am, or become, I am still* his *son. Our stories, our lives, forever entangled.*

But I don't. I can't. He is a father, a man, of his time, of his history. It would embarrass him, make him feel uneasy. The words remain unspoken.

This morning the Australian nurse told me I was not allowed out of bed. But my Dad is allowed in, allowed into my room, into a space, a landscape, where once again he can tell stories to his son. I cherish the moment. His stories soak into my bones.

Memories subside.

Now, looking down on the debris, I do something I have never done before. The little finger of my right hand creeps in and touches it. I am surprised at how rough and hard 2000 feels under the pressure of my fingertip. I had expected more give, something smoother, softer, like octopus flesh. Fragments of 1994 and 1988 are softer, but still resistant to my touch. My dead flesh offers no caress.

Suddenly I feel repulsed and ill at ease, like a grave robber disturbed in the early hours of the morning. Knowing I am desecrating holy ground, sensing someone watching me. I put the lids back on and sit very still for a few minutes.

Standing, back aching, I place the jars gently back on the shelf. Silently apologizing to my various bodies and selves that have just been invaded once again by my insensitive prodding. It will be a while before I look at them again. They will not be disturbed.

Later that day, Alexander, my six-year-old son, inquires, "Dad, can you run now?"

Back Again

"Did you enjoy that, my love?" the landlady asks as she takes my plate away.

"Wonderful," I reply, "you can't beat a good fry-up."

"Morning Michael," she says to the young man who briskly enters the breakfast room. "Same as yesterday?"

"Yeah. Thanks, Pat."

As he helps himself to cereal from the table near the window, I watch him. I am a compulsive body watcher. Michael is around six feet tall, in his mid-twenties, lean physique, slightly stooped at the shoulders, jet black, gelled hair, cut very short at the sides but curly and long on top, suntanned face and arms. There is a pink scar about 2 inches long on his left elbow. Flashy watch, crisp white short-sleeved shirt, blue chinos, brown brogues, and a bright yellow, diamond-patterned tie. I assume he's a representative for some company. Most people are who stay at bed and breakfast places like this. I silently nickname him "Rep-Man."

As he turns, I see the freshness of his skin, its tightness, and feel the energy his body contains as it moves him effortlessly toward a table near mine. As he sits, the image of my own face in the mirror as I shaved that morning comes back to me. It looked tired, heavy, and empty. Rep-Man stands easily and refills his glass with orange juice. He has no back pain, I can spot the signs. I am a compulsive observer of bodies in pain.

His ease of movement, once again, reminds me of the resistance I experience each morning as I negotiate the terms of engagement for the day with my own lower back. Today is not too bad considering the train journey up from Exeter to Leamington Spa yesterday, and the strange, soft bed I slept in last night. Just the usual dull, early morning ache, as I sit watching. Nothing unusual.

"Another beautiful day," Rep-Man says as he returns to his table.

"Brilliant," I say. Caught off-guard. I ask "On business?"

"Computers. We're doing a big show in the town hall today."

I was right. He's a Rep.

"How about you?"

"Oh, nothing special. Just a writing workshop," I lied.

Why lie to him? Why not tell him I'm here for a meeting, my second, of an Aging Men's Group? Is it because he's young? Would I have told the truth if he had been middle-aged like me? Or is it because I find it hard to explain to myself, and confront my own insecurities about being a member, the youngest, of such a group? Am I so scared of acknowledging my aging, impaired body to him and myself? After all, he can see it. Would a public naming be an admission of defeat? Am I scared of his youthful disapproval?

"That sounds interesting," Rep-Man says without any hint of irony. He sounds sincere.

"Yes, it is. We meet in the Midlands every three months to

share ideas."

This is less of a lie.

As Rep-Man eats, I think about why I joined the group. About how I read a book by its founder, David Jackson, in which he reflects on his own experiences of his body rapidly falling apart. As I sip my lukewarm coffee, I remember that even though he'd been moving in that general direction for some time, he physically fell apart, cracked up, in the middle of the 1980s. For David, this falling apart provoked an emotional crisis about his masculine identity and raised numerous questions about how gendered identities are located in bodily experience. He wrote with brutal honesty of his fears and anxieties about losing control of his body and senses of self. David opened up about how these fears and anxieties concerning who he was, and who he might become, centered very much on the hidden history of denial he had carried around in his body for so long.

David's story touched me, touched my flesh. Literally, gripped me. Across generations our bodies became connected. We communicated, tentatively at first, about our shared vulnerabilities, fragilities, fears, and sense of loss as men with "failed" bodies. He invited me to join the Aging Men's group. Nervously, unsure of where it would take me, I agreed.

I could have told Rep-Man all of this. I could have, but I didn't. As so often before, I silenced my body.

Rep-Man studies his work sheet for the day.

"Hope your show goes well," I say to him as I pick up my rucksack and take my leave.

"Thanks," he says smiling, "Have a good one."

I bet he makes a lot of sales today. He has an honest face.

Outside, the cool air of the morning touches my face. I inhale, and it slides into my lungs. The sky is a big bright blue, no clouds, just blue. As I adjust my rucksack to get the weight even over my shoulders, I stare at the blue. The street is lined on both sides with grand Georgian houses, mostly white. The early sun makes them shine. Their big sash windows, the eyes, gaze back at me. The green of the gardens is deep and lush. It is a beautiful June day. My body relaxes.

On the corner is a food store. I call in to buy some fruit and several sandwiches. It's kind of an unwritten rule that we all have to take some "healthy" food to share for lunch at the Aging Men's Group. As I pay for them I feel a little guilty about my high-cholesterol fried breakfast.

The hall we are meeting in is about 10 minutes' walk away. I opt for the sunny side of the street, feeling the heat on my shoulders and back of my head as I move on. The silence in the street is interrupted by the scream of a 125cc Yamaha motorbike with a broken silencer. The young male rider is kitted up in bright riding gear, giving it full throttle, and going far too fast. The sound screams in my head. I notice his "L" plates. Another macho ritual. "Wanker," I think to myself.

The sound recedes, and I welcome back the calmness of the morning. In the calm there is a minute tingle in my left buttock. Tiny, tiny, tiny, tiny, so brief, but there. I sense it. Automatically, I stop and adjust my rucksack. In the garden next to me a large tabby cat is sunbathing on the front porch. It stretches itself luxuriantly and its length seems to double. He rolls his head toward me and our eyes meet briefly. He averts his gaze, indifferent to all but the warmth of the sun on his sinewy body. I envy him.

I step forward. There it is again. The tingle. Like when a puppy nips with its tiny sharp teeth. Nothing malicious, just playful. Each step with my left foot initiates the nip. Perhaps I'm slouching more than normal. I imagine the top of my head attached to a string as it gently pulls me upwards to extend my spine. It's gone. For a few steps it's gone. Then, it's back. Only a tingle. "Let it go," I say to myself, "You've been here before. Let it go." Perhaps the effects of the caudal epidural injection I had six months ago are wearing off. Perhaps, there's a thorn in my rucksack that's prodding me as I walk. I check—no thorn. I also check the small compartment in my rucksack where I always carry my anti-inflammatory pills and painkillers. All there. So is the tingle when I begin to walk again. I want to let *it* go. But will it let *me* go?

Deeper now in my left buttock I feel it. Sharper, tugging, less playful now. With each left step I wait for the brief cut of pain. How far have I walked? No idea. Looking back behind me I guess at 500 meters. Make it to the hall and rest, but how far is it. Left step—*stab*. Right step—fine. Left step—*stab*. Right step—fine. Left step—*stab*. Left, left, left—*stab, stab, stab* . . . Stand still, lift left foot off the ground. Stand still, take all the weight on the right foot. Relief. Stand still. Move. Left step—*stab*.

Breathe slowly. Don't get scared. It could be a pulled muscle. The soft bed last night might have jiggled the back. It's deeper now. The glutes on the left side move into spasm as the brain tells them the spine is in trouble. Deeper now, deeper, as the electrical message moves on into the outside of my left thigh. Moving on. Smaller steps, carefully, delicately taken. The first flash into the outside of my calf. The foot hardly touching the ground now. The searing slash from lower back to left foot.

Ears listen. No hearing. Eyes see. No sight. The world, my world, collapsing, into the left side of my lower body. I *am* my left limb. I am the space between pain and no pain. I stand still. I cannot take one more step.

A low garden wall. Sit. Relief—the spasm subsides. Other parts of my body speak to me, welcome me back. Mouth dry. The taste of bacon lingers from breakfast. I hear my heart beat. It's fast. I feel it thumping against my T-shirt that clings to me with the sweat. A rivulet of sweat weaves its way down the nape of my neck. The wet patch between my shoulder blades is sticky. My body oozes a fear, a fear of pain to come. A fear of moving once again into another world of slowness, impairment, disability, and otherness.

Where am I? Did I turn left or right out of the street? Where is the hall from here? I can't remember. Time and space have dissolved. Taking a map from my rucksack, I get my bearings. I chart a course for the hall. Laughter erupts from somewhere inside me. A map, a bloody map! For what? Where is the map for where my body is going to take me? It doesn't work that way. My laughter goes quiet. I go quiet, very quiet.

Stand. No pain. Could it have been a one-off? Who am I kidding? Within twenty steps the illusion is shattered. I'm shattered, fragmented. The cycle begins to repeat itself. Thirty minutes more with stops. I make it to the hall. For the morning I inhabit a space with seven other aging men. They are kind, gentle, men who would offer me support if only I would share my fears with them. I don't. I drift in and out of the conversations. Perhaps they feel I'm aloof, not committed, not entering into the spirit of things.

Sitting and moving in the hall causes no problems. After lunch, on such a beautiful day, one of the aging men suggests that we all go for a walk along the nearby canal. Readily, I agree, having swallowed a large number of painkillers during the morning without anyone noticing. As we walk, I make excuses so I can stop and rest. Ahead, some old railway sleepers underneath a horse chestnut tree give me a chance to escape from the group. I excuse myself, saying I just want to sit and watch the ducks feeding for a while. The men walk on. I watch them get smaller. Once they are out of sight, I begin my slow, limping, journey back to the hall. To lie down, to wait, to gather my strength for the afternoon.

They're back

"Are you tired?" one of them asks.

"Yeah, a bit knackered actually. Didn't get much sleep last night in the B&B," I lied.

We decide to each write one line of our own about the walk, and then arrange the lines into a poem. I thought of them walking away from me as I sat under the tree and wrote, "Aging men walking in pairs. Their reflections follow closely behind them."

I couldn't follow, and I didn't once look at my own reflection in the water.

Pub Walking

Mike, a work colleague, stands in the doorway of my office. He looks as tired as I feel at the end of a tough academic week.

"Thank Christ it's a Friday," I say to him. "Fancy a beer?"

"You read my mind," he laughs. "How about the Fire House?"

"Sounds good. Give me ten minutes to get my gear together."

It's cold as we walk down the hill into town. As we talk work, I look at the window displays in the shops. I watch people moving around me. I notice some stars already out. In recent weeks, my gaze has extended beyond the immediate vicinity of the pavement in front of me—my "falling down" range. My universe has expanded.

I feel the rhythm of Mike's gait beside me. I'm matching him. My flesh is warming to the pace and deflects the cold February air from my face. We've already walked over 600 meters. I couldn't have managed this four months ago. There is pleasure in my movement. Of being, melted, in the moment. I turn to Mike, pro-pelling my words at him with evangelical zeal.

"All these people. They do it without thinking. It's so easy for most of them. They don't understand. It's a privilege. It really is an incredible privilege and they should cherish it. *Never* take it for granted."

"What? Sorry?" Mike says, confused at my outburst. "You've lost me."

"Walking. Just walking. Walking to the pub. It's such a wonder-ful privilege. It really is. I know. Believe me, I *know*."

Humoring me, Mike replies with a smile, "I'm sure you do, Andy."

I hope he never needs to know.

I enjoy the privilege while it lasts.

Until the next time.

Writing Autoethnographically: Some Reflections

In recent years, despite their merits in certain contexts and for cer-tain purposes, I have become increasingly dissatisfied with being the absent author, the silent voice, in the traditional realist tales I tell about others. I have also been concerned about becoming unidimensional as a researcher and as a person in terms of how I come to understand the social world around me, my place in it, and how I convey this understanding to myself and others. Against this backdrop, I have drawn strength from the narrative turn in the social sciences which has helped me realize that writ-ing is a method of inquiry, a way of knowing, a method of discov-ery and analysis (Richardson, 2000). Following Bochner (2001), this narrative turn has enabled me to move, when necessary, "away from facts and towards meanings; away from master nar-ratives and towards local stories; away from idolizing categorical thought and abstracted theory towards embracing the values of irony, emotionality, and activism; away from assuming the stance of disinterested spectator and toward assuming the posture of a feeling, embodied, and vulnerable observer; away from writing es-says and toward telling stories" (pp. 134–135).

Accordingly, I have attempted to expand my writing-knowing repertoire (Sparkes, 1995), and have experimented with alternative genres, such as, confessional tales (Sparkes, 1994a, 1998a), ethnographic fiction (Sparkes, 1997a), and autoethnography (1996, 1999a, this chapter). I'm still experimenting. In so doing, like Richardson (2001), I come increasingly to "absolutely respect the power, mystery, and complexity of writing" (p. 34).

As part of this experimentation, writing autoethnographically (see Ellis, 1997, 1999; Ellis & Bochner, 2000), has raised a number of issues for me. First, it has helped me recognize how, in my "normal" academic writing I maintain tightly secured boundaries within me and beyond me, keeping various identities and selves separate, shored up, and protected from the swirling confusions I so often experience in my daily life. In this writing I tend to privilege rigor over imagination, intellect over feeling, theories over stories, and abstract ideas over concrete events. Here, the intellect dominates the emotions. Like Bochner (2001), I become a *divided self*, in which fragments of me become distanced spectators to the lives of other people and my own, seeing but not touching or embracing each other. As Bochner (1997) observes, "The sad truth is that the academic self frequently is cut off from the ordinary experiential self. A life of theory can remove one from experience, make one feel unconnected" (p. 421). He adds, "Academic life is impersonal, not intimate. It provides a web of distractions. The web protects us from the invasion of helplessness, anxiety, and isolation we would feel if we faced the human condition honestly" (p. 421).

Over the years, perhaps like many men, I have often found it easier to cloak myself in the "web of distractions" and maintain a gulf between my academic and personal world. Various bio-graphical disruptions and interrupted body projects have, how-ever, collapsed these worlds into each other and shattered the il-lusion of separation. In the process, it became evident that my grasp of the scholarly literature and the received knowledge I gained from this did not help me as much as I hoped it would to understand the various epiphanies in my life that revolved around issues of embodiment. As such, I find myself empathizing with Bochner (1997), who realized that even though he had studied, taught, and theorized about loss and attachment for more than two decades, he didn't really begin to *know* loss until he experienced his father's death. Reflecting on this issue Bochner comments:

> And the more I thought about my experience of loss, read other people's accounts of loss, and reviewed the theoretical and research literature, the more I began to understand that the academic world was not in touch with the everyday world of experience, the ordinary world. The research literature offered me data, labels, categories, and theoretical explanations but it didn't express how loss felt and it didn't invite engagement with the particularities of the experience. (p. 424)

Similarly, my own "theories" often didn't connect to how I was feeling and experiencing life with regard to my "problematic" body over the years. A body that engaged in elite performance during its younger days, but acquired a chronic lower back problem at the age of twenty that terminated my involvement in top class sport (see Sparkes, 1996). Since then, this lower back problem has continued to interrupt my life on a regular basis and has led to numerous bouts of manipulative therapy by osteopaths and chiropractors to keep me mobile and alleviate acute episodes of pain, four series of sclerosing injections into the ligaments around my lumbar vertebrae, three courses of epidural injections, one manipulation under general anaesthetic, and surgery on my lumbar spine in 1988, 1994, and 2000 to remove prolapsed discs. Acute episodes of intense back pain come without warning, and a dull aching pain in my lumbar region is a constant companion. I have good days and bad days.

By stating that a lot of theories have not always connected to my own experiences over the years, I am not trying to devalue the use of abstract theory or deny its relevance for specific purposes in specific contexts. Neither do I want to suggest that we should never use stories as data. Researchers from a variety of disciplines are rightly interested in autobiographical tales both as a cultural product and a social act, as well as a resource for investigating changing ideas about the body, self, and identity. Indeed, I share these interests (e.g., see Dévis & Sparkes, 1999; Sparkes, 1994b, 1998b; Sparkes & Smith, 1999; in press). Rather, my plea it that, on occasions, we consider repositioning our theories and data in relation to the life as lived, and be a little more cautious about how, when, and why we turn storied lives into categories and theories.

As Frank (1991) argues, "The grounding of theory must be the body's consciousness of itself . . . Only on this grounding can theories put selves into bodies and bodies into societies" (p. 91). In challenging the tyranny of abstraction, Frank goes on to suggest that bodies certainly do have problems among other bodies, "but the point is to hold on to the fundamental embodiment of these problems rather than allowing the problems to be abstracted from the needs, pains, and desires of bodies" (p. 91). In this regard, autoethnographies can help us to hold onto the fundamental embodiment of problems and keep us closely connected to the needs, pains, and desires of bodies. Furthermore, as Bochner (2001) points out in relation to personal narratives:

> We can call on stories to make theoretical abstractions, or we can hear stories as a call to be vigilant to the cross-currents of life's contingencies. When we stay with a story, refusing the impulse to abstract, reacting from the sources of our own experience and feelings, we respect the story and the human life it represents, and we enter into personal contact with questions of virtue, of what it means to live well and do the right thing. (p. 132)

Writing autoethnographic stories has brought me into contact with "questions of virtue, of what it means to live well and do the right thing." This has provided a means for me to develop a greater sense of integration between the concerns that infuse the "private" and "public," or "academic," domains of my life. Whereas before, I called upon separate voices to engage with these divided worlds, suppressing one at the expense of the other, I now feel more willing and able to combine them in the same writing arena. Like Richardson (1992), however, I do not know where this attempt at integration will take me.

As indicated above, writing autoethnographically has also encouraged me to accept and nurture my own voice(s), and acknowledge the multiple subjectivities and positions I inhabit. For example, in constructing "Jars," "Back Again," and "Pub Walking," my chosen positioning for these stories is that of a "wounded storyteller" (Frank, 1995). As such, the stories are not just *about* my body. Rather, the stories are told *through* my wounded body. They come out of my body. As Frank reminds us, "The body sets in motion the need for new stories when disease disrupts the old stories. The body, whether still diseased or recovered, is simultaneously cause, topic, and instrument of whatever new stories are told" (p. 2).

Writing autoethnographically, therefore, provides me with an opportunity to give voice to my body (wounded or otherwise) in different ways. This in turn allows my changed and changing body to, once again, become familiar to me as a storyteller engaged in the process of constructing new maps and new perceptions of my relationships to the world. Thus, as Frank (1995) might argue, turning my problematic body into a story transforms fate into experience. Consequently, the problems that set my body apart from others becomes, in the stories that open this chapter and others I have told elsewhere (Sparkes, 1996, 1999b), a common bond of suffering that joins me with other bodies in their shared vulnerability.

This joining with others is possible because writing autoethnographically can be both a *sacrament* and a *call to witness*. For Richardson (2001) writing about one's life and producing personal stories can be a sacrament. To her, this means two things:

> Experiencing the flow of writing and experiencing *connectedness to others*. The sense of time and space as separate is undermined, re-understood as deeply interrelated. As you write, you can find yourself connected to others; the meaning you construct about your life connects you to others, making communion—community —possible. (p. 37, italics mine)

Importantly, this potential for connection, of communion, is *reduced* when the autoethnographer takes the role of *declarative author-persuader* (Barone, 1995), producing texts that are meant to impart knowledge by orchestrating selected voices in certain ways, shutting out other voices, and limiting interpretive options (see Sparkes, in press a). Thus, for example, in the story "Back Again" I could, acting as a declarative author-persuader, have begun with the following quotation by Leder (1990):

> But pain strikes one alone. Unlike the feel of the cool wind, pain is marked by an interiority that another cannot share . . . pain tends to induce self-reflection and isolation. It effects a *spatiotemporal constriction* . . . The disruption and constriction of one's habitual world thus corresponds with a new relation to one's body. In pain, the body, or a certain part of the body, emerges as an *alien presence*. The sensory insistence of pain draws the corporeal out of self-concealment, rendering it thematic. No event more

radically and inescapably reminds us of our bodily presence. Yet at the same time pain effects a certain alienation . . . The painful body is often experienced as something foreign to the self. (pp. 74–76, italics mine)

Having legitimized my text by an appeal to a formal authority, I could then have adopted a more distanced and detached writing stance towards events in "Back Again." For example, I could have written, "Walking down the street, the first signs of sciatica were felt in my left buttock. As I continued walking, things got progressively worse until I had to stop. I realized my back problem had returned and felt anxious." I could then have drawn on a range of academic theories to frame this flattened-out, surface story. Here, I would *tell* you what these events mean with regard to pain. Of course, the act of telling is not without value. However, I want to *show* you my pain, my panic, my spatiotemporal constriction, alien presence, and so on. I want to invite you to experience these sensations with me. I want you to feel them in your bodies, in mine, and the bodies of others. I want to evoke a response.

For example, in an attempt to take the reader into pain, its intensification, and the threat of pain to come, I use the incident with the noisy motorbike—an event outside my body that assaults my senses—as a counterpoint to an event within my body that signals a different kind of assault to come. Thus, in the returning calmness of the morning, "there is a minute tingle in my left buttock. Tiny, tiny, tiny, tiny, so brief, but there. I sense it." This tingle, this warning of what is to come, is described as "Like when a puppy nips with its tiny sharp teeth. Nothing malicious, just playful." But as I move down the street the pain intensifies. To give the reader a sense of this, and also a sense of how pain is connected to the rhythm of my walking, I write, "Deeper now in my left buttock I feel it. Sharper, tugging, less playful now. With each left step I wait for the brief cut of pain . . . Make it to the hall and rest, but how far is it. Left step—*stab*. Right step—fine. Left step—*stab*. Right step—fine. Left step—*stab*. Left, left, left—*stab, stab, stab* . . . Stand still, lift left foot off the ground. Stand still, take all the weight on the right foot. Relief. Stand still. Move. Left step—*stab*."

Moving on, things get worse, pain is spreading, hurting more, and I signal this to the reader by introducing new body parts and using different adjectives to describe the pain: "It's deeper now. The glutes on the left side move into spasm . . . Deeper now, deeper, as the electrical message moves on into the outside of my left thigh . . . The first flash into the outside of my calf . . . The searing slash from lower back to left foot." Thus, the rhythm of pain moves from the playful nip of the puppy to the stab. Pain moves from the tingle to something that is deep, searing, flashing, and slashing. Using such words and phrases, I attempt to invite the reader into pain.

Similarly, as with pain, I could have drawn on numerous theories and concepts about narrative, the body, self, and identity to frame my stories (see Sparkes, 1997b). For example, in considering the relationship between narrative and reality, Neisser (1994) provides four controversial categories, not accepted by everyone, with regard to autobiographical memory:

> (1) actual past events and the *historical self* who participated in them; (2) those events as they were experienced, including the individual's own *perceived self* at the time; (3) the *remembering self*, that is, the individual in the act of recalling those events on some later occasion; and (4) the *remembered self* constructed on that occasion. (p. 2, italics original)

Neisser (1994) later speaks of the *oblivious self*, and notes how "autobiographical memory is best taken with a grain of salt. The self that is remembered today is not the historical self of yesterday, but only a reconstructed version. A different version—a new remembered self—may be reconstructed tomorrow" (p. 8). Again, I could have included this as a direct quotation, adopted a more distanced writing stance, and *told* you about how these different selves operate in relation to identity construction and reconstruction within parts of my story. However, in my stories, I choose to show you these selves in action.

For example, in the story "Jars," the remembering self is signaled when, having picked up the three jars, "I suddenly get the urge to smell these remains. The lids come off, I inhale, I inhale memories." The remembered selves are there in jars that contain the corporeal debris of 1988, 1994, and 2000 and which are preserved "long after they would have rotted outside of my body." These remembered selves are connected to the historical selves created in the stories told of me when "I'm 17," "I'm 39," "I'm

45," and "Still 45," years of age. These, in turn, are informed by the perceived selves who experienced the events at the time. Thus, a number of stark contrasts are offered to the reader. For example, there is the non-problematic, performing, seventeen-year-old, sinewy, sporting body-self, that cuts air, and feels speed oozing though it. This body moves so fast "the world turns molten, melting in wavy space around me." In contrast, the thirty-nine-year-old body-self is problematic. It hobbles and limps. It feels useless, anxious, fearful, embarrassed, and guilty. "My uselessness makes me angry with my body. At that moment I hate it intensely." Thus, the various selves that Neisser (1994) talks of are actually woven into, and played out within the story of "Jars" and my other stories. As a consequence, the reader is invited to feel my various selves in action, and to engage with them in relation to their own historical, perceived, remembering, remembered, and oblivious selves as they read the text.

In providing these invitations, following Bochner and Ellis (1996), I do not want my stories to be consumed as "knowledge" or received passively. I don't want readers to sit back as spectators. I want to engage them and evoke a response. I want readers, whatever their positioning in relation to me, to feel, care, and desire when they read my stories. Clearly, such aspirations provide a number of general writing challenges that I, and other producers of autoethnographies, need to confront (see Sparkes, 1996, in press a). For example, how might I communicate the subjectivity of key moments in my life so that the world of lived experience is made directly accessible to the reader? How might I write the body-self and produce a narrative that draws readers in, engages them, and provokes their feelings so that they experience, or could experience, the events being described? How might I develop an embodied narrative that acknowledges the enabling properties that stem from me *having a body*, while also recognizing the constraints that follow from the fact of me *being a body*?

Furthermore, how might I write about my own biographical disruptions and interrupted body projects in ways that are themselves as disruptive, fragmented, and as emotionally charged as the events they describe? How might I write so that I shrink the distance between myself as the experiencing subject and my accounts of lived experience? How might I write about body-self and time-space relationships in ways that fuse the personal and the societal in autobiographical forms of inquiry? Finally, how might I write so that the warping tyranny of dualisms such as subjectivity/objectivity, masculine/feminine, able–bodied/disabled, young/old, and so on are dissolved?

Meeting these challenges is difficult. However, when they are met, when autoethnographers show rather than tell, when they call upon a variety of evocative forms of representation, such as poetic representations, ethnodrama, and ethnographic fiction (see Richardson, 2000; Sparkes, 1995; in press a), then the potential for connection, for communion, is greatly enhanced. Writers of autoethnography, therefore, need the courage and confidence to relinquish the role of declarative author persuader and write as *artfully–persuasive storytellers*. For Barone (1995), this kind of storyteller *trusts* the reader, understands the necessity of relinquishing control, of allowing readers the freedom to interpret and evaluate the text from their unique vantage points, and will coax the reader into participating in the imaginative construction of literary reality through carefully positioned blanks, or interpretive spaces, in the writing.

My intention is that my stories contain a lot of interpretive spaces, inviting the active reader to fill them with personal meanings gathered from outside the text. Here, following Barone (1995), my aim is not to prompt a single, closed, convergent reading but to persuade readers to contribute answers to the dilemmas my stories pose. Tsang (2000) notes in her attempt to convey to the reader a sense of her own varied, ambivalent, confusing but sometimes definite relationship to her multiple identities, "My belief is that an engaging story can relate this sense to you in such a way that you can identify with it on a personal level, using your own experience to understand and empathize with my experience" (p. 46). Similarly, Ellis (1997), reflecting on one of her own pieces of autoethnographic writing, comments as follows:

> My open text consciously permitted readers to move back and forth between being in my story and being in theirs, where they could fill in or compare their experiences and provide their own sensitivities about what was going on. I attempted to write in a way that allows readers to feel the specificity of my situation, yet sense the unity of human experience as well,

in which they can connect to what happened to me, remember what happened to them, or anticipate what might happen in the future. I wanted readers to feel that in describing my experience I had penetrated their heads and hearts. I hoped they would grapple with the ways they were different and similar to me. (p. 131)

My hope is that the stories I have told in this chapter, as open texts, invite readers in, enticing them to think and feel *with* the story being told rather than *about* it. In distinguishing between thinking with a story as opposed to thinking about it, Frank (1995) points out, "To think about a story is to reduce it to content and then analyze that content. Thinking with stories takes the story as already complete; there is no going beyond it. To think with a story is to experience it affecting one's own life and to find in that effect a certain truth of one's life" (p. 23). In reflecting on the possibilities of theorizing with stories and not just about them, Frank points to the need to respect the integrity of the story *as a story*.

The first lesson of thinking with stories is not to move on once the story has been heard, but to continue to live in the story, becoming in it, reflecting on who one is becoming, and gradually modifying the story. The problem is truly to listen to one's own story, just as the problem is to truly listen to other's stories. (p. 165)

Clearly, thinking with stories calls for a different kind of reading than many academics are used to, and it also calls upon them to write differently. However, combining these in the form of autoethnography can provide a valuable resource that enables another person's world of experience to inspire critical reflection on one's own. Here, readers recontextualize what they know already in light of their encounter with someone else's life. This may not always be a pleasant experience. When an autoethnography strikes a chord in readers, it may change them, and the direction of change cannot be predicted. As such, well-crafted autoethnographies can act as an *occasion for conspiracy* that, according to Barone (1990) involves, "a conversation about the relationship between present and future worlds. The reader, a historically situated self, learns from the re-created other in the text to see features of a social reality that may have gone previously unnoticed" (p. 314). At its best, when readers resonate with the story told, they borrow it for their own. When this happens, Barone suggests, there is a *breathing together* as people share ideas and ideals for the purposes of an improved reality. Hence, the conspiracy "is a plot against inadequate present conditions in favor of an emancipatory social arrangement in the future" (p. 314).

In the above sense, autoethnographic stories like mine can also become a call to *witness* for both the author and the reader. For example, speaking of those living with a chronic illness, Frank (1995) notes that becoming a witness means assuming "a responsibility for telling what happened. The witness offers testimony to a truth that is generally unrecognized or suppressed. People who tell stories of illness are witnesses, turning illness into moral responsibility" (p. 137). Frank distinguishes between the witness in the traffic court and the illness witness. Both speak on the authority of being there, but the latter's testimony is less of seeing and more of *being*. This testimony, according to Frank, *implicates* others in what they witness. Witnessing is never a solitary act, and it always implies a relationship. Ill persons, Frank argues, tell themselves stories all the time, but they cannot testify to themselves alone—"part of what turns stories into testimony is the call made upon another person to receive that testimony" (p. 141).

For Ropers-Huilman (1999) acts of witnessing occur "when we participate in knowing and learning about others, engage with constructions of truth, and communicate what we have experienced to others" (p. 23). These acts can have powerful consequences. For example, she argues that witnessing affects one's persona in its entirety, "our bodies, hearts, and souls are changed and renewed by what we witness in our lives . . . Witnessing is powerful. There are great opportunities and dangers inherent in the process of witnessing others' lives and constructing meanings about those experiences" (p. 24).

The same, of course, is true for the writer who is also called to act as witness to his or her own story once it is produced. According to Richardson (2001), we do not live lives, we live plotlines. Thus, writing autoethnographically can lead us to discover new things about our selves and our world: "we have the possibility of writing new plots; with new plots come new lives. One's life always exceeds the cultural script for it; we are not cultural clones" (p. 37). Thus, for the author comes the possibility of first recognizing entrenched cultural narratives and dominant "master" narratives, and then rejecting them by writing in ways that both resist and challenge the accepted norm. As part of this process the author might ask: What are the stories that currently shape my life? How do they constrain and empower me? How do they constrain and empower others? Do I want to change? What might be the new story? What might be the plot-line? How can I resist and alter the old ones? How do I change? How can my stories connect to those of others to become part of a new collective-story? (see Richardson, 1990; Sparkes, 1997b, 1999b).

As an active reader of my own autoethnographies, I have been forced to ask many difficult questions. For example, in what ways have I colluded with various forms of hegemonic masculinity and how has this adversely shaped not only my own life experiences, but also the experiences of those I am connected to? I am forced to ask, following Frank (1995), questions about *body-relatedness*. Do I *have* a body, or *am* I a body? I also have to ask questions about *other-relatedness*. For example, just what is my relationship, as a body, to other persons who are also bodies? How does our shared corporeality affect who we are, not only to each other, but more specifically *for* each other?

In grappling with these questions, writing autoethnographically has helped me (and others) recognize better the stories, or plot-lines, interwoven over time into my life that have shaped the construction of a specific kind of male who has been, and still is, encouraged to make significant emotional investments in a *disciplined body* that defines itself primarily in actions of *self-regimentation*. The most important action problem for this kind of body is that of *control*, and when faced with a loss of control it attempts to reassert *predictability* through therapeutic regimens. This single-minded pursuit of regimens transforms the body into an "it" to be treated and the self becomes dissociated from this "it." As Frank (1995) points out, a self dissociated from its body will rarely seek and discover terms of association with others, so the disciplined body becomes *monadic*. That is, in terms of its other-relatedness, the monadic body, comes to understand itself as existentially separate and alone.

Recognizing the storylines that inform the disciplined body, and how they have, and still do, operate to shape me, enables me to ask questions about the possibility of change. For example, how might I challenge and change the storylines associated with the disciplined body in order to negotiate a different body–self relationship that enables me to live differently in the world *as* a body and *being* a body? How might I begin to reconstruct myself in terms of the idealized type described by Frank (1995) as a *communicative or communing body*? This kind of body accepts its contingency as part of the contingency of life. Bodily prediction is regarded as exceptional, and contingency comes to be accepted as normative. Furthermore, this contingent body is fully *associated* with itself and exists in a *dyadic*, shared, and empathetic relationship to others. According to Frank this kind of body represents, "an ethical *choice* to place oneself in a different relationship to others. This choice is to be a body *for* other bodies . . . Dyadic bodies exist *for* each other: they exist for the task of discovering what it means to live for other bodies" (p. 37).

Clearly, the communicative body is very different from the disciplined body. Furthermore, as I have argued elsewhere (Sparkes, 1996), the reflexivity encouraged by writing autoethnographically does not guarantee that any new body–self relationships will arise phoenix like from the text. Attempting to change from a disciplined body to a communicative body (or any other idealized type), is an extremely dynamic, difficult, complex, delicate, and precarious process. For example, how does one begin to emotionally disinvest in one particular kind of body and reinvest in another? What kind of alternative, or subversive, body stories are available to act as narrative resources and assist this process of change? How do people gain access to alternative narratives? What support (e.g., social, moral, emotional, physical, and economic) do people need to act on these alternative narratives once they are found?

In view of the difficulties of bringing about real personal change, in one's self and others, it is important not to claim too much for autoethnographic writing. It is not a process imbued with magical properties, and even though there may be magical moments, these are not guaranteed. Having said this, it is equally important to acknowledge the potential this form of writing has to act as a powerful catalyst for both individual and collective change, as well as to recognize how such writing is able to support and inform the change process over time. If nothing else, as I hope I have demonstrated in this chapter, autoethnographies can make a contribution by generating an awareness of the stories and plot-lines that shape us, so that we can better understand these stories prior to rejecting them. In relation to this, Frank (1995) notes that the moral imperative of narrative ethics "is perpetual self-reflection on the sort of person that one's story is shaping one into, entailing the requirement to change that self-story if the wrong self is being shaped" (p. 158).

So far, in this chapter, I have tried to indicate a number of benefits from engaging with autoethnography. It would, however, be remiss of me not to mention that there are also risks involved. As Richardson (2001) points out, writing about one's life is not without its perils.

> Writing about your life brings you to strange places; you might be uncom-fortable about what you learn about yourself and others. You might find yourself confronting serious ethical issues. Can you write about your de-partment without serious consequences to yourself and your students? What about your family? Who might be hurting? How do you balance "fact" and "fiction"? How do you write a "true" ethnography of your experiences? These questions, of course, are the ones that contemporary ethnographers ask themselves when they try and write up their "data" about other people. How different it feels when it is you and your world that you are writing about; how humbling and demanding. How up-front and personal-in-your-face become the ethical questions, the most impor-tant of all questions, I think. (pp. 37–38)

Furthermore, the academic world is not prone to welcoming with open arms those within its ranks who produce alternative forms of representation such as autoethnography (Richardson, 1997). Making public my fears, fragilities, and vulnerabilities has not en-deared me to a great many scholars, particularly males. I have also been hurt by the trivializing charge of self-indulgence that is so readily leveled by mainstream academics against such work. Even though I have learned to recognize the anxieties and misun-derstandings that fuel this charge, and so gained the confidence to reject it (see Sparkes, 2000, in press b), this charge still has the power to sting and undermine my confidence.

So, in writing autoethnographically there are perils as well as pleasures, possibilities, and potentials. Certainly, many might not be drawn to this genre as a way of exploring lived experience. Others, however, will feel more connected to this form of representation and sense the contribution it can make as a way of knowing that allows both the author, and the reader, to feel and understand differently the world in which we live together as embodied beings.

ACKNOWLEDGMENTS

My thanks to Guy Faulkner, David Jackson, Brett Smith, and Peter Swan for their helpful comments on an earlier draft of this paper. A big thanks also to Jim Denison for his supportive critiques throughout the writing process and for displaying an ethic of care in his role as editor. As ever, my most special thanks goes to Kitty, Jessica, and Alexander for living the stories with me and touching me with their lives.

REFERENCES

Barone, T. (1990). Using the narrative text as an occasion for conspiracy. In E. Eisner & A. Peshkin (Eds.), *Qualitative inquiry in education* (pp. 305–326). New York: Teachers College Press.

Barone, T. (1995). Persuasive writings, vigilant readings, and reconstructed characters: The paradox of trust in educational storysharing. *Qualitative Studies in Education, 8*(1), 63–74.

Bochner, A. (1997). It's about time: Narrative and the divided self. *Qualitative Inquiry, 3*(4), 418–438.

Bochner, A., & Ellis, C. (1996). Talking over ethnography. In C. Ellis & A. Bochner (Eds.), *Composing ethnography* (pp. 13–45). London: Altamira Press.

Bochner, A. (2001). Narrative's virtues. *Qualitative Inquiry, 7*(2), 131–157.

Dévis, J., & Sparkes, A. (1999). Burning the book: A biographical study of a pedagogically inspired identity crisis in physical education. *European Physical Education Review, 5*(2), 135–152.

Ellis, C. (1997). Evocative autoethnography: Writing emotionally about our lives. In W. Tierney & Y. Lincoln (Eds.), *Representation and the text* (pp. 115–139). New York: State University of New York Press.

Ellis, C. (1999). Heartful autoethnography, *Qualitative Health Research, 9*(5), 669–683.

Ellis, C., & Bochner, A. (2000). Autoethnography, personal narrative, reflexivity: Researcher as subject. In N. K. Denzin & Y. S. Lincoln (Eds.), *Handbook of qualitative research (Second edition)* (pp. 733–768). London: Sage.

Frank, A. (1991). For a sociology of the body: An analytical review. In M. Featherstone, M. Hepworth, & B. Turner (Eds.), *The body: Social process and cultural theory* (pp. 36–102). London: Sage.

Frank, A. (1995). *The wounded storyteller.* Chicago: University of Chicago Press.

Leder, D. (1990). *The absent body.* Chicago: University of Chicago Press.

Neisser, U. (1994). Self-narratives: True and false. In U. Neisser & R. Fivush (Eds.), *The remembering self* (pp. 1–18). Cambridge: Cambridge University Press.

Richardson, L. (1990). *Writing strategies: Reaching diverse audiences.* London: Sage.

Richardson, L. (1992). The consequences of poetic representation: Writing the other rewriting the self. In C. Ellis & M. Flaherty (Eds.), *Investigating subjectivity* (pp. 125–140). London: Sage.

Richardson, L. (1997). *Fields of play.* New Jersey: Rutgers University Press.

Richardson, L. (2000). Writing: A method of inquiry. In N. Denzin & Y. Lincoln (Eds.), *Handbook of qualitative research (Second edition)* (pp. 923–948). London: Sage.

Richardson, L. (2001). Getting personal: Writing stories. *Qualitative Studies in Education, 14*(1), 33–38.

Ropers-Huilman, B. (1999). Witnessing: Critical inquiry in a poststructural world. *Qualitative Studies in Education, 12*(1), 21–35.

Sparkes, A. (1994a). Life histories and the issue of voice: Reflections on an emerging relationship. *Qualitative Studies in Education, 7*(2), 165–183.

Sparkes, A. (1994b). Self, silence and invisibility as a beginning teacher: A life history of lesbian experience. *British Journal of Sociology of Education,* 15(1), 93–118.

Sparkes, A. (1995). Writing people: Reflections on the dual crises of representation and legitimation in qualitative inquiry. *Quest, 47,* 158–195.

Sparkes, A. (1996). The Fatal Flaw: A narrative of the fragile body-self. *Qualitative Inquiry, 2*(4), 463–494.

Sparkes, A. (1997a). Ethnographic fiction and representing the absent Other. *Sport, Education and Society, 2*(1), 25–40.

Sparkes, A. (1997b). Reflections on the socially constructed physical self. In K. Fox (Ed.), *The physical self: From motivation to well-being* (pp. 83–110). Champaign, Illinois: Human Kinetics.

Sparkes, A. (1998a). Reciprocity in critical research: Some unsettling thoughts. In J. Smyth & G. Shacklock (Eds.), *Being reflexive in critical educational and social research* (pp. 67–82). London: Falmer.

Sparkes, A. (1998b). Athletic identity: An Achilles' heel to the survival of self. *Qualitative Health Research, 8*(5), 644–664.

Sparkes, A. (1999a). The fragile body-self. In A. Sparkes & M. Silvennoinen (Eds.), *Talking bodies: Men's narratives of the body and sport* (pp. 51–74). SoPhi, University of Jyväskylä: Finland.

Sparkes, A. (1999b). Exploring body narratives. *Sport, Education and Society, 4*(1), 17–30.

Sparkes, A. (2000). Autoethnographies and narratives of self: Reflections on criteria in action. *Sociology of Sport Journal, 17*(1), 21–43.

Sparkes, A. (in press a). *Telling tales in sport and physical activity: A qualitative journey*. Champaign, Illinois: Human Kinetics Press.

Sparkes, A. (in press b). Autoethnography: Self-indulgence or something more? In A. Bochner & C. Ellis (Eds.), *Ethnographically speaking: Autoethnography, literature and aesthetics*. London: Altamira Press.

Sparkes, A., & Smith, B. (1999). Disrupted selves and narrative reconstructions. In A. Sparkes & M. Silvennoinen (Eds.), *Talking bodies: Men's narratives of the body and sport* (pp. 76–92). SoPhi, University of Jyväskylä: Finland.

Sparkes, A., & Smith, B. (in press). Sport, spinal cord injury, embodied masculinities and the dilemmas of narrative identity. *Men & Masculinities*.

Tsang, T. (2000). Let me tell you a story: A narrative exploration of identity in high-performance sport. *Sociology of Sport Journal, 17*(10), 44–59.

CHAPTER 3

Body Talks: I Write

Arto Tiihonen

A Milestone to Freedom

My feet hit the wet cement with a dull thud. The impact rips through my body and stirs my memory. It's still dark. The sun won't be up for hours. The last leaves of autumn rustle as the first breaths of morning pass among the branches. And through the darkness my thoughts focus, but not on the warm café connected to the petrol station ahead of me. They turn inward as time and my journey cease to matter. Is this Finland? I ask, noticing the parked cars, petrol pumps, and lights inside the café. Yes it is, I hear myself answer. And is this me, tired and stumbling, barely awake, hung over . . . ?

It is me. And directly behind me are eight months of compulsory service in the Finnish army—exhausting drills, screaming sergeants—followed by a week of soccer matches and boozing in Poland. But now I am heading home . . .

I move closer to the café. I am stumbling along like a half-submerged canoe. My body feels fragile and vulnerable; I am keeping it under control to prevent some unexpected collapse.

My asthma is troubling me again; I have lived the last few months in a daze—marching, dawn patrols, dribbling the ball up the pitch. On this autumn morning, though, on my way home after being away so long, I am on the brink of being overcome by weariness, and so my thoughts finally begin to unravel . . . I am free, I feel deeply, I am free.

It is the first time in years that I understand what this means. I am free even as a human being. Only a few months earlier I saw my life in such different terms: I was awaiting my breakthrough, I was in magnificent shape, the winter league matches were going splendidly. During the last practice match before a measly illness I made five goals. Then a flu developed into bronchitis; even that wouldn't have spoiled things, but my eagerness led to a recurrence of my asthma. The worst thing, however, was that I wasn't ill enough to be told to rest, so instead I trained and lay awake, trained and lay awake. Finally, I found myself falling asleep at my post. Naturally, I told no one.

Now, walking alone through the dark, I feel that I am sinking. And I no longer care. Only five hundred meters to the café. I am really lumbering, though. And I become aware of the immensity of my freedom. I'm no longer a football player, no longer an athlete. I am a twenty-year-old unburdened by my past—wins, losses, successes, failures. I see my life-line drawn on the black cement; I try not to stray from its path, which right now feels like my only security. Somehow I know that this is where I must stay. It may be the first time in my twenty years that I truly realize that I am coming from somewhere and that I must go somewhere else. Before sport, school, and then the army made my decisions. I took what was passed on to me. After all, that was my job on the field too, to take the ball, bluff, dribble, shoot . . . Score! So there, pressed down against that imaginary line by the heaviness of my body, I creep on, aware for the first time that this line is out of bounds for other people, this is my rut, mine alone. Not even stray balls will bother me here.

I don't know how long the journey took, and I have almost forgotten now where I was coming from. But my goal was the service station's café—a place favored by the local youth after hours. I didn't belong to any regular gang, but still I wanted to get there. In my condition, at that time of the night, it was the only place where I could get in under a roof. But that was not the only reason; the café represented something more. It was along my lifeline, the line toward my future. That was why I continued to move one foot and then the other. It was painful, but a pleasurable pain, nearly masochistic. For once I had the courage to be so weak and insignificant. Nobody saw me, nobody was reading my thoughts. All the same, I was somewhere, I was something, something that I also sensed with such immediacy. I was.

They could well erect a milestone by that petrol station along the southern exit road from my hometown. A milestone where I woke up to adulthood, to the realization that the responsibility was mine. When I at last stepped in from the chilly autumn weather, entering the petrol-smelling café, I had decided what I would do with my life—or at least what I would not do with it. My line as a soccer player, I knew, had hit a wall. And I knew finally that it would not crush me. That was because I saw a new line: a beautiful trajectory across space, unchecked by any outside pressures. The girl at the café had given me an odd look, but I didn't take notice. I was free and confident. I took tea. Coffee would have been too much for my stomach.

A Bike Trip into the Unreality of Sport

The sun is blazing hot above my head. I pedal, pedal. The heavily forested hill rises before me, seemingly endless, and the road climbs its flank like a narrowing, only slightly meandering ribbon. I feel a pain mixed with joy in my calves as I tell my bike to travel faster and faster. My heart is pounding and I hear the rustle of my lungs roaring in my ears. I do not allow myself to slow down; I feel power in my pelvis, endurance in my hocks. The air currents cool my skin where my sweat, after flowing briefly down from its little fountains, dries. I brush the back of my hand across my temples where the salty water is smarting in the corners of my eyes. Otherwise, I am totally focused on the rotation of the axle.

The hillscapes of middle Finland, densely covered by conifers and leafy trees, and the ponds, brooks, and lakes of the low-lying stretches flit by on both sides as I, after reaching a steady pace, cycle on and on. Since I left the main road, where the passing lorries checked my going, the joy and ease of pedaling has turned me into a flowing movement, a flowing thought. Now when my body feels the pleasurable surge of a steady rhythm, and the scenes change at an equally even pace, it is easy to become aware of what is essential.

My journey goes through places where my father's ancestors originally lived a few hundred years back. I picture them, settlers, burn-beaters, fishermen, hunters, woodsmen, and bridge bailiffs for the crown. They moved north beyond the "big water." A good hundred years ago the migration turned back to the south. My great-grandfather and his male descendants lived and still live mostly in a sizeable trading center south of the big lake, engaged in various craftsmen's trades. In other words, in the same place where I spent my childhood and youth. Unlike them, I went first north to university, but found my eventual home in the south, by the sea, in the capital, Helsinki. I consider my family, myself, my history: Where I am coming from, where I am now, where I am going?

The bike moves easily, and as if without noticing I increase my speed. I have cycled nearly a hundred kilometers without a pause, it is just a good twenty kilometers farther to my childhood home, when I decide to pedal flat-out all the way. My pulse quickens, I breathe faster, I already feel the lactic acid making its foray into my muscles. I just go on, pedal and pedal and pedal. I no longer ease off even when the road is going downhill. I just work the pedals unceasingly and in a higher and higher gear.

With such intense exertion strange things happen. My body brings forth impulses that send me back to my youth. I am no longer pedaling but cross-country skiing. I am skiing at a ferocious speed; I consider dropping out but know I can't. Swearing, I hammer my sticks into the snow. I have no strength left but I have decided to fight. Even my eyes go dim, some kind of panic strikes, but I ski on. This is one of the most important ski races in my life; it is the anchor lap of the junior Finnish skiing relay race championship, and I am fourteen. Half what I am now, biking. The air currents wane, the moods of that race take over. My body rehearses a story inscribed into it. My flesh talks, and I listen. But I do not merely listen: I comment, I understand something new about myself. That race, I see it now, was much more than one competition among others. It was an initiation rite in which I fought with my father for his respect. And it was not just my father whom I was fighting with for respect, but the whole culture, a culture of sportsmen that was permeated by success and winning. I was hurting and I was about to die of exhaustion, but I knew that I could not give in.

A different force is driving me forward now as I cycle, and I want to find out if I have the strength and the courage to once more reach my extreme limits. Back when I was a young boy skiing I had no choice, but now I do. Or do I? For although I am utterly alone out here on the road, I still have the feeling that I must prove something to someone. But who? When I was young it was Father, my friends, sport. Who is it now? Is it myself, or is it the environment in which I operate? Suddenly I believe that I shall know the answer if I continue to drive myself to my extreme limits. So I pedal more and more furiously, more and more urgently. I see with absolute clarity why it was so important to ski so fast, to ski and to win. It was a route upward, it was also a route somewhere else, it was a route to self-respect.

I have recently become aware of the contradictions in my life. I must decide whether I can still live by sport and support myself in fields that I trained for, or whether I should give them up for good and look for something else. I pedal more rhythmically, more urgently. I am seeing things more clearly, feelings surface, important ideas emerge. Changing the world, the thing that I have been trying to do for a living, begins to feel hollow if I don't change myself first. I realize that I was driven to change the world by the same fury, the same intentions as when I ran that ski race as a lad—I would just be trying to show the others that I really can, that I really have the stamina, and that I really can take the world by the crank and turn it. Look, Father; Look, the men next door; Look, all the people from the sports club; Look at me!

For a moment my body feels empty and tired. I am about to give in—stop pedaling—it has all been useless after all. I have been fighting only for respect. I thought that if I did things that were respected I would myself become respected. Sport felt futile, a waste of time, morally suspect. When I abandoned sport I had abandoned my faith in corporeality. But for some reason I haven't been able to stop, the journey is not over yet. I decide to test my limits once more.

I pedal on and on, gripping the handlebars, standing on the pedals, feeling no longer the sweat and the pain but instead an infinite pleasure. I pedal on and my pulse quickens. I breathe faster, faster. It is as if I'm making love and I cannot stop. It is only vaguely now that I sense that I am riding my bike through the same topography as that time years ago—the ski track ran nearly by the roadside. But the feeling is different. Then I was full of angst, now I am moving with ease, and I'm full of joy. There is nothing that could stop me now. When the last descent opens out before me, I feel that I have understood something about myself. And I know that I shall change direction. I shall return to sport.

The remainder of my journey to where my parents live takes me along a winding Finnish gravel road with a surface like a washboard, where one must drive at a sedate pace. My body lies relaxed on the bike as I, breathing in familiar scents, pass, in the cooling summer night, places ever so familiar. But just now I am unable to pay very much attention to my surroundings, the leafy forest, the small brooks, the fields, and the open lake. When I arrive home, even the folks there must be content with brief greetings because I have to go and write the story of my bike trip. A story that has already been completed, a story whose title, too, I already knew: A bike trip into the unreality of sport.

Commentary

Readers become involved in stories when among other reasons they get attached to a set of narrated events, or when the narrative has so many signs of emphasis that it rouses itself to life. In this way, writers not only stage events but often suggest how those events are to be acted, how they should be pitched, and how they should be voiced. How a phrase is to be understood, or is understood, therefore, is often more important and can influence a reader greater than what is literally said. The life of a story is its subtext—what is revealed, what remains hidden. It can mean the difference between a voice of uninvolvement with one's own story and a sense that the story is alive. Thus, the specific choices we make as writers at every stage of the writing process signal belief and work to create a feeling of being inside a moment, and thus how we understand our own and others' lives.

In 1983 I retired from my life as a football (soccer) player. This was a hard adjustment for me to make, but in a sense I wrote myself out of this difficult time by reflecting on my past through diaries, short stories, and various forms of memory work. As I have refined my writing practices over the years—how I make specific rhetorical decisions—my demands and expectations as a writer/researcher have greatly changed. Whereas once I was satisfied with simply laying down the facts of an experience, today I am much more concerned with turning my experiences into a story that merges the past with the present in a coherent manner. It's not enough for me to write pretty sentences. I believe that prose and theory must act together, and in many ways this is what drew me to autoethnography as a creative analytical writing practice. This is what I refer to as autobiographical expertise, which is a narrative way to learn about our meanings and memories.

In Finland, I am not alone in this thinking. A number of other researchers like myself have dedicated the last decade or more of their research and writing lives to various practices of autobiographical writing. What we also share is a passion to examine through these texts our varied and diverse body experiences. With autoethnography, I find that I can satisfy a number of intellectual and emotional demands that I bring to my work. However, my skills as a writer have only come with hard work, practice, and study. Primarily, I found that to chose autoethnography as a way of writing research means shifting from typical social science telling mode into literary showing mode. This is crucial. The most elementary direction or advice. For it is largely through showing that writing gets its power and holds readers' attention. Thus, in an effort to create vital texts, autoethnographers must consider showing real people in action, and through those actions the issues of their story should become clear as ideas and positions are tested, and we come away with a definite impression of meaning. This technique can be employed through various writing genres. For example, short stories, essays, or more dialogical texts. It all depends on the mood the writer hopes to convey to the reader. In what follows, therefore, I would like to discuss some of the basics of showing as a literary device which I believe can only enhance our work as autoethnographers.

In my opening story in this chapter, "A Milestone to Freedom," I attempt to *show* my demise as an athlete. My first seven sentences offer only sensory information and description without one word of speech. Because it was my aim to bring forth a sports story of dejection and sadness, I first had to create the appropriate tone or mood. And showing as a technique is highly effective in establishing a story's mood, much more so than straightforward statements that limit our ability to imagine or feel what a situation must be like. Showing raises our attention not just to what is happening in a story but to how something is happening and how it is being experienced. For example, my slow walk alone in the dark towards the café in this story connects who I am as a man at that moment—someone seeking an identity—to who I used to be—a soldier and an athlete who obeyed others. Rich, evocative writing like this, therefore, enlarges our sense of involvement and expands how we come to understand people and issues. Showing, then, can become a powerful literary vehicle for stimulating others' critical imagination and allowing readers to grasp the relation between history and biography.

I believe that the art of showing is particularly relevant to stories about sport and movement because sport and movement are so visceral. When we are active, whether in a competitive game or a morning walk along the beach, we often lose sight of what is real, rational, and conscious as images, colors, sounds, and smells all blur. As I wrote in my second story in this chapter, "A Bike Trip into the Unreality of Sport," we heat up when we exercise, our attention narrows, and enjoyable and painful sensations present themselves. With showing it becomes possible to go beyond conscious reasoning and bring readers inside and in–touch with people's lived movement experiences. This was one of my primary aims with my two stories in this chapter.

I call writing that brings readers inside of experience "performative," where it becomes possible to go beyond textuality and make the reader "feel" what is happening. In this way I always try to write in ways that create a sense of other-worldliness. For example, in the opening to my second story I'm trying to depict my body as it moves through time and space. "The sun is blazing hot above my head. I pedal, pedal." As this paragraph continues, my sentences bring a languid, drawn-out feeling to the sensation of moving fast. "My heart is pounding and I hear the rustle of my lungs roaring in my ears." Through evocative showing, then, I want to remind readers that our bodies aren't short and angular, but long, curved, soft, and round. Like a photographer who sees shapes in images, I want the reader to experience and witness limbs extending, torsos stretching—"I feel power in my pelvis, endurance in my hocks." And such images are important to convey in our literature on the moving body, where dominant bioscientific conceptions work in subtle ways to turn us into objects or machines. With evocative writing about the body it is possible to challenge this "body as machine" representation and use more embodied metaphors that can influence readers to think differently, or should I say more humanely, about movement and physical activity. In addition, evocative writing practices bring with them certain transformational qualities. Personally, it is largely through writing that I become aware of aspects of myself that previously remained hidden or trapped somewhere inside my body.

Writing techniques related to showing, therefore, enable me to express many of the sentiments, emotions, and sensations that accompany how I move, but that go beyond what words and language offer. For example, how do we put into words the rush of speed a skier may know, or the burning lungs a swimmer may feel? How do we explain the timelessness of running for two hours, or the trance one slips into while repeatedly practicing a five foot put, or a free-throw? How do we make a reader understand what it really means to win or better yet, to lose? How do we convey physical pain? And how do we provide readers with a sense of what it's like to be in the groove, such as when a team experiences complete synchronicity almost verging on telepathy? Ironically, sport is arranged linearly but experienced circularly. It's the story of the curved line, the arc, the splash, the whoosh, and it's how this is all experienced and felt that is our job to explain and communicate, and that must influence our voice and how we are heard throughout a story. Autoethnography as a new and exciting research form holds the potential to fulfill all of these promises.

CHAPTER **4**

Initiation

Katherine Parrott

I was *so* scared. After our children's ponies this was the big time. The fact that her name was Olivia (Newton-John) didn't do anything to ease the churning in my stomach. In hindsight, I know the dusky gray horse was as gentle as mist on the hills, but back then I was too young and too scared to see past her size.

I almost said I didn't want to do it, but my brothers would have made me. It was okay for them—they were so much bigger than me and fearless, too.

Deep in my stomach I cramped with fear. My thighs quaked against the smoothness of the saddle. My hands stuck to the reins, and clutching them cautiously I buried one hand deep in the coarse salt-and-pepper strands of Olivia's mane. White-knuckled, my other hand grabbed the pommel. I felt wooden, rigid with fear, perched on top of her mountainous height. The ride took forever—we went up to the Top Paddock to shift sheep.

Would she feel my nervousness? I desperately tried to hide my fear from her. She pretended not to feel it. I'm sure of it.

"Let go of the pommel," my brother said, "don't jerk at her mouth." I tried to relax, tried to let go. This was important, I had to do it right: head up, heels down, grip with your knees. Sit down in the saddle, become one with your horse. We each led the other.

Olivia picked her way carefully through the paddock, following my brothers on their horses. She held her head carefully, ears twitching like antennae, as if asking me, "How are you getting on back there?" Slowly, slowly, the knots in my stomach melted, my hands became supple, like the leather they held. I relaxed in the saddle, swaying to the gentle rhythm of Olivia's stride.

By the time the ride ended I was floating, euphoric. I could do this! And I'd made a new friend.

*   *   *

After that first ride, I helped my brothers exercise our polo ponies every day. Even though I worked with all of them, I still had favorites I rode more than others. It was my responsibility to get the two "old girls" fit for the coming season. I rode them every day after school, gradually increasing the length of their rides. Starting out gently, staying in the paddocks you could see from the yards, and gradually going further afield into the big paddocks in the furthest corners of the farm. We improved together—the horses had a lot to teach me. Belle and Olivia were old hands at polo, and had been through the early-season routine many times. I didn't ride the younger horses so much—I was still at primary school after all—and like me, I guess, the thoroughbred youngsters were excitable as they learned their new skills. Their spirit, their energy, drew me, fascinated me, but I knew they spelled danger, and I was happy to wait. So I stuck with the old girls, and we worked together.

We'd ride all round the farm—across smooth rolling hills; descending into steep gullies where pockets of bush and huge limestone rocks took on shadows and shapes. There was nothing to stop my imagination out there—no cars or interruptions—I was free to daydream. Riding through paddocks where I knew every track, I saw smugglers and bandits in rock caves, and moas in the bush. We ducked into shelter with famous polo players—Codey Forsyth, the Heguy Brothers—and galloped home before storms with famous equestrians hot on our hooves. With Olivia kicking up divots of rich chocolate-brown earth, I'd stand in the saddle, urging her on. We'd ride the wind, faces close together as I crouched over her neck, both looking forward, rushing to meet the land up ahead.

Once Steve and Alex—my two eldest brothers—began to play polo, the other sports our family did gradually dropped away. Because we lived in the country, I'd never played a sport properly—there was no Saturday netball or hockey. The boys had played rugby at boarding school and for a couple of seasons after they left, but soon polo started taking up summer and winter, so they had to choose. We were all pretty good at sports—I used to love being as good at soccer, hockey, or longball as the boys at my school. We played *everything* at lunchtime, and I loved scoring goals, smashing the ball upfield, and the clash of sticks as we chanted, "Hockey one, hockey two, hockey three!"

Mum was pretty keen on golf, and Dad played a bit, too. I can remember Mum playing, but she stopped as soon as us kids got really into our sport. She went to golf almost right up till I was born—dragging herself round the golf course with her big tummy.

My brothers—Steve, Alex, and James—would have a hit at golf, too—not on a proper course, but in the paddocks at home. They'd pull out Mum and Dad's clubs and make up their own course. The first hole started from the small ledge of grass next to the garage—just outside the back gate in the holding paddock where the big shed was. As you faced your ball, the hill sloped away in front of you, bumping down into the gully where the pigpen was. Not much except the house cow got in this little paddock, so if you duffed the shot and hit it into the gully, your ball was lost for sure in long, leathery grass.

Just past the pigpen was the fence line between the Shed Paddock and the Goose Paddock, and along the fence ran a line of huge, twisted old pines. They were beaten and broken by harsh westerlies, several trees leaning up against each other for support. Pine cones and broken branches littered the ground. There was one gap in the trees, a clear hole through which you had to smash your golf ball. You'd hold your breath waiting to see where each shot went, and sometimes there'd be a loud crack as a ball would miss the gap and smack into the trees. You'd see the ball hit the tree and bounce off, then the clonk would sound, riding on the breeze. Everyone would laugh as the ball plopped down on the ground under the trees, bouncing a couple of times and disappearing into a heap of pine needles.

Quite often though, a glorious swing would send the ball whistling through the gap. The sweet thwack of the club on the ball would send it fizzing outwards, dropping effortlessly in the green grass of the paddock. Rolling a little before coming to rest. Once Steve, Alex, and James had had their shot they'd set off down the hill, in long, swinging strides to search for their balls. I'd be running along after them, wishing I was old enough to play, and our pet Labrador, Henry, would gallop along beside me, sniffing at clumps of grass and mounds of horse poo. If their balls were lost, the boys would get me to come and help them find them, and the farm dogs would be tearing around in front, barking and play-fighting, mad and excited to be out of their kennels.

The second hole was up the steep Goose Paddock hill, to where it leveled out on top. I remember standing on that hill one day, with others around me—my cousins maybe. The wind was the most fierce I'd ever known—it screamed all around us, pushing us east, and behind us in the distance the wild west-coast Tasman Sea heaved and churned. I lifted my arms and swore I could fly. I could feel the wind lift me, pulling me upward and out over the ledge of the hill till it seemed like my feet came off the ground. I was strong.

Most days that wind is a rasping, growth-stunting curse, but I remember that day—it's marked in my mind. I stood on the hill pointing down to our home and the wind made me feel alive, happy, and secure.

The days when we played golf seemed to happen less and less as we grew up. I had a season's hunting, and loved the freedom of wide-open country and the amazing feeling of soaring over jumps. I didn't used to mind that the hares got killed, ripped to pieces by all the hounds. I was proud to be blooded—that pagan smearing of hare's blood on each cheek which I wore all that day, loath to wash off. On a farm you get used to the death of animals, especially the ones that are pests and who have no use or aren't special in some way. The thrill of the chase, the team of you and your horse, the galloping and jumping was a wonderful day's sport. There was nothing else to think about—my senses were full. Crisp, sharp winter air, deep, damply green grass. Rich, fertile ground. The warmth of your horse and musky smell of their sweat. You were part of a pack, riders baying like the hounds, surging and flowing over the ground. Splayed like a wave we followed their lead, sniffing out prey, tracking them down.

Those days out hunting were some of my most prized—tinged with excitement and jitterbug nerves. Each new piece of country, an unknown farm—new spas and dropped wires, swamps to cross and hills to climb—was an adventure and a voyage I couldn't wait to start. The anticipation would build at the pre-hunt breakfast—talking excitedly over hot cups of soup as we stood clustered in the woolshed in our jodhpurs and coats. The pre-hunt speech from the Master as our horses stood ready, expectant, outside.

Sometimes Mum even let me off school for a special midweek hunt happening in our district. The horse I hunted was called Patches, and she was borrowed from a friend. She was gutsy and got just as excited as me, which was funny because normally she was so quiet and sedate. Riding Patches, I dreamed of jumping, hunting, and maybe even eventing, and this is when I started riding our polo ponies. It was like a new world, a magical opening, and I decided I would make one horse my own. I'd teach her to jump; we'd be a team.

I didn't know much about riding really. I was only about nine when I first rode Olivia, and I'd been to our pony club just a very few times. I'd get books out of the library, studying the pictures to see how the riders looked and what they did. My family told me what to do, too, and one lesson from my brother has always stuck in my mind. We were down on the little flat by the woolshed —James got really fed up trying to teach me how to rise to the trot. I'd sit up for a stride, then bounce back down in the saddle for a while with my black, hard hat falling down over my eyes, before rising for a stride and then bouncing again. It was very uncomfortable, and it took me some time to understand that I was meant to rise and fall smoothly to the rhythm of the horse's stride. I must have looked funny. James was standing there with his curly red hair trying and trying to make me understand. "Up and down again, Duck. Up and down."

We had some old jumps at home, from when my brothers were going to pony club. They were mostly broken or had the poles stacked up against the fence by the time I got keen on jumping. I had to hunt round in the grass to try and find the pegs that held the poles up. Grunting and red-cheeked, I dragged old drums into line, propped poles on old tires, and stuffed manuka branches that Mum had helped me find into the brush. I really wanted to do some jumping, and so I asked my Dad and my brothers which polo pony they thought could learn how to jump. I was so pleased when they said I could try teaching Olivia.

Teaching Olivia was a slow process—mostly because I didn't push very hard. I knew that you had to be assertive and show your horse who was boss, but I took it pretty slowly, building her confidence and mine. I had no real idea of how to teach her; I'd just put her at the different jumps, soothing her when she refused and praising lavishly when she did something well, exclaiming she was the best horse in the world and thumping big pats on her sweaty gray neck.

The drums that lay on their sides were about the biggest, most scary jump I had—at about two feet tall. The times when we got over them I'd feel proud enough to burst. We'd take off down to the bottom of the paddock, jumping over a ditch and then galloping back up and down the hills like a roller coaster with the wind rushing past us and my stomach doing flip-flops, coming up into my throat, turning over and then sliding down into my gut. Screaming and grinning with the excitement of it. I could spend hours working in that paddock, not getting bored, each little achievement sparking me off again. Mostly I would work by myself—and then beg someone to come and watch so we could show off what we had learned. I can remember silhouettes of my family standing up at the top of the hill by the house, watching us down below.

I was pretty proud of teaching my polo pony to jump. Looking back, we only did what probably all horses are capable of, but Olivia and I had done it on our own, and it felt like a big achievement. I had so many plans: hunting over the winter; long, misty rides; plaiting her thick gray mane and tale for ribbon days in the summer. I thought that eventually she and I would be so busy that my brothers wouldn't use her for polo anymore, and that they'd give her to me properly.

I used to ride pretty much every day—there was no hanging round inside watching TV for me. After Mum had made me empty my lunchbox and I'd had afternoon tea, I'd pull off my tidy school clothes and get into my ones for round home—old jeans and a hand-me-down shirt. I'd shout out to Mum that I was off for a ride, the kitchen door would slam behind me, and I'd dig my boots out of the cupboard. I'd shake them for spiders and put my feet tentatively in, then I'd be off down the hill to the shed and the stables. The gate to the stable had been there forever and its sliding wooden bolt was worn from our hands. Opening it automatically, you'd be looking out at the farm and the wind, planning the best route for the ride—out of the wind, hard enough for the horses. I'd turn into the stable that, like the main shed, had a dusty, dirt floor, squashed down and compacted by the treading of our boots.

The saddles are still kept on long wooden "horses" while the bridles hang side by side on the wall. Some glisten and are ready for polo, while others are dulled by a layer of sweat. So much leather for each horse—not just the simple bit, reins, brow and cheekbands—but a dazzling arrangement of breastplates, under-checks, surcingles, and nosebands—each horse with her own special recipe.

For a ride round the farm I'd choose my favorite saddle, pick up a bridle, and consider my hard hat. Sometimes my conscience said I should wear it, and a hat is a comfort if you were unsure of your horse. But often I couldn't resist the freedom of leaving it behind in the stable. It lets you *feel* the breeze so much better—it's all around you, you're not *hidden*—and so as Olivia jogged my red ponytail would swing, my hair dancing and bouncing on my back.

Gathering my gear, I couldn't wait to get out there; saddle over one forearm, bridle over a shoulder, and saddle blanket in a free hand. Then it was down to the yards tucked out of the wind, where the horses waited patiently for their turn to be worked. On hot days their covers would come off them first thing, to stop them overheating in this sheltered spot. They spent the day in their own little yard that was big enough to walk round in, big enough to relax. The yards kept the horses from eating too much, so they spent their time dozing or nibbling each other over the rails of the yards.

There's a rhythm that goes with saddling up a horse. Smooth fluid movements made thousands of times get you in touch with your horse, and you're ready in no time. First, reins overhead and the bit slid gently between teeth; cheek band buckled firm, and forelock set free from the browband. The blanket and saddle placed over the back; girth fastened as tight as the horse will allow. A few last–minute arrangements adjustments, checking that everything fits.

I'd check myself last, put on my hat, and give a last pull on the girth when I was up on Olivia's back. Then head down the hill past the woolshed and through Number One Flat, jogging up the first hill into freedom at last. Relaxed and at peace, but a twinge of excitement at what the ride might bring. Some days I'd work hard on my riding, concentrating on my seat, my hands, or my legs. But other days I'd just enjoy riding along, with the greenness of spring, or the brown heat of the summer. Chatting to Olivia, telling her what had happened at school, pointing out things and planning our next move.

I loved being in charge of Belle and Olivia and doing my bit—it seemed so busy on our farm then. I loved the responsibility of looking after some of our oldest and best polo ponies, and I didn't care that I didn't watch the same programs as the other schoolkids or visit their houses. I thought my special jobs were more important, more fun than going to Brownies, visiting places, or watching TV. When my friend Karen asked me to visit, I said "Sorry, I can't—I have to ride the horses."

None of my friends at school had families that played polo—and none of them had even been to watch. Apart from polo, our whole family never used to go to town much. Mum would go once a month to stock up. She'd come home with the car laden, and we'd help to unpack it, making trip after trip to the car and back. There'd be groceries, stuff from Wrightsons, and Mum always used to bring us kids something, too. She'd carry her handbag and shopping through to her room, then call us in to see.

"I've got you these, so see if they fit . . ."

I used to run out in my bare feet saying, "What did you get me? Did you get something for me?"

One day Mum came home with nothing for us. After that I still used to run out and ask if she had, but we didn't get presents from town anymore. She'd look at me and say, "No, I'm sorry Duck, I didn't bring you anything today."

On the farm we all had our own jobs to do. I was about eleven now, and we had some more land and lots more horses on the farm—about twelve polo ponies—things were really busy at our place. Other things seemed to have changed, too. Things I didn't quite understand.

One day on the school bus, Damon said, "What's your family got to worry about—you're rich."

"We are not," I yelled back. "We're really hard up." I thought of our house with no pictures on the walls. I thought about Dad, and how mad he got when he sat at his desk.

"Ohh, rubbish. You've got everything. You've got a really big farm, with two trucks, a ute, *and* a motorbike. Plus you've got all those useless horses running round—you're rich." The bus pulled up at the Babingtons' gate, and before I could reply Damon had gone. I didn't really know what to say anyway. It was like trying to explain to Karen why I couldn't go and stay.

Damon had never been to our house. And it wasn't long after that day on the bus that his family sold most of their farm and moved into their cottage. Damon's Mum and some of the other Mums in our district started working in town during the days, in offices or at the bank. My Mum didn't go out to work—we just worked harder on our farm and our polo. In the winters my brothers started going away overseas to work as polo grooms. The rest of us waited at home for them, and in the summer my brothers played and we worked on the horses, gradually getting more gear, more horses, more serious.

For a very small time in the year, there is magic all around on a farm. Misty spring mornings see mushrooms sprout up and out of the ground. Sometimes Dad would come in for morning tea and say there were mushrooms up in the Top Paddock. After we all had morning tea, we'd take little knives and buckets and disappear into the mist, like sheep and cattle melding into the bush. Shadowy figures, eyes fixed on the ground, we'd search and search for the perfect mushroom.

I never even liked mushrooms then, but I loved going out searching for them. Different ones were exciting—I liked finding really big ones, but the little buttons were cute—and their flesh was so pink and perfect. I'd race from one to the next, searching for faultless, flawless mushrooms to put into my bucket, gently placing them bellies-up so they wouldn't get broken.

There's something so magic, so utterly enchanting, about mushrooms—and the mystery of the fairy circles that they grow in. I used to like riding and looking for them. I'd just start by seeing one or two growing somewhere. Usually I'd ride on past them—thinking I wouldn't see any more. But soon I'd be getting off Olivia to pick small amounts hiding in their ones and twos—just enough for Dad's tea. Once I started I'd go back to the ones I saw first, and then Olivia and I would be zigzagging up and down all over the paddocks: checking secret places where I knew they grew, building a bundle, cradled in the front of my shirt that I held with one hand, riding with the other, and dropping the reins when I came to a gate, maneuvering Olivia with pressure from my legs.

Sometimes the mushies would be growing on a hill, so I'd get Olivia close, talking to her, and I'd lean down as far as I possibly could. She was so patient, standing steady as a rock, moving a little when I asked, trying to get me that tiny bit closer. I'd be groping around in the air, reins dropped, abandoned on her neck, perilously close to falling off if she moved. If the hill was quite steep I could just about reach the ground, but despite being swiveled in the stirrups, more off Olivia than on, I never quite managed to pick mushrooms from horseback.

I'd go home when my shirt couldn't hold any more, gently riding back so the mushrooms didn't get broken.

"Look, Mum, what I got when I was out for a ride. Mushrooms for Dad's tea." Mum didn't like mushrooms either, but she'd always admire them and then make me peel them. I'd show Dad when he got in, and he'd ask where I found them. Mum fried them, with butter and a little bit of water that made them steam and smell good—earthy and woody—mushies on toast.

While I rode round the farm I dreamed of becoming a famous rider—or the world's best woman polo player. Back then the best woman was English, Claire Tomlinson, she was on a four handicap and supposedly hard as nails—tougher than most of the men. I dreamed of being admired by everyone, for being tough, but fair, treating horses and people with respect. I never played in any polo games, but I used to love having practice chukkas with everyone at home, or stick-and-balling in the paddock by myself. The boys and I used to stick-and-ball in the Number One Flat or in the hay paddock after it had been mown. Some horses were really funny in the hay paddock, because it was across the road from the old woolshed that we used to keep the pigs in. Horses hate pigs, and even though we hadn't had any in the woolshed for years, the smell of them must have lingered, because some of the horses would go all stupid when they got over by the road fence. One of the old horses, Fortune, must have had an especially good nose, because she used to go really silly. She'd snort and throw her head round, jogging sideways to try and avoid going toward the shed, so you'd have to give her a good kick in the guts to get her to behave. Once you did that, she was pretty much all right, though she'd make me laugh by still mucking round.

I remember one day down there when everything went right and it seemed like my dream of being a famous polo player could come true. I cantered Fortune in a wide circle, the two of us moving easily over the ground as she clumped along, relaxed. Our pitch was the freshly mown hay paddock, not even flat, but with dips, curves, holes, and power-poles to keep both of us on our toes. I raised my stick as we swept round the curve, eyeing the small white ball in front of us. I steadied Fortune, touching her lightly with my heels and squeezing gently with my thighs—making sure she was paying attention. She responded, and together, we faced the ball. Spotting the ball, she took charge of lining us up, and I concentrated on the ball and my swing. The stick swung like a pendulum, meeting the ball with a satisfying THWACK, which sent it arcing out in front of us. Focused now, we single-mindedly pursued it, successively stroking it downfield until we reached the edge of the hill.

Again I checked Fortune, easing back on the reins, gripping with my legs, then lifting forward to play a backhand shot. I was quite strong at backhands, but this time I miss-hit and the ball skewed pathetically a few feet to the side.

"Bugger," I muttered, looking back to see where it had gone, as I swung Fortune around to face up again. The edge of the hill faced us back toward home, and this end of the paddock always had the horses straining to get back to the stables. "Oi," I said, giving her a good-natured kick in the ribs, "Not yet you don't." We wrestled around the corner to face the ball, and Fortune grudgingly gave me her attention. She perked up a bit once she saw the ball, and we threw ourselves forward to meet it.

Off we went, back to the other end of the paddock, this time with me trying to tickle the ball round in a circle at the other end—imagining myself taking on defenders in the final of the Savile Cup or the New Zealand Open. I succeeded—a little crookedly—and the ball ran into the long grass near the road fence. I pulled up to swipe the long grass with my stick, ferreting out the ball and stopping Fortune moving away from the hated shed with the pressure of my legs. As I looked, Dad appeared up the road on the motorbike. He stopped at the gate into the hay paddock and came to retrieve my ball.

With him was Henry, the young English guy we had staying with us that summer. He was different from our normal grooms —wealthier, and was only here for six weeks, on a sort of polo exchange. He was a young player, getting some polo experience in another country, and had been left at our place by his parents a few weeks earlier.

We all chatted for a minute, then I turned to continue stick-and-balling. It was something I never got sick of—I could stay out there for hours practicing by myself, till my horse was in a lather and was thoroughly bored. Fortune was pretty good, she was one of the old hands, and very patient with all my mistakes. She helped me really, doing half the work, lining us up for the ball so I could concentrate on hitting it.

Dad and Henry stayed to watch as I tore round the paddock, making run after run from end to end, imagining myself wiping the superior smile off Henry's face as I beat him to the ball. Now and again I'd go over their way and catch a glimpse of their faces. Dad laughed and looked quite chuffed when he told me afterward that Henry was impressed with how I could play—he wasn't used to seeing me do anything other than help exercise the ponies. I'd obviously surprised him, which made me feel great, and I knew I'd looked good out there. I also knew I could be quite good if I had a chance. But girls didn't play polo.

Fortune was my favourite stick-and-ball pony then; I didn't really stick-and-ball Olivia because I was always so keen to go and do jumping with her.

It was the middle of the week before the season's biggest polo tournament, and I couldn't wait to get home and go riding with Olivia. I'd had a pretty standard day at school—hot—and when I hopped off the bus it was so good to get into the shade of the pine trees. I was walking up the drive when a sudden breeze rushed past me. I looked up through the trees in time to see a silver-gray glider almost the color of Olivia's coat swoosh its way overhead. Through my surprise I knew enough to realize what it was. We often got a top-dressing or an air force plane on maneuvers roaring over the house, but this aircraft was totally silent. It skimmed over the trees in its quiet eerie way—like a marker—and disappeared from sight leaving me in silence. I ran up the drive, my schoolbag banging against my back, racing inside to tell Mum what I had seen.

The house had that feeling like no one was home—the air was still, as if everything had just stopped and was waiting, poised, for all the people to come back. I ran around calling, "Mum, Mum? Muuuum?" I called out the front door and then out the back, sending my voice into the different corners of the garden. No one replied.

In my room I stripped off my school clothes and quickly pulled on the pile of home clothes in my wardrobe.

The house felt funny with no one in it, and it made me impatient to find out where everyone was. There was no note from Mum, and they never went out without telling me—unless something was wrong.

I charged through the kitchen, ignoring the biscuits on the bench, and headed out the back door to find my gumboots. I gave each boot a vigorous shake upside down, and stuffed my feet into them, wrapping the legs of my jeans round my ankle.

The afternoon was quite warm but the breeze made it cold enough to need a sweatshirt. I looked up and around for any sign of the glider, but all I could see were some magpies dive-bombing.

Rushing down the driveway I could see a strange car—shiny and new—parked by the tractor. The rubbish basket from the kitchen was sitting on top of the strainer post by the double gates—Mum must have gone down to burn the rubbish. Standing on the garden fence I could see a small group of people on the flat by the woolshed. I could easily pick out the shapes, Mum, Dad, Steve, Alex, plus two strangers. One of them was standing holding onto one of the horses—a gray. For a second I thought it was Olivia, but then I realized it was Lucy.

Getting down from the fence, I ran down the drive, through the gate, and down the track to where they were all standing. They all turned to look as I came down the hill, except for the short man holding the horse who was talking. I pulled up just short of them, so as not to scare Lucy.

Dad introduced me to the two men, who nodded and smiled. One of them asked me how school was, and even though he was quite a small, round man, he had a big booming voice and a twangy English accent. He wore a cap with a polo player and horse logo embroidered on the front—I hadn't seen the design before so he hadn't got it in New Zealand. I stared back at the men and wondered what were they doing here. No one offered to explain.

Attention switched back to the horses—they were examining a small scar on Lucy's back leg. Mum and I moved away up the hill a bit and sat down in the grass. I asked her what was going on.

"We might be selling one of the horses. I'll tell you about it later," she replied in a low voice.

I sat there, digesting this piece of information while a funny feeling rose up inside me. The middle of my stomach felt tight, and I glanced quickly up to the yards at the top of the hill. "Is it Lucy we're selling? Why are we selling her?" I liked Lucy—she was a nice horse, and she was a pretty good polo pony. I couldn't see any reason why we should have to get rid of her.

"We don't know which one yet," Mum whispered, ignoring the second part of my question. By this time they'd finished inspecting Lucy, and Alex was taking her back up the hill to the stable. A minute later Steve ran up the hill after him, and in a few minutes came back down leading Olivia, saddled up ready for a ride. This made me sit up.

"What's Steve doing with her? What are they doing? We don't want to sell her—she's *mine*."

Mum didn't say anything, just told me to "Shhhhh." She looked kind of angry, like she did when she and Dad had a fight, so I did what I usually did and shut up. By this time Steve had reached the men, and he handed Olivia's reins to the one that had spoken to me. He turned Olivia so he was on the uphill side of her, put his foot in the stirrup, and swung aboard.

I felt numb, and confused, like I was about to explode—what was this guy doing riding my horse? He swung her around and walked, trotted, then cantered—schooling her round in circles on the flat. I squirmed on the bank, fidgeting, picking handfuls of grass. He put her through her paces; up and down, up and down. I watched them, unblinking, as Olivia broke out in a sweat. She started to puff, but did as she was told.

The man kept going in circles for about ten minutes, then pulled up by the others. Steve handed him a stick, and chucked a polo ball out onto the flat. Now I sat very still and watched as the man worked Olivia, stopping and turning on the ball, delicately tapping it around and around. Olivia outdid herself—stopping and turning in a flash, neck reining superbly from side to side, anticipating where he wanted her to go.

After he had finished Steve asked me to go and untack Olivia. I walked her up the hill and mechanically unsaddled and hosed her. Questions raced round in my head as I let Olivia go in the yard. I gave her a hug and a bit of feed for a treat. Then I sat on top of the gate and watched everyone walk up the hill. The men shook hands all round, said goodbye and that they'd be in touch. As they walked to their car I heard Alex ask how long it would be before the horse left if they sold one. I didn't hear what they said in return. Mum was pretty quiet, but after the car had driven away she said to me, "Come on, come up to the house, Duck, and do your music practice."

After that day I kept waiting to hear if one of the horses had been sold—I was too scared to ask, and thought that somehow, if I didn't mention it, maybe everyone would forget the men had even been here. I just tried to carry on like normal, riding and practising my jumping until one day after a ride, the boys told me I better not jump Olivia anymore.

"Why not?"

"Because she might get hurt," Steve said.

I can't really remember exactly when I found out that Olivia had been sold, but I figure it was kind of like how I found out if one of the old animals had been put down. Nobody would tell me because they'd think I'd get upset, and it wouldn't be till ages later that I realized they were missing and would ask where so-and-so was. They didn't think that I could hack it—they thought I'd make a fuss—but they didn't realize that I wanted to be treated the same as them—and I deserved to be told when something was happening.

I wasn't involved in the decision to sell Olivia—I don't know when the phone call came, and I don't know who was brave enough to finally tell me. Olivia was my best friend. We'd never sold a polo pony before, and the thought that we were selling Olivia was the worst thing I could imagine. I didn't understand why of all our horses, it had to be her. I didn't even understand properly why we had to sell any horses at all.

When I asked Mum, the answer was pretty simple. We needed the money.

Olivia was the ideal "patron's horse"—quiet, kind and reliable, and virtually able to follow the polo ball herself. That same nature that had helped me with my riding and made us such a good team.

Before I knew it, there were only a few weeks left until Olivia went. I hated sending her away to a place she didn't know, with God only knew who to take care of her. We'd never even be able to make sure her new home was okay, because she was being sold to someone in England. It was so unfair—she was good, *too* good, and we were being punished for it by her being sent away.

I tried to think of ways to get her to be able to stay. I knew the vet was coming to make sure she didn't have any injuries. Could I do something little to her, hurt her just enough so that she would still be okay, but enough so she wouldn't be sent away? I thought of all the different things that could happen. She could hurt a tendon, or get a cut somewhere, come lame somehow. But I could never have hurt her. I imagined myself cutting her, or riding her hard over uneven ground, and knew that she wouldn't understand why I did it—she would only feel the pain and know that it was me.

Then of course there was my jumping. Now all we could do was go for rides around the farm. How could my Dad and my brothers sell the one horse that I had adopted as mine? There were *hundreds* of others—why her? I couldn't really believe that it had happened, and my plans for Olivia didn't seem to matter.

And even though it really hurt, I somehow kept most of my protests to myself. I'm not sure why.

The dread I felt about Olivia leaving grew over the weeks as time got shorter and shorter. And even though I prayed it wouldn't, the day still arrived. I was determined to have one last ride.

Mum got me up well before my usual time, and I can remember that fresh autumn morning in crystal clear detail. It was a little misty, but warm. I went to the stables by myself, caught Olivia, and soon set off through the paddocks. Everything was very quiet, even the birds weren't really awake. I wanted to ride into every paddock on the farm so she could see them one last time—and I nearly managed it—but I made sure we went into all the ones we liked best. I talked to her as we rode.

"Do you remember the time we jumped the big log in the Bush Paddock?"

"Don't let anyone ride you badly or use their spurs too much—buck them off if they do."

We galloped up the hills with the cool morning air rushing past us, and walked quietly down the gullies. Sometimes I cried, and the tears dried, sticky on my face, but it was a wonderful ride. I wracked my brain to try and think of a place where we could hide, but there was nowhere to escape—they'd find us anywhere.

It was getting late—I could tell—and I knew we'd been out there for ages. The morning didn't feel new anymore, and everything had settled into the heaviness of the day. I turned us toward home—I had to go to school. I couldn't even be at home to say goodbye.

It was playtime when our old orange Ford finally drove past the playground and stopped at the T-junction. I sprinted to the end of the playing field, breaking school rules by climbing over the fence. I can't remember who was driving—I think it was Alex. The morning was still a little foggy, and the birds still hadn't bothered to get up. An eerie silence and a damp gray mist surrounded me and the battered orange Ford with its green wooden crate. I reached up through the gaps in the wooden slats, standing on tiptoes to get to Olivia. All I could see were her pretty gray legs and her soft, round belly. She put her head down and gave my hand a nudge with her nose.

The silence was broken as the engine roared into life, and the Ford sputtered away down the tree-lined straight. Olivia stood steady and quiet in the crate. The gaudy green and orange faded into each other as the truck got smaller and smaller, until nothing was left except gray mist and shadowy green trees. I watched them, standing still long after they had disappeared and the roar of the truck had faded away.

Someone asked me what was happening. "One of our horses is going away," I said. And I walked slowly back up the field to the classroom. The rest of that day's a blank, and when I got home, something had changed. Everything was empty, and there was only Belle for me to ride.

Initiation . . . continued

My initiation into the world of autoethnography began in 1997 as a master's student in Leisure Studies at the University of Waikato, when I was faced with writing my thesis. For my topic I wanted to examine my own and my family's involvement in polo in New Zealand. As an undergraduate studying sport and physical activity, I had carried a nagging sense of dissatisfaction with the traditional academic methods of conducting research and representing people's lived experiences—positivism, empiricism, realist tales. To me these approaches felt flat, impersonal, and passionless. In graduate school I could not reconcile the issues I wished to examine with a research methodology that I felt ignored subjective interpretations. However, as I read about the growing body of autoethnographic research, I was inspired to investigate more experimental qualitative research and creative writing techniques in my own research. As a result, my days as a graduate student became a time of enormous learning and growth; both in my knowledge of research methods and in my understanding of my own life.

As my thesis progressed, I realized that writing it would be a process of bringing together experiences from different spheres of my life—growing up as a "country kid," being part of a polo family, going to university—to create what Bochner (1997) calls "a continuous life of experience" (p. 418). This process helped me understand my experiences, helped me understand myself and where I was headed, and helped me see the ways in which different facets of my life were connected.

Through my compulsory research methodology course, I was exposed to authors such as Sparkes (1992), Henderson (1991), and Denzin and Lincoln (1994). Laurel Richardson's (1997) *Fields of Play* was another book I resonated very strongly with on my uncertain journey towards autoethnography. Her book is a reflection on her life so far, and she also discusses her past experiences, the different turns her life has taken, and the way all our experiences affect our lives and beliefs. In particular, Richardson writes, like Bochner (1997), about her experiences inside and outside of the academy, showing how the two have been separated, but also how her experiences have led to a reconciliation of these two spheres of her life. Her book is deeply personal as well as artistic and sociological. In fact, Richardson opens her book with a quote from T. S. Eliot, which I found myself identifying very strongly with:

> We shall not cease from exploration
> and the end of all our exploring
> will be to arrive where we started
> and know the place for the first time (p. 1).

In *Fields of Play*, Richardson (1997) explores her process of coming to know her world differently, and she talks about aspects of her life that have contributed to this process. One of the most powerful features of her book is that she is seeking a way to reconcile her relationship with her parents. And although she uses *Fields of Play* to discuss a number of important academic issues, I felt her reflections on her personal experiences were the most effective parts of the book.

Richardson writes in her own voice, as it was at the time of the experience she is recounting, and she uses her family's childhood holidays as a metaphor to describe, "her place." She reveals how on returning to the same holiday camp some forty-two years later, everything looked different, but the same. Richardson's experiences since she had been there with her parents made the camp and the meanings she associated with it different, but at the same time she could recall many activities that they did there, and was still affected by how she felt all those years ago. The juxtaposition of these two perspectives is what makes Richardson's writing powerful for me, as she shows vividly the impact autoethnography can have. Richardson's writing went beyond the mere words describing her experience to a point that was closer to the meaning of the experience for her. I found this type of research so inspiring, and immediately I realized it was what I hoped to do with my own study. For example, I wanted people outside of polo and outside of my family to understand something of the joy, sadness, conflicts, and contradictions that polo held for us.

Autoethnography allowed me to go beyond words and describe my experience closer to the actual meaning of the experience. The positivistic research methods I had used previously did nothing to explore the almost spiritual connection I felt was an important part of the movement experience that is riding a horse. My story about Olivia discusses my own and my family's involvement in polo, but the experience that is at the heart of the story is my relationship with, and connection to, a horse.

To me, riding a horse is unlike almost any other sporting experience. In many ways it is like being part of a team, but the team consists of one human and one other living creature—an animal you must form a close bond with. There are very few sporting pursuits where a person must work in partnership with another living creature, and where each partner contributes his or her own strengths and weaknesses to a relationship that must be based on mutual trust.

To participate in an activity where I direct and control the other member of my team, yet at the same time can be so inferior to that teammate, is an amazing and humbling experience. And the feeling of that teammate's strengths and mine coming together in unison, to create movement that is graceful, fluid, fast, and strong is a bewitching experience. For this reason, I wanted my writing to contain a sense of this special relationship between a person and a horse, as well as some of the feelings and meanings that go with the experience. To achieve this, one of the writing techniques I relied on throughout my story was inflection. And it is a discussion around how to use inflection to go beyond mere words and capture some of the hidden meanings of our experiences as physically active beings, to which I would like to devote the remainder of this commentary.

Inflection assists the writer in bringing a sense of verisimilitude to his or her writing, and creating a feeling that what is written can be believed. Inflection is how one brings a larger meaning to the words. Or as Baxter (1999) says, it assists in drawing readers into the story, making the writing seem real enough for them to become involved in the story and hence believe in it. Baxter also indicates another meaning for inflection. He explains, "Inflection is two things: an indication of life-in-the-moment and an indication of how a phrase is to be understood" (p. 185). Inflection then, became one of my chief tools for indicating what horse riding meant to me.

In "Initiation", an inflection tool I turned to quite often to build a sense of the relationship between horse and rider was my choice of phrasing. There were myriad of ways that this relationship could be portrayed, yet I deliberately chose phrasing to emphasize the team-like relationship between my horses and me. Throughout the story, I deliberately refer to us as *a team*, and I make reference to the fact that we worked *together*. One of the most obvious inflection tools I use here is the fact that the horses and I would *talk to each other*. In the scene where I ride Olivia for the first time, she asks me, "How are you getting on back there?" as if she is caring for me, making sure I'm okay. When I am stick-and-balling

Fortune in the hay paddock, I kick her "good-naturedly" in the ribs, saying, "Not yet you don't," when she tries to turn toward home. My intention here is to conjure up an image of friendly "joshing"; the horse-and-rider equivalent of a dig in the ribs or punch on the arm. In essence, wherever possible, I humanize the horses and describe them as if they were my friends.

Inflection can be many things; simple strategies such as italicizing words that need emphasis, the ways in which speech is written and emphasised, or the pace of one's writing, and the emotions assigned to characters or scenes. Inflection can be done subtly, and appear seamlessly in your writing, but strongly direct readers towards particular meanings. When writing my autoethnography, how to inflect my writing often seemed completely obvious to me because I was so familiar with the characters I was writing about and so familiar with the tone I wanted to create. As an analogy, each scene was practically painted in my head before I even sat down to write. Yet for readers, who would come from outside my experience, the way in which I inflected my writing was absolutely crucial. This was a real challenge for me: to step outside myself and put myself in the readers' shoes and examine my words and phrases from another's perspective, all in an effort to check whether my intended meanings have been expressed clearly.

A second inflection tool that I use in this story is to change the pace of my writing depending on what is happening. Changing the pace of one's writing is an excellent way to bring readers into a story. We can all think of exciting times in a book where the writing seems to drag our eyes along the page; we read as fast as possible to discover what happens next. Similarly, in quieter, more restful times, our writing can be slower. To achieve changes in pace, the writer needs to pay attention to every detail. This includes the length of sentences, use of words and phrasing, the sounds of words, imagery, and puctuation. An example in my own autoethnography where I write quickly ocurrs when I talk about teaching Olivia to jump, and in particular our joy when we manage to jump the drums. I describe how we would "take off down to the bottom of the paddock," going "up and down the hills like a roller coaster." Here, my use of the roller coaster simile is deliberate. I want the reader to think of a long, looping ride that takes your breath away with its speed. And I construct my sentence like a roller coaster too, using a long chain of linked statements that draws the reader along at speed. I use punctuation and phrasing to assist with the effect, too. For example, the sentence, "Coming up into my throat, turning over and then sliding down into my gut." The short words in the first half of this sentence lead the reader to the crest of the roller coaster's ride at the comma, then "turning over and then sliding down into my gut" has the reader plummeting towards the next sentence. The whole paragraph is designed to lead the reader at speed through a series of written tosses, turns, pitches, and rolls in an attempt to give him or her a sense of the frenetic, exhilarating pace at which Olivia and I rode over the rough terrain. All of this variation and change, says Baxter (1999), adds to the color and depth of a story and keeps the reader awake and alert. The light and shade of our writing, therefore, is what will often hold readers' attention, and these changes don't have to be earth-shattering to be effective. In fact, quite often it's our most subtle effects that have the greatest impact.

I tried to move subtly into the climatic scene in my autoethnography where Olivia is sold, by first describing my arrival home from school that day as if it were just another normal day. As well as introducing the sale scene, this passage is instrumental in other ways, and the emphasis of my writing here changes accordingly from slow and heavy to fast and frantic. My description of the glider and the empty house are attempting to describe the heaviness, the pensiveness of the scene; I want the reader to pause a little, and feel the silence and emptiness in the air in anticipation of the knowledge to come. This is achieved by the way I describe the scene: my phrasing. At the same time, I need to alert the reader to the fact that something is not right, and to hurry up, read on and find out what it is. I do this via what I describe—the foreign glider and the strangeness of Mum's absence from the house and garden. Thus, throughout this scene, I am working on the pace of my writing. The reader hangs in silence at particular points, such as after the sentence, "No one replied." The short sentence and subsequent paragraph break momentarily makes the reader pause, listening for the reply to my call, before rushing onward to discover what's wrong. Aside from the short sentences that are thrown in to keep the reader on his or her toes, my writing is "fast." I use simple sentences of similar length that list my focus on the thoughts and actions required to get out of the house and track down the source of the danger. I juxtapose the fact that I am in a hurry (I "run up the drive," "charge through the kitchen," and "rush" down the driveway) with the fact that everything around me seems to be still and barely moving. By doing so, I hope to create a sense of discord that sparks the reader's interest and entices him or her to move quickly through the page.

I've also found that injecting emotion into my writing is another excellent inflection tool that gives the reader many clues as to how to interpret a passage. An indication of how a character is feeling is an enormously powerful tool. And often as readers we identify with characters, pick up on their emotions, and even feel them ourselves. The opening scene in "Initiation", where I ride Olivia for the first time is a good example of a place where I have used emotion to inflect my writing. Here, the dominant emotion is fear: I am terrified at the prospect of riding this seemingly enormous horse for the first time. The images I use, therefore, are all designed to emphasize my fear; my stomach *cramps* with fear, my thighs *quake, white-knuckled* as I grab the pommel. I try to show how insecure I felt on this first ride; when you are not confident on a horse, you feel as though you are sitting perched on top of a very tall, thin precipice. To ride a horse well, you need to be relaxed, you need to meld yourself to the horse in order to move with it rather than against. When you are tense and afraid, it may seem as though your only point of contact with your horse is via your thighs and your hands. You apply pressure with your thighs and your hands hold the reins, but you feel desperate to find more contact with your horse, thus the reason for grabbing the mane and hanging onto the pommel of the saddle. In this first scene, I deliberately use images relating to that feeling in order to convey my fear and feeling of insecurity. I also say "The ride took forever," in an attempt to convey how time seems to slow down when you are in the midst of a frightening experience.

Once again, it may seem obvious to illustrate the fear I was feeling in this scene. It seemed obvious to me, because I remembered so clearly the fear that I felt. But of course, for the reader, who wasn't there and who knows little about horses, it is not obvious, and the inflected fear is an essential part of the scene. Imagine if I had simply described the ride, without adding any emotion to it. The scene would have been sadly lacking, and the reader would have had no sense of how monumental the experience was for me.

The last scene in "Initiation" is a place where I also use inflected emotion, yet my technique here is slightly different. Having got to this point in the story, the reader is likely to assume that the emotion I will be feeling is sadness. And indeed, that is the atmosphere I try to create, but rather than painting myself as feeling sad, I infer sadness in a slightly different way. I try to create an eerie feeling in this scene, a sense of numbness and unreality. Baxter (1999) makes the interesting point that an uninflected voice can have just as much impact in the right situation. In particular, Baxter says, "There is something about uninflectedness that suits trauma very well," (p. 195).

In the final scene of "Initiation", I deliberately keep my own actions uninflected, describing the scenery around me to inflect the situation. Even though I run to the end of the playground, climb over the fence and reach up to touch Olivia, I don't add any emotion to my actions. I want the reader to feel my sense of numbness, as if I'm thinking, *This can't be happening*, and that any minute, the mist will clear and I will wake up. I deliberately make the surroundings misty and heavy: "there was a damp gray mist, and the birds still hadn't bothered to get up." The gaudy green and orange is the stark focal point in the otherwise heavy scene. Once again, I hope to contrast the trauma of this scene by leaving myself emotionless while the scenery carries a heavy sadness. I think this works, too, in conveying just how desperate I was. The depth of my despair went far beyond any words, in which case I decided why try to capture my feelings. As musicians also tend to say, silence can be the loudest note.

Thus, the use of emotion, change of pace, and choice of phrasing are three useful examples of how inflection can assist the autoethnographer's aim to go beyond words and arrive at closer approximations of lived experience. In "Initiation" I tried to go beyond words towards something that would illustrate the meaning that raising polo ponies had for me and my family. Of course, representing an experience completely is impossible, but I hope that my writing does come close, well, at least closer than more traditional social science writing styles. Because by doing so, I believe I can invoke a response from my readers. I want them to be actively engaged in my writing, and involved and consumed by the story. Without doubt, inflection is a key component in achieving those aims.

REFERENCES

Baxter, C. (1999). You're really something: Inflection, tone, and pitch. In J. Checkoway (Ed.), *Creating Fiction: Instruction and insights from teachers of the Associated Writing Programs*, (pp. 182–196). Ohio: Story Press.

Bochner, A. P. (1997). It's about time: Narrative and the divided self. *Qualitative Inquiry, 3*(4), 418–438.

Denzin, N. K., & Lincoln, Y. S. (1994). Entering the field of qualitative research. In N. K. Denzin, & Y. S. Lincoln (Eds.), *Handbook of qualitative research* (pp. 1–17). Newbury Park, CA: Sage.

Henderson, K. A. (1991). *Dimensions of choice: A qualitative approach to recreation, parks and leisure research.* State College, PA: Venture.

Richardson, L. (1997). *Fields of Play: Constructing an academic life.* New Brunswick, New Jersey: Rutgers University Press.

Sparkes, A. C. (1992). The paradigms debate: An extended review and a celebration of difference. In A. C. Sparkes (Ed.), *Research in physical education and sport: Exploring alternative visions* (pp. 9–60). London: Falmer Press.

PART II

Crafting Ethnographic Fiction in Sport Research

Imaginative writing always holds a stake in the truth. For whose imagination can exist beyond the constructions of thought and language? Fiction, fantasy, fable . . . each enables us to discover in an unique way who we are and what it means to be human. Ethnographic fiction as a social science writing genre locates research on a stage where disciplinary divisions blur and boundaries surrounding "truthfulness" disintegrate. With this comes a sense of freedom to invent and play; the measure of success, too, lies as much in the telling—characterization, plot, diction—as it does in the message—coherence, relevance, impact. Ethnographic fictions direct us to think and feel narratively, where reality is not what it is, but what we make it into. The contributors to this section expound on issues and circumstances found in natural settings, but their style moves us into the realm of Story, where interpretation, analysis, and aesthetics become fused into one grand evocative, reflective presentation that performs to us and for us as itself.

CHAPTER 5

A Fan's Life: Lost and Found

David Rowe

The Fiction:
Amour Impropre, or "Fever Pitch" sans Reflexivity

When I first saw her I was gobsmacked. I hadn't had the old trembling knee thing since the last minute at Mausoleum Park in '94, when that wanker Broadbent side-footed wide from three yards and the whole End went ape 'cos we knew were "going up, going up, going up, up, up!" Not only was Charmain a real looker, she was also wearing—I reckon it was fate, or maybe just good taste—a dress that was the exact same shade of red as our away strip. It was like we were made for each other, and this time I might really meet my mascot for life.

I snuck up on her blindside, sold the bloke who was chatting her up a dummy and gave her the patter. I couldn't help noticing that she looked a bit like Mandelson's sister, who I met a couple of times before he got transferred to that French club, Abattoir-du-Pres or something. When she said that she'd go to the flicks with me on Saturday, I can tell you I was over the moon. Every cloud, silver lining and that—I didn't have my usual commitments that day. Getting knocked out of the Cup in the first round can have its compensations—I was available for selection, you might say—and for once I could give the reserves a miss. They were playing mid-week anyhow.

She was a great girl, good as gold. Never said much, mind, but she just loved my lounge-room shrine to the Manglers, and all those knickknacks from the club, some of them going back nearly seventy-odd years. I'd tell her all about each one—where the team finished that year, how the grandstand burnt down, and such—and this misty look would come into her eyes like she was really moved. We had the odd row about my nights out with the lads, and the away trips, but I said to her "Come along if you like, you'll love it." But she was never that keen on the game, although she did come to a few of the home matches, and wanted to see what Gavin Badcock looked like in the flesh after he got engaged to that chick from the *Cynical Marketing Vehicles*.

Her heart was never in it, I'd have to say—she used to grumble a bit about how I'd never go shopping at weekends with her, and how we'd often find ourselves at home with a curry watching *Match of the Day* and my "Manglers Greatest Moments" compilation videos on Saturday nights after the pub, but I said we had to save some dosh somewhere for the deposit on the terrace just a couple of streets from Entrance G. This wasn't like me—when I start out in a new relationship I like to take it one game at a time, not thinking of the big prize at the end of the rainbow. But it was different with Charmain. As far as I was concerned, being with her was like winning the League and Cup double when all the media pundits predicted you were for the drop that year.

Things were never that great between the sheets, I do concede, but I didn't think that was the be-all and end-all, and I thought it would get better with practice and a few more training sessions. Janice Nugent never minded my thing with the scarf, socks, headband, and rosette—used to laugh like a drain sometimes, actually—but this one never seemed to go for it. I'd be really getting going and she'd say something that would put me off—like to turn my crowd chant tape down, or switch off the 100-watt lamps that I'd positioned above each corner of the bed for a bit of on-pitch atmosphere. I felt really humiliated, and I've got to admit I really lost it (and in more ways than one, if you take my meaning) when she said that she couldn't concentrate with my giant poster of Max Bootle on the ceiling.

I guess I began to realize that something was wrong when she became a bit distant, and couldn't seem to be bothered comforting me the night Mangle Town drew at Slaughterfield, and I knew that, barring mathematical miracles, we were down. But when I bumped into Tracy Fole in the pub, who'd had a few, I just couldn't believe it when she sniggered and said that Charmain had been playing away with Edgar Frost. I was sick as a parrot and a whole lot more. I was going to go right round there and then to confront her, but it was only twenty minutes until kickoff, and I had to wait over two hours till I could tell her just what I thought of her. Mind you, the game took my mind off it pretty well (as bloody good a scoreless draw as I can remember), and it wasn't until I was in the car park afterwards that I had that sinking feeling in my stomach and I remembered what Tracy had told me.

When she answered the front door she seemed a bit sorry and shamefaced, but after I started to yell at her she gave me all this crap about priorities and stuff. Kept using big words like "obsessed," "fixated," and "fetish," which she'd obviously just found about in that stupid psychology course she's doing round at the Tech. I nearly wept when I told her about all the trouble I'd gone to getting the signed team photo for her birthday, but she just said "That's the whole point, you myopic idiot!" and slammed the door right in my face just like that.

Well, I was gutted, I can tell you, and I could hardly concentrate during *Question of Sport* that night, and I even got a couple of the answers wrong. He must have turned her head, that Edgar, with his poncy university degree and all those dumb things she told me that they did together—like day trips to the Moors when I was travelling with the team, Saturday afternoons in the art gallery (no wonder she hardly ever came to the match), and dinners out in trendy restaurants eating that foreign muck (when I thought she was washing her hair)! What a waste of time, and how selfish and narrow when our lads were sweating blood for the reputation of the town, and she couldn't even be bothered to go along and give them a cheer.

I'm well rid of her, that's what I think. There's plenty of other players in the squad, lots of other scoring opportunities. She'll be sorry. One day Charmain will see a front-page splash in the *Daily Bounder* about how the blokes have done the place proud by winning the UltraSuperCelestial League. A bit of that glory could have rubbed off on her. Now she's just a loser and a pseud doing one of those fancy MBAs and working for the OmniCash Corporation. If she'd stayed solid and the two of us had stuck it out till the final whistle—even if it meant extra time and penalties—she could have been a real winner. Just like me.

The Rationale

There is a good deal of advanced theory and research on sport, sex, and gender, especially concerning women (for example, Birrell & Cole, 1994; Guttmann, 1991; Hargreaves, 1994; Lenskyj, 1986). The tendency to associate the concept (and, implicitly, the "problem") of gender with women and femininity in the analysis of sport has also been counteracted (as in other areas of social science) by a growing critical literature on men and masculinity (for example, McKay, Messner & Sabo, 2000; Messner & Sabo, 1990; Pronger, 1990; Rowe & McKay, 2001). There is much more to be done on this subject on a number of fronts, not least by giving greater attention to the masculinist manifestations of sports culture at levels other than the elite and at sites beyond the locker room (Tomlinson, 1997). Sport is, clearly, much more than a self-enclosed, self-sustaining professional institution. It is vast, sprawling ensemble of organizations, practices, and identities that can only exist as a popular cultural form because it reaches deep into the recesses of everyday life. It encompasses the lifeworld not just of the "athlete worker" but, crucially, of the sports *aficionado*—the fan.

This cannot be a world of direct, unmediated experience in contemporary society. The much mythologized domain of village sport under what Ferdinand Tönnies (1963) calls *gemeinschaft*—if it ever existed at all—has been steadily replaced by what I call "the media sports cultural complex" (Rowe, 1999). By this I mean that the relentless interwining of the institutions and experiences of media and sport since the late nineteenth century has had profound phenomenological consequences, whereby our ways of seeing and "feeling" sport have become inextricably entangled with how it has been represented to and for us by the media industry. This is not merely a question of the spread of sports reportage—the sports news in newspapers and on television—nor even one of the popular reception of "live" or recorded sport-at-a-distance through the broadcast media. It is that for sports fan, the partially interested, and the hostile observer alike, sport is substantially apprehended through the prism of visual and verbal language provided by the media sports industry and, in turn, mediated through socio-cultural experience—of class, gender, locality, and so on.

For those researchers working within sociology and cultural studies seeking to extend knowledge and understanding of sport as social institution and as site of cultural politics, it is useful to deploy Weber's (1949) concept of *verstehen* (understanding from the social actor's operational point of view). In this task they are also striving for a fuller appreciation of how the very representational materials human subjects employ to describe what is seen and felt have been deeply influenced by the readily available framework of the popular sports media. The dynamic relationship between news media sports coverage and its manifestations in the everyday life of groups and individuals is worthy of close scrutiny, revealing as it does an intricate feedback loop of information, dissemination, interpretation, and adaptation. The complex and reflexive nature of this process is further revealed by the popular fictional representation of sport—the cartoons, novels, and films that simultaneously draw on, articulate, reinforce, and distribute sports mythologies across space, time and social strata (Rowe, 1999). Of particular interest here to the hermeneutics of sports texts, identities, and practices is the point of intersection between interpretive sociology and the representation of the social world in fiction. It has been long established that analytical social science can "mine" expressive art for insights and source material. The conventional direction of analysis in this chapter is, however, reversed. It is not merely a sociology of art (Duvignaud, 1973; Wolff, 1993) but also proposes an art of sociology, or, more intriguingly, an attempted fusion of sociology as art—and of art as sociology. By using the tools of popular art, the fictional text presented above seeks to function within aesthetic and analytic discourses usually kept separate until the latter is used to decode the former. In this regard, the technique bears some resemblance to "ficto-criticism" in literary studies, in which the fictive text and the criticism of it are deliberately conflated (see, for example, Kerr and Nettelbeck, 1998).

What is to be gained from this technique of taking a sociologically and fictively informed approach to the critique of sport? Clearly, one advantage is to enhance the degree of analytical reflexivity—a correction to the misconception of the academic text as somehow less manufactured, more "real" than its literary equivalent. A further clue to answering this question lies in the capacity of literature, through its formal codes, conventions, and degrees of license, to illuminate human experience in a more vivid and absorbing manner than most sociology texts. This is both a question of audience appeal (readability) and also the working of the text in such a way as to break down a dualism of logic/reason and affect/irrationalism. Of course, scientific sociology has a different major purpose to that of literary fiction, but it can surely learn a little from the latter's capacity for reader engagement at other than the technical level of theory and data analysis. This is another way of proposing a "passionate sociology" (Game & Metcalfe, 1996), but in this case inscribed within a fictive text.

The impulse behind this shift of register is familiar. Publishers and undergraduate students alike favor more sociology texts becoming more reader friendly. "Language debates" that perennially crop up in some of the more traditional journals and in newspaper education supplements are usually clarion calls for the practitioners of sociology, cultural studies, literary criticism, film theory and like areas of scholarship to renounce their perceived willful obfuscation. The argument of this chapter should not be confused with such straightforward populism. As Toby Miller (1997) argues, even the most elementary scientific text (in his example an undergraduate economics "primer") contains highly technical language. It is sheer fantasy to believe that the sophisticated theorizing and empirical analysis necessary for even partial understanding of the massive complexity of the world of humans, objects, and symbols can be easily and satisfactorily reducible to simple propositions and words. Indeed, as the street argot and English vernacular of the above fictional piece reveals, jargon (a closed, group-oriented subset of language) is as much a part of everyday speech as it is of scientific discourse—and can only be decoded after appropriate "instruction." Although not a prescription for all sociology texts to incorporate fictive techniques, I am arguing for an acknowledgement that all texts have a style or styles, and that each has an implied reader who, it is assumed, it is not intended to alienate.

In the twenty-first century (perhaps even more so than before) it is incumbent on practicing sociologists to find new ways of plying their intellectual trade under conditions where the value of their discipline and academic labor is by no means self-evident. Higher educational systems increasingly wedded to the concepts of choice, flexibility, portability, relevance, and application can be uncomfortable places for sustained, cumulative intellectual exploration. Contemporary sociologists need increasingly to find effective ways of engaging students in a manner that will first intrigue and then inspire deeper, unfoldingly reflexive inquiry. To illustrate this point I cite my own undergraduate experience, wherein it was as much the literary skill as the sociological acumen of C. Wright Mills that encouraged me to struggle through and out of the textual molasses of structural functionalism. Mills's seminal work *The Sociological Imagination* (1959), it should be recalled, contained an instructional appendix "On Intellectual Craftmanship." Similarly, it was the fiery Marx of *The Communist Manifesto* (1967) that absorbed me rather than the stern political economic technicism of *Capital* (1946). This is not an attempt to turn sociology into a "literary beauty contest" nor to deny the importance of plainer, measured, and intensively detailed works. But it is to assert the importance of easing the point of entry for the reader and the capacity of a sociological text to inspire further intellectual work in what might otherwise be a forbidding or unlikely area of study.

In my own case, it was Stan Cohen's (1980) *Folk Devils and Moral Panics* that, after a good dose of classical sociological education via the "Founding Fathers," gave me the first inkling that what was of undoubted relevance and importance could also be a pursuit of passion and even pleasure. It must be conceded that its subject matter and "cast list"—youth culture, media, police, and the judiciary—were uncommonly compelling and exotic, and the temper of the times and my own stage in the (gendered) life cycle encouraged an affinity with the book. But Cohen's ability to make the analysis and his research subjects come alive, as Howard Becker (1963) and other subcultural theorists had done before him, opened up new possibilities for "doing sociology" for this uncertain student. Cohen, an admirer of the "Gonzo Journalism" of Hunter S. Thompson (1979) and the "New Journalism" of Tom Wolfe (1975) that promoted idiosyncratic first-person as opposed to omniscient third-person reportage, self-consciously developed the sociology-fiction linkage in the "Last Seminar." In this brilliantly self-reflexive nightmare scenario published in *Sociological Review* (Cohen, 1978), the "othered" objects of much sociological discourse—the impoverished and the marginalized—become man fest in the groves of academe. Cohen's intervention was but one small eddy in a much wider current in social science and the humanities. Feminist research and scholarship, with its emphasis on the personal-political and embodiment, has consistently favoured a much more overt declaration of authorial identity and purpose (for example, Gottfried, 1996). In Francophone postmodernism, the end of the "grand narratives" (Lyotard, 1984) produced by sociology and other totalizing systems of thought was proclaimed, along with pronouncements of the "death of the author" at precisely—and contradictorily—the moment when authors such as Jean Baudrillard (1988) were achieving celebrity and even genre status. Considerable license was being extended to the once all-powerful, all-knowing textual "enforcer"—the author—to step out from behind the magisterial shadow thrown by the objectivist text and embrace their inevitable subjectivity.

While this "deregulating" of register and point of view has undoubtedly resulted in some excesses, it has also enabled sociologists to re-engage with their discipline on more flexible terms (see, for example, the special 1993 issue of *Sociology* on "auto biography"). For sociologists of popular culture, this has been a particularly useful cleavage in helping to breach the schizophrenia-inducing schism between their mainstream professional practice and their activities as reporters and critics in the mass media (see, for example, Frith, 1988), or merely as fans whose fascination for the subject matter had led them to research it in the first place (see Grossberg, 1988; Lewis, 1992). In this way, non-sociological material (both popular and otherwise) could be utilized not only as source material, but adapted as a technique to explore, analytically and simultaneously, the research object and the sociological apparatus that sought to produce authoritative knowledge about it.

In the case of the short story's treatment of the relationship between sport and masculinity, source material and writerly technique from outside sociology were deployed inter-textually as a means to develop insight into the phenomenological logic of "excessive" fandom. The textual stimulus for this piece was, as the title suggests, Nick Hornby's 1992 best-selling autobio-graphical book *Fever Pitch* (the 1997 film of which has a screenplay by Hornby). This rite of passage story about obsession with a British football team (Arsenal) can be said to have reflected, constructed, and reinforced various forms of "lad" culture (such as "soft" and "hard" lad) within British expressions of masculinity. Hornby's self-mocking take on a world he represents in documentary fashion is also extended to another form of popular culture—music—in his semi-autobiographical work *High Fidelity* (1996, also filmed, 1999).

Much of what Hornby describes and comments on in *Fever Pitch* appears intuitively valid for those with situationally-based knowledge of men, football, and Britain, sitting reasonably comfortably with reports of ethnographic sociological research into football culture (for example, King, 1998; Giulianotti, 1999). Such a successful book obviously had significant resonance for its readership. But however empathetic Hornby's work might be, its representativeness—an issue for any work that seeks to capture the experience of a generation of a nation's men—is in question. What, we might ask, if our "lad" had not, like Hornby, had a materially comfortable middle-class upbringing in a southern English commuter town, attended the University of Cambridge, become an English Literature teacher and, ultimately, millionaire author by "realizing" this cultural capital through literary reflection? In other words, what if our male football fan was more like, for example, Keith Talent, the odiously moronic character in Martin Amis's slice-of-metropolitan-lowlife novel *London Fields* (1989)? By means of this imaginative leap, "Amour Impropre" seeks to create a tool for sociological analysis that works as sociologically informed literature—and provides some clues to the craft secrets of the trade in the process.

The Craft

By taking the obsessive sports fandom of one character (historical, self-reported) and comparing it to that of another (fictional, naturalistically represented), different patterns of masculine sports culture can be thrown into relief. In methodological terms, it is a process that exchanges "real" data (self report, quantitative survey, interview, focus group, ethnographic observation) for the "imagineered" text of the literary novel. In this way, there is some clarification of how the "real" and the "imagined" intertwine in everyday life and of the role of literature and of other creative cultural forms in making, reflecting, and refracting the societies in which they are produced. It also enables the dream-like work of condensation, displacement, and projection that temporarily frees the researcher from the responsibilities of orthodox data collection and analysis so as to apprehend the full extension of the logics of specific types of practical consciousness. This creation of a composite phenomenon almost certainly unobservable within the field—for generations sociologists have called it a Weberian "ideal type"—is intended to aid the understanding of the elusive-because-familiar qualities of popular cultural practice.

Amis's character Keith is distinguishable from Colin (the Hornby character in the *Fever Pitch* film) in structural terms by class and through its existential realization as *habitus* (Bourdieu, 1977). What I attempt in the short story to do by fictive means is to take this manifestation of class and masculinity and develop it *ad absurdum*, for heuristic and literary purposes, in order to reveal, with unusual clarity, its all–encompassing, self-reproductive nature. It is its very imperviousness to alternative logics—such as instrumental rationality—that characterizes this discourse, despite its superficial similarities with Hornby's self-reflexive and sensitive meditation on the meaning of Englishmen's relationship to football. It is a discourse recognizable to sociologists who have read the ethnographic work in Britain on male youth cultures and subcultures, notably that produced by the Centre for Contemporary Cultural Studies (for example, see Hall & Jefferson,

1976). It is the staged return, in Stuart Hall's (1982) terms, of the "repressed"—the darker, dysfunctional, intractable side of masculine life seemingly untouched by the anguished quest for self-knowledge and self-improvement that marks such anxious masculine texts as *Fever Pitch*.

Sport in the case of the enunciator of the monologue in "Amour Impropre" is not just "like" life or a metaphor for it, but instead supplies the specific language frame and form—a synthetic combination of sports media catchphrases and snatches of everyday speech of variable origin—that envelops this human subject's experience and way of seeing the social world. This language is both wide-ranging and directly related to vernacular. It is for this reason that I have insinuated many expressions that are comprehensible only within a given context, to the extent that perhaps a glossary should have been supplied. Such subcultural language is readily diffused within the mainstream or parent culture by means of the accelerated circulation of images and texts in an increasingly mediatized—and even globalized—society. The appropriation in this case of the novelist's ear for everyday speech is itself something of a *trope* functioning to trace the multidirectional circulation of the signs of sport throughout the media sports cultural complex, which I take to incorporate everyday, media, literary, and academic speech. The intent is dialogic in seeking to engage both men and women in debates about the role of sport in contemporary masculinities (Tomsen and Donaldson 2001), and also reflexively extends to the writer and his own, sometimes bathetic embrace of sports fandom (not to mention the larger minefield of human relationships). As with any text, nonetheless, how it works—and whether it works at all—is the province of the socially situated reader.

The monologue comprises fragments assembled from a variety of sources, such as a modified interview snatch from one of the research subjects in Paul Willis's (1977) *Learning to Labour*, "outtakes" from my interviews on a range of research projects, "caught" utterances of the various orders of chatter (Eco, 1986) in and outside sports stadium, speech imported from other social domains such as bars and living rooms, various products of the sports media, and passages fabricated by the author. The ethnographic element contained herein is intentionally synthetic, attempting to create a textual assemblage or *bricolage* (Levi Strauss's influential concept notably deployed, among others, by Hebdige, 1979) that would probably be impossible to find so neatly packaged "in the field." It has long been argued that a more profound form of "truth" may be found in non-realist works of art because they do not rely on the faithful recording of the surface appearance of the real (for example, Brecht, 1978). But "estranging" the reader too readily would undermine the relentless, blinkered and concentrated nature of the unnamed narrator's tirade, and so obstruct the elaboration of the possibilities inherent in the very excessiveness of fandom when coupled with a particular form of anachronistic masculinity. The story, then, seeks to simulate the real while enabling its inherent absurdism to speak through it.

A key element of craft here is stylistic consistency—the monologue must be allowed to run with the minimum of imposed extraneous elements, so allowing the extraordinary features of the character's mind set to emerge within the narrative itself. The insinuation, for example, of "magical realist," "alienating," or postmodernist devices that draw direct attention to the artificiality of the text and the instability of authorial, readerly, and textual relations would detract from the text's principal purpose of representing a bizarre mode of being-in-the-world using language that is in wide everyday circulation and use. In this way, the text refuses to adopt the increasingly *de rigueur* de-naturalization technique ("look, this isn't real, it's a media construction"), the use of which has become somewhat formulaic in contemporary literature, film, and television when claims to radical and progressive status are made. To "interrupt" the protagonist with some stylized reminder that he is a literary creation, or that his views are absurdly misguided, would weaken the attempt to develop understanding of the self-enclosed and self-perpetuating nature of his world, and would slow the narrative momentum that, in the *denouement*, starkly reveals the almost inevitable outcome of his myopic inability to break out of his social isolation and recover his loss.

One aspect of the text that is deliberately absurdist lies in its use of nomination. "Charmain," "Gavin Badcock," "Edgar Frost," "Mandelson," "Mausoleum Park," "Manglers," "Slaughterfield," "Abattoir-du-Pres," "Cynical Marketing Vehicles," "Daily Bounder," "UltraSuperCelestial League," and "OmniCash Corporation" are all highly connotative vehicles. These are intentionally comic, evoking real people or institutions, and lampooning contemporary brand imaging. The main purpose of this technique of using mythical names is to prevent the limitation of the text to a single, constrictive historical instance as occurs, to a degree, with the use of Arsenal Football Club in Nick Hornby's *Fever Pitch*. Instead of asking the reader to extrapolate from a single empirical case study, the aim is to use the broader phenomenon of British, male soccer fandom to incorporate a more universal condition not too closely tied to a specific organization or sport. This required a delicate balance between specific, "authentic," and perhaps arcane cultural knowledge and the possibility of extension to other countries and sports.

The "deadpan" nature of the text's humor is also intended to accommodate different cultural competencies in relation to its empirical object—for example, mention of the narrator's ritual recounting of "how the grandstand burnt down" is a reference to a real tragedy—the Bradford City Football Club grandstand fire in 1985 in which fifty–five people died. This evocation of an instance of football fans placed in jeopardy by inadequate safety in antiquated facilities refers, in turn, to other instances of death and destruction at soccer matches involving British teams in the 1980s, notably the Heysel (1985) and Hillsborough (1989) disasters (King, 1998; Lawrence, 1990). Reader apprehension of this linkage enriches the point being made (by specifying the institutional site of British soccer), but is not essential to the text's purpose. As noted above, supplementary notation in the manner of literary criticism may prove useful in such cases, but in this sense critical writing involving fiction is no different from any other textual practice—readers are essentially unknowable and have differential capabilities of decoding the text, irrespective of authorial intention. The craft imperative here, however, is distinctive—the evocative use of language makes it possible for the reader to uncover aspects of the text by means other than its literal translation through traditional social scientific rules of logic and evidence.

Some assistance in navigating this shifting space between social scientific realism and fiction is obviously afforded by the publishing sites in which such work is made available. Placement in an academic journal or book indicates just how important in any form of writing is the positioning of the text in relation to readers, writers, and other texts. No reader of any poem, play, novel, autobiography, critique or history engages with the text entirely *ex nihilo*—they are always already "cued" and "clued up" to it. No author can completely control what the reader makes of the text, but most try—sometimes discreetly, sometimes overtly—to manipulate the text in such a way as to steer the reader towards their prescribed hermeneutic. The writer of "fictive social analysis" is, again, no different in this respect to any other literary producer. Failure of the reader of a mystery thriller to follow the plot is as dispiriting for the novelist as misinterpretation of presented theory and data is regrettable for the social scientist. By keeping "on message" in this short story the author attempts to lead the reader toward an appreciation that the profoundly ordinary and common social phenomenon addressed—excessive masculine sports fandom—needs to be challenged, interrogated, and illuminated. The story's application of the character's logic occurs with a literary intensity and sensibility, while the inherent ironies in his utterances and strategies are displayed through action and reaction rather than by means of "sideline" commentary from the author. Whereas social scientists in orthodox mode would find it difficult to restrain themselves from asserting their proprietorial role in the text by offering comment and critique, the social-scientist-as-critical-fiction-writer constructs the scenario and affords the reader greater interpretive space.

What distinguishes the fictive social scientific craft from other forms of academic writing, then, is paramount awareness of the text working at multiple levels. Most writing for academic books and journals is (or should be) carefully crafted in its own terms. Theory is explicated, data are presented and analyzed, argument is fashioned, logic sustained, and formal style maintained. The author may deploy metaphor, irony, and other literary maneuvers to make a single, "crowning" point or a related series of points in broadly operating at a consistent textual level. In most academic works, disjunctive devices, such as personal confession, are usually carefully structured outside the main body of the text as foreword, acknowledgment, footnote, or appendix. The craft imperative, however, of a fictive approach is to integrate such disparate textual levels and registers, working upward through a poeticized language (animated by literary aesthetics and the pleasures of the text) to enhance the commonly de-poeticized language of social science. This is an ambitious task, and complete failure must result in bad science, bad writing, incoherent texts, and/or bemused readers. But at its best it takes acceptable risks in pursuit of a more comprehensive analytical project, risks that can be minimized by the application of craft skill that might produce something daring and exciting rather than scientifically solid but run-of-the-mill and even banal. This task requires the development of what we might call "bi-aurality" and "bi-orality"—the simultaneous hearing and transformation into speech of the contrasting voices of the conference room and of the spaces beyond held in productive tension.

The idea of "moving" in this book is intentionally ambiguous and multi-faceted. Sport is founded on the physical movement of the body, but it is only of interest because it emotionally moves participants and spectators alike, while writing about sport in a fictive manner informed by social science entails movement between comfortably delineated authorial and readerly positions and practices. This is a task that is more than usually demanding even for writers well equipped with the standard "rhetorical techniques" suggested by trusty writing primers (such as Wasson, 1975). The conventions of academic writing have made it difficult to be read for pleasure rather than out of duty. Successfully encouraging more readers to turn the page in pursuit of a vibrant sociology is a move worth making.

NOTE

Grateful acknowledgment is made for permission from Human Kinetics to reprint sections of this chapter that originally appeared in, Rowe, D. (2000). *Amour impropre*, or "fever pitch" sans reflexivity. *Sociology of Sport Journal, 17*(1), 95–97.

REFERENCES

Amis, M. (1989). *London fields*. London: Jonathan Cape.

Baudrillard, J. (1988). *America*. London, New York: Verso.

Becker, H. S. (1963). *Outsiders: Studies in the sociology of deviance*. London: Free Press of Glencoe.

Birrell, S., & Cole, C. L. (Eds). (1994). *Women, sport and culture*. Champaign, Illinois: Human Kinetics.

Bourdieu, P. (1977). *Outline of a theory of practice*. Cambridge: Cambridge University Press.

Brecht, B. (1978). *Brecht on theatre: The development of an aesthetic* (edited and translated by John Willett). New York: Hill and Wang.

Cohen, S. (1978). The last seminar. *Sociological Review, 27*, 5–20.

Cohen, S. (1980). *Folk devils and moral panics: The creation of the mods and rockers*. Oxford: Martin Robertson.

Duvignaud, J. (1973). *The sociology of art*. New York: Harper & Row.

Eco, U. (1986). *Travels in hyperreality*. New York: Harcourt Brace Jovanovich.

Game, A., & Metcalfe, A. (1996). *Passionate sociology*. London: Sage.

Frith, S. (1988). *Music for pleasure: Essays in the sociology of pop*. Cambridge: Polity.

Giulianotti, R. (1999). *Football: A sociology of the global game*. Cambridge: Polity.

Gottfried, H. (Ed.). (1996). *Feminism and social change: Bridging theory and practice*. Urbana: University of Illinois Press.

Grossberg, L. A. (1988). *It's a sin: Postmodernism, politics and culture*. Sydney: Power.

Guttmann, A. (1991). *Women's sports: A history*. New York: Columbia University Press.

Hall, S. (1982). The rediscovery of ideology: Return of the repressed in media studies. In M. Gurevitch, T. Bennett, J. Curran, and J. Woollacott (Eds.), *Culture, society, and the media* (pp. 56–90). New York: Methuen.

Hall, S., & Jefferson, T. (Eds). (1976). *Resistance through rituals: Youth subcultures in post-war Britain*. London: Hutchinson.

Hargreaves, J. (1994). *Sporting females: Critical issues in the history and sociology of women's sports*. London: Routledge.

Hebdige, D. (1979). *Subculture: The meaning of style*. London: Hutchinson.

Hornby, N. (1992). *Fever pitch*. London: Victor Gollancz.

Hornby, N. (1996). *High fidelity*. London: Riverhead Books.

King, A. (1998). *The end of the terraces: The transformation of English football in the 1990s*. London: Leicester University Press.

Kerr, H., & Nettelbeck, A. (Eds.). (1998). *The space between: Australian women writjng fictocriticism.* Nedlands, WA: University of Western Australia Press.

Lawrence, G. (1990). Football hooliganism: Australian media representations of the Heysel stadium riot. In D. Rowe and G. Lawrence (Eds,). *Sport and leisure: Trends in Australian popular culture* (pp. 40–58). Sydney: Harcourt Brace Jovanovich.

Lenskyj, H. (1986). *Out of bounds: Women, sport and sexuality.* Toronto: Women's Press.

Lewis, L. A. (Ed.). (1992). *The adoring audience: Fan culture and popular media.* New York: Routledge.

Lyotard, J. F. (1984). *The postmodern condition: A report on knowledge.* Manchester: Manchester University Press.

McKay, J., Messner, M. A. and Sabo, D. (Eds.). (2000). *Masculinities, gender relations and sport.* Thousand Oaks, California: Sage.

Marx, K. (1946). *Capital: A critical analysis of capitalist production* (edited by Friedrich Engels). London: Allen & Unwin.

Marx, K., & Engels, F. (1967). *The communist manifesto.* New York: Penguin.

Messner, M., & Sabo, D. (Eds.). (1990). *Sport, men and the gender order: Critical feminist perspectives.* Champaign, Illinois: Human Kinetics.

Miller, T. (1997). Actually existing journal-ism. *Social Text, 50,* 147–148.

Mills, C. W. (1959). *The Sociological Imagination.* New York: Oxford University Press.

Pronger, B. (1990). *The arena of masculinity: Sport, homosexuality and the meaning of sex.* New York: St. Martin's Press.

Rowe, D. (1999). *Sport, culture and the media: The unruly trinity.* Buckingham, UK: Open University Press.

Rowe, D., & McKay, J. (2002, in press). Sport: Still a man's game. In S. Tomsen and M. Donaldson (Eds.), *Male trouble: Looking at Australian masculinities.* Sydney: Pluto Press.

Sociology, Stanley, L., & Morgan, D. (Eds). (1993). *Special issue: Auto/biography in Sociology, 27* (1), February.

Thompson, H. S. (1979). *The great shark hunt: Strange tales from a strange time.* London: Picador.

Tomlinson, A. (Ed). (1997). *Gender, sport and leisure: Continuities and challenges.* Aachen: Meyer & Meyer Verlag.

Tomsen, S., & Donaldson, M. (Eds.) (2002, in press). *Male trouble: Looking at Australian masculinities.* Sydney: Pluto Press.

Tönnies, F. (1963). *Community & society (Gemeinschaft und Gesellschaft).* New York: Harper & Row.

Wasson, J. M. (1975). *Subject and structure: An anthology for writers* (fifth edition) Boston and Toronto: Little, Brown.

Weber, M. (1949). *The methodology of the social sciences.* New York: The Free Press.

Willis, P. (1977). *Learning to labour: How working class kids get working class jobs.* Farnborough, UK : Saxon House.

Wolfe, T., & Johnson, E. W. (Eds.). (1975). *The new journalism.* London: Pan.

Wolff, J. (1993). *Aesthetics and the sociology of art* (second edition). Ann Arbor: University of Michigan Press.

CHAPTER 6

Pass

Toni Bruce

After the game, coated in a film of moisture and warm all over, they burst into Saville's bar, a whirl of noise and motion. Popular with the university student drinking crowd precisely because of its unfashionable décor and battered furniture, it was always quiet on Sunday afternoons. The dim lighting, dark wood paneling, and a brown carpet of impossible-to-define style were in stark contrast to the glow of the late autumn sun outside. The odor of decades of Saturday night spilt beer so much part of the atmosphere that they barely noticed it.

Sweaty bodies squeezed into the well-worn booths, reliving the best passes and stupidest shots, catching up with the latest women's basketball news, and ordering pizzas to refuel after nearly two hours of exercise. Sam's team were in their regular formation, tall player opposite short player on each side of the table with Diana, the captain, in a chair pulled up at the end. Sam was squashed in next to her roommate Claire, Big C to her friends. Wisconsin born and raised, C's Swedish ancestors had passed on their size, pink skin, and strawberry blond hair. Opposite Sam was Andie, a second–generation German American, the biggest and slowest of the forwards. The space next to her was saved for Bobbie, who always arrived last, being one of the few who insisted on showering before hitting the bar.

Snug as a bug in a rug, Sam thought, slurping soda and initially paying little attention to the voices swirling around her. It didn't seem to matter if she was hanging out in this near-empty, beer-soaked Midwestern bar, fighting for space in a crowded southern New Zealand pub, disrupting the understated ambience of a fern bar in West London, or knocking back wines in a suburban Italian diner in Australia—this was basketball, this was home.

They all heard Bobbie arrive.

"What the fuck are you looking at?"—directed at two guys leaving the bar—was followed by her unmistakable hoot of laughter as the guys scurried out the door. Even without makeup, Bobbie's startling green eyes, perfect triangular jawline and taut, compact sprinter's body always attracted attention. She and Sam met in New York. When they took lunchtime jogs up Madison Avenue to Central Park's more open and foot friendly paths, men's jaws dropped. Sam thought she could have run naked and attracted no notice at all, so striking were Bobbie's looks.

It had been a great afternoon of pick-up basketball in the back gym that Diana booked every week—one of the rare times the women could get uncontested access to a court. Even then they almost always had to kick guys off. Luckily, few were willing to argue when Diana, all 6'2" toned muscle, suggested it was time for them to leave. Sam's team used the time to practice and challenge themselves—often splitting up to balance out the teams. Of the core group of fifteen women who turned up regularly, almost everyone had played college ball so the standard was high. Women who had little experience were welcome but few came regularly. They realized they didn't really fit in, even in these social games.

Sam loved passing to Diana. She'd give up the glory of scoring for the intense pleasure of the pinpoint pass any time. Like today. Even with Bobbie shadowing her every move, Sam had managed to find Diana. At one point, with her back turned to the basket and Elise, a new player, in perfect position to catch the easy pass, Sam had caught a glimpse of Diana cutting towards the hoop. After a quick fake down towards the baseline, Sam had rifled a no-look, bullet pass backwards over her right shoulder in Diana's direction. A shocked Bobbie had to jerk her head away as the ball grazed her right ear. No one but Diana would have expected a pass like that. Probably no one else could have caught it. The basket scored and the team shared high fives. Diana mouthed, "I love you" when no one was looking. Sam gave her the thumbs up. They weren't worried that Bobbie had already scored at the other end on a runaway lay-up. A pass like that needed savoring.

"Hey, did you hear about Sam's dream last night? She was . . . Oooooooooph." The sharp gust of air escaping from C's diaphragm after Sam's elbow to the ribs only slowed her down momentarily. "She dreamed she was kissing another woman!"

"Good on you girl. That's the second time this month isn't it?" Andie's attempt to high five Sam across the table went begging. "Was it the same woman?"

"Oh shut up both of you. And no it wasn't the same one. It was no one." Well, not exactly no one. But no one she knew at least. In the dream, Sam had been at a party, leaning against a hallway wall, observing a parade of young, beautiful women flow from room to room as if on an imaginary stream. One had stopped. Sam's lips tingled again as she relived the sensation as their mouths made contact. Her kiss had been soft, tender, warm, and her breath gently fanned Sam's face. As her tongue slipped between Sam's lips, she had woken with a start, long moments passing as her heart rate slowed to normal and she became fully present in the darkness.

"Well, did you like it?" Andie leaned forward, her knees knocking Sam's beneath the table.

"No!" It came out almost as a shout. She dropped her voice as heads turned towards them. "It felt strange. I didn't even know who she was."

"But weren't you tempted to kiss her back?" Andie was insistent.

"Oh stop it. No. I mean . . . No. Of course I wasn't."

"Are you sure?" Andie picked up on Sam's hesitation.

"Maybe she's coming around to our way of thinking at last," Diana said, smiling.

"Don't get your hopes up." Sam shook her head in mock despair. "It was only a dream. A bit like that three-pointer you took at the buzzer in last week's game, eh Diana?"

"Do you mind if I join you?" The tentative request by Elise, who turned up for the first time today, temporarily put paid to Diana's reply.

"Sure. No problem," she said. "Elise, isn't it?" Elise nodded her head. "C'mon Bobbie, squeeze up to Andie and there'll be plenty of room." Elise perched on a spot at the end of the bench as the conversation continued.

"Did you see that game on ESPN last night?"

"Yeah. Wow. What about that three-point shot from Chamique in the last second? It was unbelievable. I've never seen anything like it in a women's game."

"I did that once in college. Two seconds to go and we were down by one . . . "

"Yeah. Sure. You saved the day again, Diana, right?"

"I wish." Diana shook her head. "But I took the shot and missed."

Everyone laughed. They couldn't all be heroes, or should that be heroines? Anyway, it didn't matter now. Diana had been on fire today. With Sam's passes finding her even in the most congested situations, no one had been able to stop her. Who knows what the score was but it must have been a blowout. That's why they made Sam and Diana split up after half an hour. Not that Sam minded too much. She'd managed to convince Andie to swap assignments. So it had been Sam on Diana. The tallest and shortest players on the court. As usual, Diana got the best of the contest but Sam made her work for every shot, refusing to give her anything easy. They didn't say anything. All communication was through their bodies, quads tensing to hold position or initiate an explosive drive to the basket. Hard muscles on hard muscles, long arms against short, a dance of force and balance, nuance and power.

The dinging of a bell rang out as a male voice yelled from the bar: "Number 25. Your order's ready."

"What about that time that woman tried to punch you out to make you miss?" C, a dentistry student, had only recently seen the result of that punch.

"Ah. A new story." Diana kicked back in her chair. "I haven't heard this one before."

"Yeah, well a girl has to have a few secrets, you know." Sam's coy tone was enough to send Andie to her feet.

"Well, I've heard it before. I'll get the pizzas. Anyone want to join me?" Elise and Bobbie scooted aside to let her out but no one else moved. All eyes turned to Sam as Bobbie slid down the bench to face Sam and Elise spread out a bit.

"OK. Well, I was playing on the baseline against a girl who was about Diana's height . . . "

"Yeah, we all know about your fetish for playing with big girls," Diana joked.

"Yeah, yeah. It's only because you're so easy. Anyway, I'm scared of the little people. Take a look at Bobbie—who'd want to come up against all that muscle?"

Sam's "Ow!" closely followed Bobbie's kick under the table. "See what I mean? That hurt."

"Get on with it!" Diana was used to being obeyed.

"OK. OK."

"Show them your tongue," C said. "It's totally disgusting."

Out slithered Sam's tongue, long and pointed at the tip, with its noticeable scar slashing across the front third.

"Oh my God. That's enough to put me off eating," said Andie returning with a large combination pizza in each hand.

"Not much chance of that," said Diana who shared an apartment—and food bills—with her. Andie giggled as Diana took possession of the pizzas but stayed standing, waiting for the rest of the order to be called.

"Fucking hell." Bobbie was hooked.

"Your mother must have been a lizard." Diana laughed.

"Yeah, well," Sam said, "lizards know when to pull their tongues in, and I didn't."

"What happened?" Elise's eyes lit up. She reached for a slice of pizza and settled back against the booth.

"OK. Well, it was on a club team tour to New Caledonia. We were up against the best team on the island and they weren't used to losing so the big girl on their team was getting pretty pissed off. I heard later she'd been punching people in the stomach off the ball, stuff like that. So, it's two minutes from the end, running clock, and we're up by twenty points. It's not like they can make a comeback or anything. Someone got fouled going to the hoop so we have shots but in international rules you can take the ball at halfway instead. So that's what we do. The other team are all lined up waiting for a free throw and I get the ball at the top of the key so I think, 'What the hell, I'll just have to do a layup.' The next thing I know, this big arm comes out of nowhere and smashes me under the chin."

By now, Sam is standing and her right arm curves round, hard and fast, with a clenched fist. It's a good thing no one is at the end of it. C hunches lower as Sam's arm just clears the top of her head.

"Anyway, in those days I played like Michael Jordan, with my tongue out. And my lower jaw clamps shut on it. The final whistle goes—no foul—and I'm straight into the bathroom at the end of the court, too surprised to think anything really, just knowing I need to get off the court. A teammate comes in and when I try to explain what happened, she screams and says 'Don't say anything. Just stay there.' So I take a look in the mirror and half my tongue is flapping loose."

Groans all around as each person creates her own image.

"Yeah. It was pretty gross. Anyway, she came back and slapped a hunk of vaseline on it to stop any bleeding and they carted me off to the local hospital. The next thing I know, I'm having two stitches in my tongue without any anaesthetic!"

"No way," Bobbie said. "No anesthetic. What the hell were they thinking?"

"Well the guy said it would take two pricks of the needle and ten minutes for the anaesthetic to kick in so he convinced me it was the same difference just to put the stitches in straight away. I think he must have realized I was in shock. So there I am lying down watching this huge needle come down towards me, trailing black string, and then I feel it pulling all the way through my tongue."

"To hell with that. Didn't it hurt?"

"Yeah, quite a bit really, but I just sort of tried to commune with the pain, you know, and not think about what was coming next. Anyway he put one stitch in and then said, 'Ooops. I think I need to do another one,' so I had to go through the whole process again. And that was it. I didn't play for a few days and couldn't eat normal food for a week." At that, Sam started smiling and grabbed for a piece of pizza crust. "I had to pick off bits of bread like this and roll them into little balls and throw them down my throat." She choked badly on her demonstration, coughing and flailing for a soda to swill down the bread ball.

Everyone laughed. Elise wiped tears from her eyes. Gasping for air, she said those fateful words. "Oh yeah, that's nothing."

Sam realized then that everywhere she had played and every competitive team she'd ever joined had loved injury stories. The more gruesome the better. They'd display deformed fingers and bare their scars with unabashed pride. They were the marks of battle, the marks that branded each as one of an elite group. She had heard the rugby players do the same things—boast of playing games with concussions, remembering nothing of their tries or goals. Social players didn't seem to tell these stories. It was always the elite athletes, the ones who put their bodies on the line at the top levels of sport.

Elise moved closer to Bobbie to let Andie sit down with an oversized plate dripping with corn chips, nacho sauce, and sour cream.

"Let me tell you about the time a girl tried to break my windpipe," she said. "I was playing in England when I was at university over there and ended up marking a woman who'd played in the England Juniors team. She was about half a foot taller than me but I was having a good time."

"Ah hah," said Diana, "another one with a big girl fetish."

"No way," said Sam, "and I thought it was only me!" Elise leaned back. "Sorry Elise. Carry on. Don't take any notice of us."

"Oh. OK. Anyway, I was definitely getting the better of her because she picked up three fouls in the first half and I had none. Basically I think the ref took pity on me because we were going at it pretty hard. So then she started getting bitchy, saying things like, 'You can't do that, you're not allowed to push me around,' and things like that. And me, having picked up a bit of sarcasm after three years living over there, said, 'Oh really? Well the ref seems to think it's OK.' I guess that really annoyed her, especially as she'd hardly touched the ball and she was used to scoring thirty points a game—so the next thing I know I'm dribbling up the court and pass off to someone and then I can't breathe. She basically used the outside edge of her hand to chop me in the throat."

Bobbie flinched against the end of the booth as Elise demonstrated on her, making a short, sharp, chopping motion towards her windpipe.

"Fucking unbelievable," Bobbie said, cocking her hand into the shape of a gun and pulling the trigger. "I hate players like that."

"Yeah. Well it hurt so bad I could hardly see. So there I am grasping my throat and desperately trying to suck in some air and my coach is yelling at me to get back on defense. By the time I struggled over to the sideline and could actually talk, the other team had called a time out and I was so mad there was no way I was going off." Elise paused to grab a mouthful of beer.

"So what happened next? I would have sat you down." Diana was hoping to become a coach once she finished her Ph.D. in sport psychology.

"No way. I wasn't going off. Instead I dogged her every move. A couple of minutes later she got a runaway layup and I just sprinted down the court and shoved her in the back as hard as I could when she went up for the shot."

Gasps filled the booth as everyone envisaged Elise's actions. This was the most dangerous thing you could do on a basketball court and was grounds for immediate dismissal.

"She flew out of court and landed in a heap about three feet past the end line. As soon as I hit her I was calm again and I knew I was in a heap of trouble. So I went over and offered her a hand up and said, for the benefit of the ref, 'Oh, I'm sooooo sorry. Are you OK?'"

"Good thinking." Andie's gaze was full of respect, and understanding of what a player can be driven to do. "And then what happened?"

"Well, the ref must have thought I was serious because all he gave me was a shooting foul."

"So what did your coach do?" Diana had a one-track mind on some issues.

"He sat me down at the far end of the bench for the rest of the game. I think she would have killed me if she'd got near me again and I definitely would have lost that fight. Anyway, that was my first and last game for that team. They didn't ask me back!"

"I'm not surprised," said Diana.

"And on that note, let's have some more beer to wash down those nachos," Bobbie said. Universal agreement. "Hand over your money then," she said, "I'm not the effing Bank of America." Everyone pulled out a couple of dollars and put them in the middle of the table. She scooped them up and squeezed past Elise. Andie joined her at the bar to help carry the three pitchers.

"How's the season going, Sam?" Elise had taken Bobbie's spot opposite Sam.

"Good. Yeah. We're winning most of our games, looking good for the finals actually." It was true. With Diana at center, backed up by Andie and C, and Bobbie and Sam handling the ball, the team was on track to repeat as women's intramural champions.

"Great. I wish I had a team." Elise sounded wistful. "I've seen you guys playing in the women's competition and you always look like you're having so much fun."

"Well, we do. But it's easy when you're winning."

"But you all seem so tight. I miss that. I mean look at you here. Almost your whole team is out tonight."

"Well we like one another . . . "

Sam's answer was drowned out by Andie, returning with a pitcher of beer in each hand. "That's what you think! Did you see what she did to me today? She nearly blinded me!" Andie was giggling hard enough that the beer was in imminent danger of slopping over the sides.

"Well, if you'd just cut your hair short like everyone else, you wouldn't have any trouble, would you?" Sam remembered the incident clearly. Losing the battle for position as Andie's greater size and weight won out, Sam had pinched her on the butt—something a coach taught her years ago but she seldom used. Andie had let out an "Eeeek!" and leapt forward a foot, the end of her blond ponytail swinging round to poke her in the eye.

"No, you're right," Diana pitched her voice to reach Elise, ignoring the other two. "We generally get along well."

"Yeah," Elise said. "You all seem to be on the same page, if you know what I mean. You're all good ball players and you seem to understand each other so well on court. And it's pretty clear you spend time together off the court too. I really miss that. Since I got back home from London six months ago, I haven't been able to find a team."

"I know what you mean," Diana said. "It's taken about four years to get our current crew together. We've all played college ball, and even the Aussie opposite you has a few skills." As Diana nodded in her direction, Sam executed a half bow in recognition of the compliment.

"Well, what about softball?" Diana asked Elise.

"Oh yeah," Elise's face lit up. "That hasn't been a problem. I found a team in the first week but they don't play over the winter, so I'm feeling pretty lost right now."

"I hear you," Diana said. A few heads nodded in sympathy.

"Do you play?" Elise's question to Sam rippled around the table. Another one of those statements, Sam thought. Out of the corner of her eye, Sam caught the rest of the team hiding smiles as best they could.

"No. Actually I don't," Sam said. "In fact I don't even like softball."

"Oh," said Elise as she dropped her gaze to the table, showing a sudden interest in the many carved initials scarring the varnish.

"It's too slow for me," Sam went on. "All that standing around doing nothing for most of the time just isn't my thing."

Elise turned towards Diana. "But I thought . . ." She paused, apparently seeking the right words.

"Don't worry Elise," Diana said. "The rest of us play, don't we?"

"Yeah." "Yep. For sure." "Absolutely." The chorus of positive answers was quick and vehement.

"Sam's interests don't lie in that direction."

"You mean . . ." Elise was still hesitant.

"She's not like the rest of us."

"You're right there," said Sam. "I'm the only one with a decent accent."

"You know what I mean," Diana said.

"Yeah," said Sam.

Elise took a long look at Sam. "I'm sorry," she said. "I didn't realize."

"No worries," Sam said. "It happens all the time. It's no big deal."

"So how come you play with these guys?"

"Well, I wanted to play basketball and," Sam arched an eyebrow in Diana's direction, "as well as appreciating my prodigious talent, apparently they think I have 'potential' despite my best efforts to convince them otherwise."

"We still do," Diana said as all Sam's teammates raised their glasses in unison. Elise smiled and relaxed.

Unbidden, a conversation from ten years earlier leapt into Sam's mind. "How come you picked me?" she had asked the two women who selected her for a touring representative team. There were a couple of other guards Sam had thought would make the team ahead of her. "Because we thought you were cute," had come the reply. At the time, the underlying message had gone straight over Sam's head. Now it suddenly made sense. She told the group. As one, they burst into laughter.

"Oh yes," Andie sputtered. "You were supposed to be the next baby dyke. No doubt about it."

"But I was twenty-six at the time," Sam said. "No baby."

"It doesn't have anything to do with age," Diana said. "It's about experience."

What a mistake they had made, Sam thought. At the time she was living with a man. And what a mistake her team was making too.

"But you know I'm straight," Sam said.

"What about those dreams then?" Diana said. "And anyway, how do you know until you've tried it?" Diana's questions were half joke, half challenge.

"Look," Sam said, "don't get me wrong, you know I love you guys but women just don't do it for me."

"That's not how it seems when you're posting up against me," Diana said, a smile softening the thrust of her comment.

Sam realized Diana was right. In the space of the basketball court, there was nothing more pleasurable than bumping body-on-body with another woman, particularly one who was strong, athletic, skilled. Competition and inclusion fused together. The acceptance that you needed an opponent to play the game, combined with the knowledge that playing against each other only made you better. The understanding that only thousandths of an inch marked the difference between success and failure. That's why she loved playing with Diana.

"OK. You got me there. But it's only on the basketball court, all right?" Sam's question carried all the weight of a statement.

The moment passed. Conversation started again. Bobbie got up to buy more pitchers of beer.

Game Plan: Reflecting on Writing Ethnographic Fiction

For me, ethnographic fiction is a mix of memory, research, and imagination that grows out of my experiences—including those I have absorbed in the course of my daily life. Drawing upon more than the results of research, I integrate stories from many sources—my family, friends, books, movies, magazines, newspapers, radio, the Internet, and academic writing. My work reflects that of other ethnographic fiction writers who, unlike many fiction writers, usually "encase their story—whether about themselves or a group or culture—in a setting they have studied ethnographically" (Richardson, 2000, p. 12). Further, in contrast to many forms of traditional social science writing, I use ethnographic fiction to represent realities in ways that recognize how people make sense of their lives—through telling stories (Richardson, 2000).

For those wanting to explore new writing practices, the options are almost endless. There are books to help you, to provoke you, and often to confuse you! Writers can use multiple styles ranging from poetry to short stories to drama (Richardson, 2000). Within those styles, there are many techniques that can help create vital texts with which readers want to engage.

In writing "Pass" I drew upon two fiction craft techniques that can work well for writers of ethnographic fiction: dialogue and recollections (or flashbacks). The recollections are attributed to only one character, Sam, which creates a limited omniscient point of view, meaning that she is the only character whose mind we can enter. Because Sam's experience is the center around which the story turns, readers can only come to know the other characters through their speech or actions, or Sam's observations about them.

My aim in this story was to have the dialogue and associated actions carry the story forward. Dialogue keeps writers honest by challenging them to "show" rather than "tell." As Janet Burroway suggests, characters "reveal themselves in the way they speak and think, and the revelation is more profound when they are also shown in these ways" (1996, p. 135). The characters' actions—what they do and don't do, what they say and don't say, how they say things, and their responses to the conversation—help reveal individual women's personalities and the relationships between them. For example, the ongoing banter between Diana and Sam indicates not only their close friendship but also an unacknowledged or denied attraction between them. Dialogue also permits the writer to leave gaps and holes in what is said, leaving readers freer to make their own interpretations. And this freedom is important for an evocative sociology of sport that tries to move beyond the traditional objective accounts of stripped down reality that make up the bulk of research repre-sentations in the field.

Done well, dialogue should provide several layers of meaning. First, it needs to carry the history of other conversations and interactions between the characters. For example, in one case Sam deliberately misreads Diana's meaning by saying, "I'm the only one with a decent accent." It is Diana's reply ("You know what I mean") that should show readers—without telling them—that the characters have been over this ground many times before. Second, the conversations must express a particular vision of social-scientific truth (Richardson, 2000). Revealing this vision is important to qualitative researchers/writers who already acknowledge their work is always embedded in particular cultural and historical contexts and views of the world. In "Pass," Bobbie's reaction to being ogled (by men) embeds her in a culture that constructs women as sexual objects available for the male gaze. The ongoing power of an historical understanding of sport as a male domain is revealed in the need for the women to book a court each week and ask male players to leave.

Writing dialogue that rings true is a challenge that fiction writers suggest can be mastered by developing your "ear" to hear the distinctive ways that different people speak. Using dialogue means you have to attend to the voices around you. Some writers suggest studying conversation transcripts to identify particular phrases or idioms that individuals use. I know I have my own pet phrases and try not to impose them on all my characters. Flannery O'Connor says you don't want all your characters to sound as if they have only ever heard the language that comes out of a television set. But if, as in this story, most of your characters are of similar age, education level, and upbringing, it can be challenging to make their voices distinctive enough to be identifiable. The language people use can reveal much about their class, background, upbringing, and personality without the author having to tell the reader. For example, Bobbie, who comes from New York City, is much more "in your face" than the laid-back Midwesterners. Her language and actions have more of an edge. Diana didn't become team captain by chance. Her leadership of the group shows in her comments ("Get on with it!") and the way she controls much of the conversation. In other stories where it might be important to explore issues of oppression or abuse, the way the characters speak—showing a lack of education, for example—can suggest much about their ability or inability to resist.

But dialogue doesn't take place in a vacuum. While privileging speech as the way to move the story forward, readers still need enough concrete information to be able to place the characters in a specific place and time. It helps me to think about the setting as a film set and to try to provide enough description that a director could cast the characters and find a suitable location from the story alone. In "Pass," descriptions of the ambience, physical space, and some of the characters are provided at the start of the story. More is integrated later.

Although I focus on dialogue, it is seldom possible in a piece of ethnographic fiction for dialogue to do all the necessary work of showing what's happening. This is where recollections fit into the story. Through flashbacks or memories the author can introduce key background information, and provide the kind of context that the characters (who are talking and doing things) take for granted. To do this effectively, writers must have already come to understand their own world views and the social-scientific truths that will define the world within which the characters operate. For it is these truths that the characters take for granted and that create their social realities. The writer must attend to the cultural and historical contexts in which the story takes place, for they are as vital to the story as the specific context (e.g., the bar and basketball court) in which the actual story happens. A couple of examples suffice here. At the specific level, since Sam is the only character who has flashbacks, it is she who must remember the incident when Andie's ponytail nearly poked her eye out. At the cultural level, Sam recalls a conversation from ten years earlier that suddenly makes sense to her. Without her involvement with this specific group of women, she might never have understood the meaning of that conversation. Additionally, this memory allowed me to expand upon one of the central themes of the story—sexual identity. Thus flashback and memory become devices to embody theme, perspective, and even theoretical orientation—in this case feminist—through the characters' thoughts and actions. Through their own socially constructed realities, these women challenge cultural ideas about femininity and masculinity by, for example, rejecting the male gaze, challenging the male domination of sport, and actively creating a safe community for lesbian women.

In this story, like others I have written in formats as varied as newspaper columns and traditional academic texts, I find myself exploring "the questions that itch" my life (Murray, 1991, p. 73). Don Murray perhaps puts it best when he says, "I suspect that most writers have a few obsessions they must investigate with language" (1995, p. 2). For me, the larger obsession is trying to make sense of my experiences of being female in the traditionally male world of sport. More specific obsessions represented here include the importance of team, the seductive power of "flow" experiences, and the exploration of sexuality. Basketball is the ground on which I explore these issues because it has played such an important part in my life.

The story took many forms and, like stories should, ended up surprising me. Among other things, I wanted to explore the tension of insider-outsider status and the many dimensions along which this can run. In an early draft, Sam was on the "outside"—as the only heterosexual player she didn't fit in completely. In revision, Sam became an "insider"—with skill level becoming more important to team membership than sexual identity. In the final version, although Sam initially appears as an unproblematic insider, her different sexual identity is later revealed, albeit humorously, as a tension within the team. At the same time, through her involvement with this specific group of women, Sam has been forced to face herself and to question her sexuality and what basketball means to her, as revealed through her dreams, dialogue, actions, and thoughts. In addition, the ways a player might try to become an insider are revealed through Elise's character, who tells her injury story and tries to subtly probe the team members' sexual identities and reveal her own as part of this process.

I also wanted to explore the sensual aspects of moving and perfecting skills in competitive sport—pleasures that so often seem to be lost in the overwhelming focus on winning. I believe that these sensual elements of movement are key reasons why people stay involved in sports. Yet they are not easy to reveal through dialogue because they are not things we talk about. They are seldom the things we share with others. It may be that the cultural context of competitive sport precludes or makes less likely this kind of conversation but, whatever the reason, achieving this aim proved difficult when I wanted to use dialogue as the primary technique for revealing the story. The characters have little trouble discussing good shots or exploring body issues through injury stories but the pleasures, the sensuality, of testing their bodies against one another is completely absent.

And it is here that using ethnographic fiction becomes a powerful method of representation for social scientists interested in examining such hidden topics as pleasure and sensuality. It is in dealing with issues that often are not or cannot be articulated that ethnographic fiction may come into its own. When trying to explore, for example, the sensuality of movement in sport, other methods of research (such as surveys, questionnaires, or interviews) often fail to capture or deliver the depth that can be achieved in ethnographic fiction. As Laurel Richardson argues, "because narratives of the self are staged as imaginative renderings, they allow the field worker to exaggerate, swagger, entertain, make a point without tedious documentation, relive the experience and say what might be unsayable in other circumstances" (1994, p. 521).

And it may be the opportunity to represent what might otherwise be "unsayable" that is ethnographic fiction's greatest strength. It lets researchers take risks and go places that would not be possible in other forms of research. In part this is because the challenge is not to provide evidence but to create verisimilitude—the sense that something that could have happened even if it didn't actually happen. "Accuracy is not the issue; rather, narratives of the self seek to meet literary criteria of coherence, verisimilitude, and interest" (Richardson, 1994, p. 521). Therefore, unlike autoethnography, the stories told in ethnographic fiction do not have to be represented as "true" stories, only as stories that could have happened.

Ethnographic fiction is also valuable when researchers want to reach readers on several levels. I have experimented with multiple ways of writing up the same research into the lives of women sportswriters (see Bruce, 2002, in press; 2000, 1998, 1995) and, although all revolve around the same issues, I find my fictional representation (Bruce, 2000) carries more weight at an emotional level. This does not, however, mean that the work lacks analytical or intellectual rigor.   Good ethnographic fiction must meet the standards of both science and creative arts (Richardson, 2000). Good ethnographic fiction must, as Denison and Rinehart explain, "contribute to our understanding of social life while also being artistically shaped and satisfying" (2000, p. 3). The difference is that, in contrast to traditional social science research, the theoretical orientation, themes, and evidence are embedded in people's actions, words, and emotions rather than spelled out. Readers, whether students, the public, friends, family, or other academics, can "live" their own ways into the experience. For me, the success of "Pass" as a piece of ethnographic fiction depends largely on whether or not you, the reader, while reading this story managed to hear your own.

ACKNOWLEDGMENTS

I would like to thank Jim Denison, Barbara Carr Taylor, Steve Leichtweis, Pirkko Markula, and Emma Wensing for their comments on earlier versions of "Pass".

REFERENCES

Bruce, T. (1995). *What we talk about when we talk about the locker room: Women sportswriters' stories.* Unpublished dissertation. University of Illinois.

Bruce, T. (1998). Postmodernism and the possibilities for writing "vital" sports texts. In G. Rail (Ed.), *Sport and postmodern times* (pp. 3–20). New York: SUNY Press.

Bruce, T. (2000). Never let the bastards see you cry. *Sociology of Sport Journal, 17*(1), 69–74.

Bruce, T. (2002, in press). Supportive or hostile? Teasing or professional? Women sportswriters categorize locker room interactions. *Women in Sport and Physical Activity Journal, 11*(2), 49–76.

Burroway, J. (1996). *Writing fiction: A guide to narrative craft* (4th edition). New York: HarperCollins.

Denison, J., & Rinehart, R. (2000). Introduction: Imagining sociological narratives. *Sociology of Sport Journal, 17*(1), 1–4.

Murray, D. M. (1991). All writing is autobiography. *College Composition and Communication, 42*(1), 66–73.

Murray, D. M. (1995). *To write well*. Unpublished paper. Durham, New Hampshire.

Richardson, L. (1994). Writing: A method of inquiry. In N. K. Denzin and Y. S. Lincoln (Eds.), *Handbook of qualitative research* (pp. 516–529). Thousand Oaks, CA: Sage.

Richardson, L. (2000). New writing practices in qualitative research. *Sociology of Sport Journal, 17*(1), 5–20.

CHAPTER 7

On "Sk8ing": Reflections on Method

Robert Rinehart

Introduction

In 1998, I wrote the following piece, published with permission from the *Waikato Journal of Education*. At that time, I had specific intentions for the form and method (or form and function) of "reporting" my thoughts. I sought to enter the world of the teenage North America skater, to let the reader "feel" tangibly this world, including the triumphs and the despairs. I wanted the work to be effective so that readers would not merely "understand" cognitively what the protagonist Bennie and his friends were going through, but they would take Bennie internally and feel his world. They would begin to have true knowledge of how and why Bennie might react to something; what Bennie would deem to be "phat," or acceptable and good; how Bennie would relate to his friends and family and teachers; what kinds of situations would be prideful for Bennie; what Bennie's attitudes toward mainstream culture might entail.

For the present chapter, many of those intentions still remain, so I have left the story "Sk8ing" as is. However, I have included a commentary where I reflect upon the process of writing ethnographic fiction. The story, then, has itself become a vehicle for discussion of uses of fiction within ethnographies.

I intended this story to present to the reader those kinds of knowledges of human movement that would be sensuous (that is, stemming from sensory experience) and embodied (with specific actors creating spatially and temporally specific actions). In my commentary, I specifically discuss how it is a writer may *begin* a story, and why good evocative fiction may be a suitable venue for scholars to convey certain types of knowledges.

I will say here that I think the fictionalizing method answers much different questions than most scholars engaged in studying physical activity are willing to ask. To venture forth into that which is immeasurable—to eschew the development of measuring tools that are themselves perhaps arbitrary, capricious, and socially constructed—is, I believe, an act of courage in the midst of a climate of scienticity. But, as writer Jessamyn West (1973) writes, "Fiction reveals truth that reality obscures." The "truths" that fiction may reveal include ways of being, complex processes that, when broken down to their component parts, are no longer of the same stuff as the original object. As scientists have discovered even on the molecular level, the very act of observation may affect the actions of the observed. (This clearly has bearing on the truth-claims of a variety of avenues of inquiry currently extant in the "social sciences.") Similarly, using numerically based measuring tools to gauge affect, or to discern *how* something proceeds—to me, this is wrong-headed.

But to the story:

Sk8ing

He dropped in smooth-like off the slanting concrete, took a quick last puff, then tossed his Marlboro aside and went for the grind. They were skating on the concrete abutment to the library building at the state university. It was 2 a.m., a Wednesday morning, and the pinkish orange halogen lights reflected dully off their faces. A light drizzle fell. The air was thick and wet. He could see the fading lights of the two bicycling campus rent-a-cops as they left for the other side of the school. They had about a half an hour between the cops' rounds.

Three others—Sandy, Josh, and that blonde girl Corky—watched him. The tossing of his smoke was deliberate, and the timing was essential: too early, and he looked like a feeb; too late, he'd miss the trick. Same with the Ollie: to get good air, to ascend magically up to the slight rise of the coping, he timed the heel and toe pops just right, carrying the board, no hands, up with his jumping body.

He'd rented *Rebel Without a Cause* seven times, and he loved James Dean. Loved his in-your-face, "fuck you" style. And loved his timing.

Timing, and style—in lots of ways, they were everything. His friends understood this, but his mom and dad didn't. Usually, non-skaters didn't, either. His teachers definitely didn't. Claimed that he would never amount to anything . . . blah blah blah . . . same old story. James Dean, and Marlon Brando in *Streetcar* got that spiel, too.

He hit the steel handrail about mid-board on the deck, balanced easily, careful to let the backside up. He balanced, front and back, then dropped down the coping for the three-foot slide, deftly popping the board off in a heel flip, and settled down on the smooth concrete, continuing down the three-foot-wide concrete ridge. They called it "black ice," it was so slick and welcoming. He'd practiced this move thousands of times on quite a few sets of copings. But this pipe was what he considered "home," so what looked difficult was not.

He continued on for a few feet, then drove himself up what they used as a half-pipe: a gentle arc of concrete rolling up into a platform with a sculpture of some guy pointing in the distance. He ran the half-pipe, pushed his right hand down at the crest, and did a nice invert, holding the handstand pose just a second, then came back down the pipe and smoothed out, finally dropping over the edge of the concrete ridge to the pavement below. He'd hit both major tricks perfectly. It felt good. Clean and good, like a good high.

He didn't smoke dope anymore. Stopped cold on his sixteenth birthday. Learned that the hard way when he tried to attract a major: two corporate execs checked him out and found he was a major doper. Asked him about the extent of it, and he had said, semi-truthfully, "A couple joints a day." Figured everybody knew, why lie? They never called him back.

Now, he just tried to perfect tricks. Short tricks, build them up into long extended bunches. Failing to make was more fun than making. He wasn't self-taught, though. He listened to what the others saw in his stunts, tried to repeat the good and dump the bad; he watched guys like Tony Hawk and Steve Cabellero, and saw what they could do, imagined himself doing it. Then tried it. Over and over again. Listened. Watched. Practiced.

Corky, he thought, looked at him admiringly. She was young, about fifteen only, but she had what it took. She held herself proudly, and tried tricks that Sandy wouldn't always try. He liked it when she concentrated, the tip of her tongue protruding, her brow concentrate and set. She acted as if mistakes, or blemishes, or whatever, were other people's problem. He liked that she saw herself a bit defiant and that she didn't live and die by what others thought of her.

"Cool, Bennie," said Josh. "You held it longer that time." Josh, like Corky, glanced at him genuinely as he talked. But, with Josh, there already was the beginning of a challenge. Bennie sensed that Josh was appraising him, looking for weakness.

Josh meant that he had held the trick, not the smoke, longer. Holding the smoke was a bit of style; no one would consciously point that out. But riding the pipe farther down: that was skill. And Bennie usually listened to Josh; Josh knew tricks. Josh was only thirteen; his brother Sandy was, like Bennie, seventeen. Josh went to middle school, and had hung out with them for years. When Bennie and Sandy began skateboarding, Josh wanted to try it, too. So he did. And he was good at it. Josh would probably be the one to go up through skateboarding, if anyone from here could. From an early age, he lived the life. The others merely chose the life.

But Bennie had worked to get a sponsor for his skating. First, he watched older skaters. Then, he bought a couple of magazines—*Thrasher, Big Brother*—and read 'em, cover to cover. Sometimes there was advice on how to turn pro. He didn't want to owe anybody anything, but he realized that getting a sponsor would mean he could work a couple of tournaments, get paid, and live easy. So he popped off a couple of e-mails to potential sponsors.

They were interested, but wouldn't commit to an unknown. He got a friend to videotape him, and sent the tape in to twelve companies: two T-shirt manufacturers, three "truck" companies, two board makers, and five snack companies. Two bit, and offered him $750 each. He thought it was a king's ransom. He was fifteen.

In the ensuing two years, Bennie discovered that the money he could get from sponsorships let him buy things he wanted. But, somehow, skating was not as much fun.

An executive type from ESPN showed up, asked him if he'd like to get involved with this idea they had for an Olympic-type alternative sports carnival. Called it the eXtreme Games.

"Nah," said Bennie. "Skating ain't a sport. It's a lifestyle. It's an art form. You guys'll take it over."

Corky broke his thoughts. "Listen, guys. It's late. I'm heading home. I'm tired."

They drifted to the street, talking. The rent-a-cops waved to them; they waved back. Corky said, ". . . and I'm all, 'You can't take my paper! I wrote that!' And she's all, 'When you figure out which one of you was cheating . . .'" Bennie smiled and took a last drag of his smoke and tossed it down, deftly rolling over it. He was tired too, but these were his friends.

* * *

"You're late, Chambers! Sit on your numbers, people! Come on, now, hustle up there . . . So, we got a non-suit here, huh, Mr. Chambers?"

"Uh, yeah. You got it."

Walking to his spot, head down. Walking round Neuffers' spot, Neuffer commanding the space, head down avoiding . . .

"Fag."

"Asshole."

"Nice shirt, fag." Whispered. "Nice fucking shoes." Pause. "Fag."

"Fuck you, asshole." Looking up, braving the stare. Neuffer is big. "Still on 'roids, asshole?"

"Still skating, pussy?"

"Awright, girls. Who's gonna lead? Neuffer, your turn?" Assumptions, prior assumptions. Head down, taking roll, walking the numbers, head down. Flashback to third grade, when Neuffer was still big, but Bennie was fearless.

"Jumping jacks! Ready, set: one, two, three, one! one, two, three, two!"

Neuffer was teasing Kelly Stokes, running with her backpack, opening it and reading her notes to Bennie. Things were spilling out all over the playground. At first Kelly tried to get it all back but then, frustrated, she sat down plop on the asphalt and just cried. Pulled at her socks. That's what Bennie remembered. He could still feel her resentment and anger and frustration. Could still feel the choke hold he put on Neuffer.

"Get it going, Chambers!" Just like Neuffer to point out that Bennie wasn't exercising.

"Chambers? You want to sit this dance out? Let's get it movin' and shakin', girls." The coach liked to call the p.e. classes "girls."

As he began shuffling his arms and legs, Bennie hawked up a big loogie. Still handy enough to project accurately, but he could tell it was dense and foul. When Neuffer bent to tie his shoe, Bennie shot it out.

The ball of phlegm was a thing of beauty. It softly arced toward its target, hard and fast and aerodynamically perfect. Bennie watched its flight as if he were watching a football in slow motion, perfect spiral winding down. Time slowed. And then, suddenly, decisively, it hit Neuffer on his left exposed arm, and normal time returned.

"You fuck!" For Neuffer, there was no mistaking who had done it: everyone around Bennie laughed and pointed as the wet phlegm slowly made its way down his arm. Neuffer started to wipe it off with his other hand, but then reconsidered. He leapt toward Bennie, and slammed his arm across the red glistening tongue on Bennie's Rolling Stones' T-shirt. The sudden forearm shiver slammed the breath from Bennie, and he fell with the force of the blow. "Don't you ever," Neuffer hissed, "fuck with me again!"

"Knock it off, ladies," warned the coach. *"Dancing class is next period."*

* * *

Soft velour, retro-sixties material, the bean bag chair set jauntily in front of the television. Volume turned down. Motion on the screen: mountain bikers careening down a steep dirt path, dodging trees and limbs and rocks and rivulets of water and each other, the motion fast, faster than real, as if the camera were speeded up. Finally, all five bikers coming to sudden stops at a precipice overlooking a magnificent canyon. Pulling out cans of Mountain Dew. "Do the Dew!" reads the screen, as each biker mouths words, one imitating with his hand the sliding motion of a surfboard over water. Dissolve to one biker, head thrown back, riding his bike down deep into the canyon, sucking greedily from a can of Mountain Dew.

Bennie barely raises his head. These commercials are exactly what's wrong with this eXtreme Games, in fact with ESPN and most commercial television. Yet he watches for two reasons: to see if skateboarding is treated fairly and honestly, and to see if he can learn anything. After the first day of this thing, he stopped being critical and just enjoyed the show.

Corky had seen him in school the next day, and he'd enjoyed recounting some of the stunts they'd both seen. So he continued to watch it.

"Bennie?" his mom called.

"Down here, mom."

The heavy, tired tread of her white nursing shoes coming down the three steps to the rec room; the mixed aroma of sweat and grease and hairspray and old makeup and an almost sickening smell of her perfume, something called Sunflower, meant to ward off the other human smells. The quick tiredness in her eyes, the long-gone anger at his father for abandoning them, the crow's–feet imploding her face like a scrunched–up ball of paper.

"What're you watching?"

"Nothing," he says. His eyes follow her as she drops into a reclining chair, scoots the legs up, pushes the head back. He knows the answer "nothing" irritates her, but doesn't care. He's bored, waiting and saving his energy for tonight's skating.

"Oh, ESPN? Is this that X Generation thing?"

"Gen X, mom. Yeah."

"Is it good? Any skaters?" She's tried to feign an interest in his passion. Took him to AYSO soccer practices, baked brownies for the bake sale, and worked out ride-sharing for him when he took drum lessons. But she's also, he knows, worked full time, and not gotten any support from his dad after the first year.

"Yeah, the skating's usually at night, though. Not in the afternoon. They tape it, and put it together for the night audience." He's been on TV at some events, and knows how they can change what it is you did. Some of the best tricks are lost because they're following the stars.

"Oh." This is the most he's said to her in three days. Apparently, his snit is over. She wonders if she should bring it back up. Decides to. "Bennie?"

"Yeah?" Something, the tone of her voice, the way she lilts the last syllable of his name falsely, rings a warning bell: he is instantly wary.

"You think we can talk about the late nights now? And that girl? And your English assignments?"

"Jesus, mom!" He is alert now, fighting. "You know I've got to practice. And Corky's just a skater. Nothing going on." He pauses, reflecting. "And Mr. Olson is stupid, and those assignments are asinine." He falls back on the bean bag chair, satisfied. He usually tries to be sensible, or to avoid conflict with her.

"Honey. Bennie? Please don't talk to me that way. And don't do your Mowgli face. I got a call today. At work."

"Yeah?" Acting disinterested, but highly wary.

"The counselor—Mrs. Apanishaud?—called. Said they've identified you as an 'at risk' student? Could you tell me what that means?"

* * *

"You know, Mrs. Chambers, this at-risk classification is reversible, of course. We've found that we can take kids on adventure—um, well, like Outward Bound? That research has shown," Mrs. Apanishaud takes her tortoiseshell eyeglasses off, carefully striking a scholarly pose, "that, um, kids who participate in Outward Bound return to school more self-confident, self-possessed, and ready to continue with their studies—more motivated, I guess you could say?—than, um, before?"

"Yes, that makes sense."

"So we've got this 'ropes course' for our physical education classes that we're experimenting with? And it seems to get similar results to the Outward Bound program. So, having identified Benjamin—"

"Bennie. He goes by 'Bennie.'"

"Bennie, then. Having identified him as at-risk, it naturally follows that he would be a prime candidate for this 'ropes course.'" She smiles placidly; it is as if she has asked a question, though of course she has not.

Bennie is there, sitting next to his mother. At seventeen, he is mildly humiliated by this treatment. The school seems to have no clue. But he simply doesn't care enough about their opinion of him. So he has found himself silently repeating "Whatever" to everything Mrs. Apanishaud says.

"How much does it cost?"

"Normally, Mrs. Chambers, the ropes courses are an extra forty-five dollars per student; but for this special group, this population, the school district has consented to forgo any extra costs. It will be offered," she flips her wrist, "free."

"Why?" This is Bennie.

"Excuse me?"

"Why? What's in it for the district?"

"Why, the administration sees this as a potentially valuable tool for retaining students? Plus, of course, um, they will gain some useful information regarding at-risk students?"

Bennie's mother turns to him. "What do you think?"

Instead of answering her, he faces Mrs. Apanishaud. "Who's gonna teach it?"

"Well, Bennie. That's a decision for the administration to deal with? But, as of now, our current liaison with the ropes course—it's run by the park district?—is Mr. Cole, Coach Cole?"

"Just curious, Mrs. Apanishaud. Is this a part of Coach Cole's master's thesis?"

She blanches, but recovers quickly. "Why, yes, Bennie. Yes, it will be. He has subject consent forms for you and your mother to fill out? Right here?"

"What do you think, Bennie? Sounds kind of fun to me," says his mom, hopefully.

"Tell you what. Here's an idea: have me teach classes in skateboarding. Kids like it, I know it and can teach it. Let's see if that helps the 'at-risk' population."

"Bennie, you know the district can't do that. The liability is much too prohibitive," says Mrs. Apanishaud.

"Well, let me think about it," he says. He understands the game.

You don't ask anybody for anything. You work your tricks, they're all that really matter anyway. Once, you remember, in fourth grade, you won the spelling bee, the school-wide spelling bee. You beat fifth- and sixth-graders. Your final word was "infantilize." And, you guessed at the second "i," choosing it over an "a," but you got it right.

But then, things started getting weird. Your dad wanted you to play Little League Baseball, and you'd never even hit a pitched ball. But you tried. Sat on the bench most of the time, but you were a proud member of the championship Winter League Cubs. Still have the trophy to show for it. And your mom started insisting you go to church, to Sunday School. When you said you didn't like it, she took it personally. When you told your dad you didn't like baseball, he looked at you. Stared right through you with his piercing gray eyes.

At first you thought their fighting—rumblings that woke you up at night, sometimes a sudden shout—was just arguing, that they still loved each other, that it didn't have anything to do with you. They both told you that. Insisted. But, one night, your dad threatened your mom. And you heard your dad say, "I don't want him in that goddamn Catholic school. You hear me?" You heard a soft, reasoning reply. A murmur, higher pitched, conciliatory. Then you heard muffled slaps and punches, and she gasped, then sobbed high and loud and clear. And you knew that, at least marginally, it *did* have something to do with you.

So you tried harder to please. To somehow keep them together. And, for a while, it worked. Your dad smiled at your attempts to throw a spiral deep; he said, "Way to go, man!" and the word "man" felt very right in your chest. Your mom stopped taking you to church, but she taught you the piano. The left hand was clumsy, but you could pick out tunes with the simple noted right hand. Life was calm, stable, good.

Then, you couldn't keep doing better and better. Everyone kept asking for more and more from you. You took swimming, and the first day you felt like you'd swallowed ten gallons of water. The chlorine burned your nose, your goggles kept fogging up, and the girl in front of you kicked you in the head three times. At the dinner table that night you cried, frustrated, and your mom and dad fought again.

"Why does he have to be such a—jock?" she asked.

"Men do sports," said your dad. "He wants to be a man—he'll do 'em, too. That music and cultural stuff is fine," your dad said, reaching to fork a potato, "but sports'll see him through. Right?" He looked at you, and the pressure broke you. You began crying again.

And ran from the table, from dinner, from your mom and dad, and that was the beginning of the end.

Commentary

So that was the story. As with all stories, it began with a blank electronic screen. Years ago, I would have written, "It began with a blank white page," but who uses a typewriter anymore? And that breaking of silence, I guess, is where the exploration of making-something-out-of-apparently-nothing begins.

Creating ethnographic fiction is different from envisoning a scholarly thesis only in the end product. The gestation process is largely the same. In graduate seminars on research methods that I taught at Idaho State University, students would constantly have problems "coming up with an idea." And yet, ideas are every-where. It is a cast of mind, a set of attitudes, to scrape beneath the surface of what we hear, what we see, what we read every day. This kind of questioning is the beginning of establishing a good research question, but it is similarly (at least for me) the beginning of solving the puzzle of writing a story. Brenda Ueland (1987), a brilliant writer and teacher, wrote that writers need to have a questioning and eager stance, which results in a sense of "ego." But as she also pointed out, there is a difference between human ego and the Divine ego:

> By self-confidence and boldness I do not mean conceit (the human ego). Conceit is very different. It is a static state where you rest on some past (or fancied) accomplishment. Then you rest on your oars and say to all (in so many words): "Look at me. I did that!" But self-confidence never rests, but is always working and striving, and it is always modest and grateful and open to what is new and better. I think that is why boasting is vaguely disagreeable and one always regrets it: "Why did I boast? That is done. Why rest and smack my lips over that? Do something new and better." (p. 88)

But the quest for "new and better" knowledge, for more certain knowledge of the "other" and self, of a means of accurately re-engaging with the experience of another person, never ends. So discovery is a fuel for getting past the blank page.

How we report what we find, what we've discovered, is critical though. Just as there should be a fit between the form of discourse and its intended function, so too should there be a fit between the questions we ask and the form our responses may take.

Norman Denzin (1996), himself curious about the realist texts which have proliferated within social science discourse, about the "stories" that ethnographers have privileged as modernist "truths," points out that, if it is "true" that,

> As Doctorow asserts, there is no longer any such thing as a distinction be-tween fiction and nonfiction, only narrative, then all narratives assemble their respective versions of fact, fiction, and truth . . . . Every work con-structs its version of what is truthful and factual, what could have hap-pened, what did happen, or what will happen here. So truth is a social construct. (p. 238)

The "truth claims" of writers are the messages they hope their audiences will receive. But just as *writers'* "truth claims" are a social construct, so too is the nexus created between writer and *reader*—so that a multiplicity of sent messages, received messages, and much in between becomes the resultant. Readers of non-fictionalized ethnography generally do not take in writers' "truth claims" wholly. They contest some of the messages sent, they struggle with others, and they find a comfort zone between their own lived experience and the relatively minor impression most writers' work has made upon them. Readers of fiction, however, understanding that the writer sees "truth claims" as social constructions, as contested territory, and as negotiated space between author and reader, enter into the dialogue more readily.

It may be helpful here to discriminate between various types of narrative, especially fiction-based narrative. In an earlier piece, I wrote of three kinds of ethnography: "academic ethnography; fiction; and fictional ethnography" (Rinehart, 1998, p. 210). Briefly, I was trying to show that there are differences between those who write with the *intent* to tell the "truth," those who aspire to be literary, and those who use fictional *methods* to convey feelings, to express the magic of life, or to somehow instruct others.

Whether the intent is to proselytize or to illuminate, Denzin's point is that it is all constructed narrative. It all reflects a writer's worldview. How, then, with such variety in worldviews of both authors and audience, does a writer or reader check for authenticity? John Gardner (1983), concerned with standards of judgment within fictional discourse, writes

> A fictional element can be appropriate or not by only one of two stan-dards: It is appropriate to the work as an art object without reference to reality, or *it is appropriate as we test it against our sense of the actual* . . . . Our comparison of the work and reality is automatic and instantaneous. To say that *a style feels appropriate to a subject* is to say, then, that we be-lieve *it in some way helps us to see the subject truly.* (p. 79, emphasis added)

So, too, does *fiction* help readers of sociology discourse—of the stories we tell ourselves about experiences different from our own normative experiences—to see the whole subject, in its own logic of complexity, more "truly." And of course this includes stories and discourse surrounding movement, where much of what is experienced remains beneath the surface, needing to be similarly "experienced" by the reader. Evocative ethnographic texts within sport and movement may then expand upon traditional research writing genres because they paradoxically allow for a closer fit between that which is "real" and that which is written. In this way, perhaps, the evocative ethnography may serve to interconnect the body and the mind of audience and creator alike.

However, for the writer, the daunting task of beginning is everpresent. But just as some writers write in longhand with a number 2 pencil on a legal yellow pad, and others write ideas on scraps of napkins to be transferred to a more legible and cohesive mode later, and still others use a computer—and each of these methods shapes the resulting writing—so too do various writers find differing ways of facing the blank page.

For me, in "Sk8ing," the question of conveying what it was like to be a white, suburban teenager in the late 1990s was the key thing. I don't believe that all the studies, with all the statistics at hand of "at-risk" kids, could convey the kind of affect and process of growing up as such a child accurately. For as soon as we break down component parts—the working single parent, the cadre of peer group influences, the importance of media effects, and so forth—much of the totality of being a teenager is lost.

But how could I, a forty-something middle-class white, convey some of the angst of growing up in America in the late twentieth century for adolescent males? Would a listing of their concerns be sufficient? "Memorize this list, and then you will understand." No. Somehow, I had to, while connecting with the "angry (adolescent) male" tradition in the United States, convey the isolation and fear and roots of their "outsider" status, and convey it to the very group that they were resisting. It seemed that storytelling would be more effective than preaching. Fictionalizing and amalgamating some of the characteristics that made these youth who they were might just work. As well, I had to try to make it ring true, so that the "fiction" of Bennie (an amalgam character based on many hours of fieldwork) would stand in for many different kinds of Bennies. I wanted to create a "universal singular," a specific character that was unique and yet had many characteristics in common with other boys of his age and background. I wanted to have the reader identify with the characters in the story, and perhaps see in these characters some of the struggles they went through, some of the daily trials they faced.

So I began with a bit of a stereotype: a skewed, offhanded reference to Bennie's smoking, and to his rebelliousness. Facing the blank page wasn't hard, once I had let percolate all the ideas about who Bennie was, what kind of family life he lead, how he carried the marks of what "normative" society would make as "at-risk" youth. I just started writing about a kid who was trying to grow up and trying to keep some dignity in the process.

I was mindful of the culture in which he'd immersed himself—but actually, when I began writing, I wrote. What would he do? What were the group dynamics, how could I point out the lower-class status of the girl in the group—the objectification of her—without hitting the reader over the head with it? Questions, and their solutions, wormed into my thoughts as I wrote, and rewrote. I checked with kids, with young adults who had gone through this process, for accuracy—of terms, of attitudes, of gestures even.

To create verisimilitude, to create realistic effects, to convince the reader of my "arguments," what was enough "evidence"? When choices are alive and need to be made, there is little time for worrying about a blank page—or screen, for that matter. And, of course, the luxury of knowing that this writing is not permanent, that it can and will be fixed and coaxed and polished, allows me to make so many many mistakes in breaking the silence of the first page to enable the story to begin.

I wanted to experiment with voice, as well. So the breaks in the fiction, the starred sections, signified varying points of view, different angles of voices—even in the omniscient view. The protagonist, Bennie, could be seen through his own eyes, through others' eyes, and perhaps a more clear picture of what he meant would begin to emerge. I wanted him to reflect a postmodernist worldview, one in which polyphonous interplay existed, even within his own uncertainties.

So I played with the work, telling stories about Bennie, about his lifestyle, hinting at his attitudes and reasons. I hoped for engagement from the reader, so that the reader could be drawn into Bennie's world, taste a bit of it safely, and come from the experience a bit wiser.

NOTE

Grateful acknowledgment is made for permission from The University of Waikato to reprint sections of this chapter that originally appeared in, Rinehart, R. (1998). Sk8ing: "Outsider" sports, at-risk youth, and physical education. *Waikato Journal of Education, 6*, 55-63.

REFERENCES

Denzin, N. K. (1996). The facts and fictions of qualitative inquiry. *Qualitative Inquiry, 2*(2), 238–245.

Gardner, J. (1983). *The art of fiction: Notes on craft for young writers.* New York: Vintage Books.

Rinehart, R. (1998). Fictional methods in ethnography: Believability, specks of glass, and Chekhov. *Qualitative Inquiry, 4*(2), 200–224.

Ueland, B. (1987). *If you want to write: A book about art, independence and spirit.* Saint Paul, MN: Graywolf Press.

West, J. (April, 1973). Quotable quotes. *Reader's Digest,* 113.

CHAPTER **8**

Ecstasy on Skis

Martti Silvennoinen

It may be our minds that govern us, our souls that guide us, but it is our bodies on which our histories are written, in which our stories are embedded.

—Fiffer & Fiffer, *Body*

A Jump

Dad climbs down from his lorry and beats the snow off his trousers with his leather mittens. The lorry is parked next to the fence in the backyard, quite close to me, steam still rising from the bonnet. I stand on a mound of piled-up snow; I have skis on my feet, no sticks, a fur hat which covers my ears, and my legs are caked in icy snow. The afternoon winter light is turning blue. It always evokes a feeling of melancholy. The day is drawing to a close. I see far off behind a pond and the empty space of a field, where towering above the trees looms the silhouette of the tall tower of the famous Puijo ski-jump. There it is.

"You'd better be making your way home now, son. It's suppertime and you've still got your homework to do."

"In a minute," I answer hastily.

Dad walks over to the gate. I stare at the limping gait of this big man. He wouldn't be able to jump a yard with legs like that, I think, feeling a twinge of pity at the same time.

"I think you've finished jumping for one day." Dad says in a firm but not angry tone as he opens the gate.

"Yeah, just one jump more. The others are all allowed to stay out longer."

As Dad's footsteps fade, the sudden silence takes me by surprise. It must already be after four o'clock because the gravel mill at the bottom of the quarry has stopped grinding. Alone amid all this whiteness a siren sounds faint and unreal in my ear. A strange fear? Mum recently told me that many years ago she saw me in the street in front of our house standing, on my skis, poised on a mound of snow piled up by the snowplow and, through the open window, heard me chanting, "I am me!"

. . . Now here I am again on skis and standing on a heap of snow. Is this really me?

How long are they going to be on that landing slope? They must still be filling in and tamping down the snow where the last jumper fell. Waiting for your own turn is excruciating. Your fingers start going numb with the cold . . .

"Get on with it," I shout.

Now it's my turn. You can't see the jumping-off point. It's there behind the slight rise of the ramp. That is what is always so exciting. It seems as if it were hiding, laying in wait to swallow you up . . . . Ought to be heading off for supper now if I don't want to be told off when I get in . . . But that's not the most important thing right now. What's most important is this next jump: that passionate desire to slide down and execute a well-timed push-off and soar into flight. The anticipation is intense. Feeling relaxed is out of place at this critical stage. I can feel the pounding of my heart all the way up to the base of my neck.

I know where the jump record is—marked by a willow branch stuck upright in the snow—Topi has jumped almost onto the level ground—sixteen and a half meters—it's been measured with a rope—Topi's a big fellow—he's already got a thin growth of hair sprouting on his upper lip—his voice swoops between a growl and a shriek—last summer he shot Tapsa in the forehead with a spiked arrow—Tapsa got a white bandage put on it in the hospital—he was a hero—even if he didn't dare to jump—his father was the doorkeeper at a restaurant—big—a strict man—which is why you sometimes found Tapsa crying—of course, if he got hit in a fight, or if his ski snapped—he might get a good hiding for breaking a ski, especially if they were new—I know that Dad would join a piece of metal cut from a coffee tin onto the broken tip of my ski—that's a good thing—even if he curses about it—except that on the track a patched ski sprays snow almost up into your eyes—that's a bad thing—I don't feel ashamed—nearly everyone has skis like that.

There's the slope. Straight ahead. I really feel the tension building up. From down below I can hear the shrill cries of my mates. What can they be playing at?

"Come on, blast you!"

What if I push off carefully—I'll be able to jump without falling—but I want to break the record—I want at least to beat my neighbor Pekka—Pekka's got real ski-jumping skis—you shouldn't do it with the proper skis—they're too wide for the track—they mess it up—they're far too good—Pekka's got almost everything—Pekka's afraid to fight—he runs away immediately to tell his mum—Pekka doesn't really dare to jump—but his grandad owns the yard—on both sides—does he own the pile of snow against the fence as well . . . ? But the ski-jump is ours!

"Ready, come on!" I hear from below.

I suck nervously at the tip of my frost-stiffened woollen mitten and slide my skis frenziedly back and forth in the tracks. This is necessary to get rid of the snow that builds up underneath. I check to see that my bindings are properly secured. I feel a churning in the pit of my stomach as if a gang of cockroaches were scuttling around inside. I glance out of the corner of my eye at the distant jumping-off platform of Puijo ski-jump. Then I throw myself forward and take a couple of acceleratory strides.

"Coming!" I yell.

I crouch down—hands held in front just above my knees—the track begins to carry me along as if on rails—as it levels out I lose momentum—then accelerate again—there is a hissing in my ears—here it comes—the jumping-off point—remember to push upward—an explosion of breath and straight into the air—hands now obliquely upward—my mates swarm before my eyes—now for a long flight—I can hear a buzzing in my ears—a hollow in the snow flashes past—the marker trees—my stomach contracts—I land—on my side—not on my head—skis—in my nostrils, ears, eyes— cold . . .

The feeling after falling is always the same. At first you feel numb and speechless—disappointed. It feels as if you had been off somewhere else and now suddenly you're here. Falling really gets to me and the sense of shame it brings with it is only eased by the fact that the jump itself was truly a long one. Falling after a short jump keeps you awake through the night and makes the following day at school unbearable. You don't get over it 'till the afternoon, after what seems an eternity.

. . . My side hurts—and my shoulder—and my hip—my eyes search for my skis—they are intact—both of them—then, glancing around, I see it—where I came down—this time I made a real dent!

Only after making all these minute observations do I notice the snow hanging from my cuffs and trapped under the waistband of my trousers, in boys' language, round my ballocks—and my fur cap is there next to my feet.

"Bloody hell, what a hole you made!" someone shouts up at me.

"Look, you landed on Topi's mark!" comes another voice.

So here it was, what I had cautiously but earnestly dared to hope. A jump, which despite falling could no longer be shrugged off as a pure fluke. I could read the look on the boys' faces and I knew what they were thinking: *Gathering together his gear in that crater in the snow is a sportsman who has given it all he has got.* Remaining upright would have demonstrated the last word in skill, but this is surely enough to satisfy my friends. Falling after landing is nothing to be ashamed about, it is just the unsuccessful form taken by a test of courage, but plowing the whole way down the slope on your backside is straight out of Oliver and Hardy.

"Martti, are you deaf or something? Come straight in to supper, right now!" My father's dark outline shows on top of the hill.

"Yes, all right!" I bawl back, resentfully.

And he wouldn't of course understand the pleasure it would have been to have stayed on to talk, to measure the jump with the rope—to see whether it would have been a new record—to describe where it felt sore, to lament my bad luck.

Slowly, I hoist my skis onto my shoulder, tips pointing forwards, like the men at Puijo, and start trudging off up the slope. The dent I had made could this time be filled in and tamped down by someone else.

A Dream

Kuopio, a town in central Finland, situated on one of the major Finnish inland waterways about four hundred kilometers from the capital, Helsinki, was the town where I spent my childhood and youth. It had much in common with other small towns in Finland. Still in the 1950s Kuopio could be described socio-geographically as a place in which one was never far from nature, either physically or in the sense of one's mentality. The town was also characterized by a large number of wood-framed homes and other buildings with their own front and backyards.

But in one respect Kuopio was better than any other town, at least from a boy's point of view—Puijo and its ski-jump. It stood as a symbol of the native area we knew and loved in the same way as those other cities whose hills and ridges could boast a wooden jump that rose to tree top level, or even higher. Pride in locality pays scant respect to equality, however. Puijo had the biggest ski-jumping hill in the Nordic countries. That's why it was a cut above the rest. It was no wonder then that when I went somewhere else for a visit and someone asked, "Where is this young man from," I would reply without a second thought: "Puijo!"

The competitions held on the hill in March sorted the goats from the sheep. On these occasions top jumpers and less well known names took turns coming down the hill. They launched themselves into flight from the mouth of the ramp, so high up, and flew through the air in pants that flapped gaily in the breeze. When the competition was over there was a feeling of sadness, but also relief. The hill was soon devoid of spectators and remote national heroes alike. Ahead of us lay many a late winter afternoon in the company of our own heroes.

I remember how fidgety we were at school during those last lessons of the day in February and March. Waiting for the jangle of the bell to free us from our desks. After that there was nothing to stop us. School bag slung over my shoulder, I would pedal home toward the skis leaning against the wall of the cellar. At home a few vague words about homework, a quickly grabbed sandwich, and off on my skis. The sun still had some warmth left in it. Skiing a trifle hurriedly past our home-made ski-jump, the pond and over the fields towards Puijo, would I get there in time?

Immediately on arrival I would make a quick glance to ensure that there was no wire strung across the part of the hill where the jumpers landed. That would mean no jumping. Then a look at the jump itself. Is there someone already coming down the ramp or getting ready to jump? My heart would start to beat more evenly, but my sweat-soaked vest still managed to push out steam from around my neck.

If there was nobody in sight up on the hill, then the jumpers were in the hut warming up—a wooden shack with an iron stove painted red glowing in one corner. In the hut there was always the smell of woollen socks and woollen mittens. It was an exciting place. You could get close to the jumpers, hear stories—amazing ones—of jumps, of falls, of trips to competitions, of boozing, of women, too.

None of the jumpers ever greeted us or knew any of us by name, but we knew them all. Between us reigned a mutual understanding that was unspoken. We were allowed to share their company. There was no need to chase us off like troublesome puppies. If more wood was needed for the stove, one of us went and got a large armful, buoyed by a feeling of pride at being useful.

When the cigarettes were smoked, toes and fingers warmed sufficiently, and stories told, then it was time to go. Hearts started to jump. Now we'll see who gets to carry whose skis to the top of the tower. These were real Norwegians, enormously long and heavy, and they all had Kandahar bindings and varnished bottoms.

Jumping skis left distinctive tracks in the snow. They were to be found criss-crossing everywhere, particularly at the bottom of the landing area and around the hut. I've had dreams about them. Those triple-grooved tracks have a terrible significance. There was something mysterious about them—power, daring, unattainabilty. Our own narrow skis left just a pathetic single groove.

The icy steps up to the tower and the heavy skis on my shoulder would put me into almost complete panic. I'd feel like giving up and turning back. The higher we climbed, the more careful my footsteps and the tighter my grip on the wooden railing became.

Up top it was always windy. The first thing to do was to glance dizzily over the wooden fence at the drop, to convince yourself that you were really up here. The tops of even the tallest trees were well below. Then I'd look at the run leading down the ramp. It would be straight in front of me—frightening but at the same time appealing. Two triple-grooved tracks running in parallel its whole length. "When will the day come," I would whisper in silence, "when will I find myself standing at the top of the tower ready to go?"

Virtually every jumper had a quick drag on his cigarette before making the hop onto the run. The wave of a hand from the judges' tower was followed by a grunt as the next jumper got himself ready. The figure of the jumper diminished steadily and disappeared completely as he descended below the brow of the hill after making his jump. Up top we waited tense with excitement to see whether he would reappear on the upslope. Quite often he didn't.

The end of the ramp was the best place to see and experience what ski-jumping was all about. There heroism and courage flew past just a couple of meters away. Various thoughts would come to mind: Will he stay in the tracks, will he time the jump right, how in general could anyone cope with a stream of air which just about freezes your eyeballs?

I have often wondered why us lads didn't identify with those skiers of international repute or other top-class jumpers battling for first place but instead admired the local boys, who received far less publicity. Was it enough that they jumped from Puijo's Big Hill—set off down the ramp without a thought for the lower starting gates and covered such a distance in the air that for us boys there was left only ardent yearning and daydreaming? Daring achievements are not the only yardstick by which to measure one's models. For us it was particularly those "eagles" whose names appeared in the middle or toward the bottom of the result sheet—in other words our heroes—with whom we felt most empathy. Many of them lived in the same part of town, some just a few doors away. They had a swaggering way of talking and in the evenings headed off in their trendy flat caps to hang around on street corners. These were not gentleman gymnasts, or fleet-footed sprinters, or slalom enthusiasts in designer gear.

This familiarity was largely due to the fact that the jumpers almost without exception did heavy jobs, just like our own fathers. It was not at all surprising that these men escaped the daily grind by playing as hard as they worked. This was a fact which at home or with friends out in the yard could not be expected to change. But it did still grate on my ear from time to time. How could such big-name jumpers behave in such a mindless way in their spare time?

After-Images

A few years ago, in clearing out my garden shed, I came across a familiar-looking exercise book in a cardboard box. It was a thick affair with full-sized pages. Its blue cover had badly faded and its pages were dog-eared. My eyes were attracted to the cover. There, faintly discernible, drawn in pencil, was the Olympic flag, but more clearly visible was the logo, cut from a periodical, which read: *A Treasury of Sporting Pictures*. Of course, I knew what I was looking at: the scrapbook into which as a boy I had pasted pictures of ski-jumpers and gymnasts. I didn't immediately remember that the last few pages also bore images of the female form. Diana Dors and Jayne Mansfield, at least, were still identifiable, despite the fact that the larger part of these pictures had been scraped away with a fingernail. Pre-pubescent feelings of guilt?

But there were many familiar male figures on the book's pages, childhood heroes. There they were staring back at me, Finland's and Puijo's eagles, with the occasional foreigner—flying through the air on their heavy wooden skis or just leaning on their skis being inter-viewed by journalists, in their striped woolly caps, V-necked sweaters, loose-bottomed trousers, white ankle-bands, and leather ski-boots.

Could it be that this moment relived and so readily reincarnated on the threshold of the garden shed was the trigger for writing the stories in this chapter? It was, however, an initial flashback that led to a whole series of flashbacks—of the most powerful memories of sport and models of masculinity that left their mark on my child-hood and early youth. Was it in the nature of a primal memory which goes back and forth, forever returning to the past, each time taking on new nuances—won't let it rest—like a reminder of a long-ago yearning to become something that one never did become? Is it the same thing as Proust's *Mémoire Involontaire*, which is not gov-erned by reason and which cannot be compelled into the conscious mind (Benjamin, 1986, p. 15); it is there somewhere, waiting for its moment.[1,2]

This book, an anthology of writings by different authors, is in essence a storybook and a text book, and still yet an academic forum. The purpose of this book is to bring new perspectives to sport research, to its autobiographical and ethnographic branch. The issue is not just one of presenting stories pertaining to sport and the body, but also entertaining how they are examples of "moving writing."[3] What does moving writing mean? In my view it means that the stories do not leave one cold. They are poignant, even when the reader has never had direct personal experience of the particular subject matter or events of a story. My texts are grouped with other stories of the same type on the theme Crafting Ethnographic Fiction in Sport Research. Although these stories have all been written individually by their respective writers, they complement each other by all appearing on the same "reading stage." And it is precisely here that the power of texts written on the same theme lies. It allows for their sympathetic reception in the academic community. They interact while preserving their own individual characteristics.

An autobiographical story approaches ethnographic crafting in the sense that the theory of the text is inscribed in the stylistic choices adopted by the writer. According to Arthur Bochner, who recently presented a paper in progress on my campus, the concern is with

> a shift away from the predominantly textual and semiotic concerns of those who focus primarily on narrative production (most notably literary / linquistic works) to move toward a focus on narrative as a *communicative activity*, where the emphasis is on how humans use language to endow experience with *meanings*. Then, the main focus is on the "narrative fabric of the self," and in the "poetic dimension of narrative," reflecting every person's human struggle to make language adequate to experience. (Bochner, 2001)

Philippe Lejeune (1989, p. 221–222) sees the moving first person narrative as a catalyst and its writer as a catalyzer, "whose only offer is that of listening or of reading, without giving advice and without intervening, triggering in others a desire to write and make them act on it." A similar stance is taken by Walter Benjamin in his essay entitled *The Storyteller* (see Ricoeur 1992) where he recalls, in its most primitive form, still discernible in the epic and already

> in the process of extinction in the novel, the art of storytelling is the art of exchanging experiences. By experiences, he means not scientific observations but the popular exercise of practical wisdom. This wisdom

never fails to include estimations, evaluations that fall under the teleological and deontological categories that will be developed in the next study; in the exchange of experiences which the narrative performs, actions are always subject to approval of disapproval and agents to praise or blame. (pp. 163–164)

In the first of my narratives I have aimed at creating a here-and-now atmosphere. It is written in the first person in the present tense and is from a very specific perspective—that of a child. The second story has been selected from material previously published in Finnish and English (Silvennoinen, 1992, 1994). It, too, contains much that is personal, but also describes something more general: the mentality of sport-mad boys' world in a small town in Finland. "A Jump" is presented in the form of a dialogue between two generations, those of father and son, about the differences between them, in other words, what is most important. The second story ("A Dream") focuses on experiences shared with my friends and their importance to us. In this story the metaphorical message runs from my childhood to adulthood: to become something and to give oneself a different meaning, one given as if from the perspective of an outsider—a struggle which is still going on (e.g. Silvennoinen, 1999, 2000).

In their structure both stories are short and told in flashes. This is intentional. For me they exemplify that variety of ethnographic fiction which, by means of brisk, minimalist expression, aims at revealing the very essence and nuances, "That is one historical form of existence for things that are small and ephemeral but far from negligible" (Benjamin, 1982, p. 257). For me this means that, especially in flashes, one is talking about events which are repeated over and over in the memory, that can be clearly delineated and which condense around them a strong sense of reality and powerful emotions (e.g. Richardson, 2000, p. 937).

However, when it comes to representing a child, which is what I have tried to do, how would we best describe that voice? For example, is it a real event or a fictional reconstruction? Lejeune (1989) deals with this issue quite clearly:

In the classical autobiographical narrative, it is the voice of the adult narrator that dominates and organizes the text; although he/she stages the perspective of the child, he/she hardly lets him/her speak. This is completely natural: childhood appears only through the memory of the adult. We talk about it, eventually we make it speak a little bit, but it does not speak directly. To reconstruct the spoken word of the child, and eventually delegate the function of narration to him/her, we must abandon the code of autobiographic verisimilitude (of the 'natural') and enter the space of fiction. So it will no longer be a question of remembering, but of making up a childlike voice, this dependent on the effects that such a voice can produce on a reader rather than on a concern for fidelity to a childlike enunciation that, in any case, has never existed in this before . . . It is due less to the realistic evocation of a childlike word that is spoken, than to this game of voice, to these methods of fusion, of reluctance, and of shifting between the spoken word of the child and that of the adult. (pp. 66–67)

When I constructed my text, I looked for words, and I tried out different beginnings, endings, and titles. It was as if I was in a no-man's-land between the subconscious and conscious, particularly when the words refused to come. What I would do in this case was leave off for a while and try to provide a space for what one might call free association. For a good narrative cannot be forced into being. A particular memory important to oneself often, at the moment of writing, lies waiting for one like a fish hiding at the bottom of a river. To find—to lose—to find again is to me an important psychodynamic, even therapeutic process. That is why I ask the questions as I write: Why do I have a memory, memories of a long-ago childhood, why an imagination, which is allied to the world of fairy stories, why dreams?

Perhaps the practice of moving writing is at its simplest an exchange of gifts: I read you and you read me. A certain close friend of mine, who has read many of my stories, once came to me with a version of my story in his hands and said, "Look, why don't you take this bit away from the ending and put it at the beginning of the story?" "Well, here you are!"

ACKNOWLEDGMENTS

My warm thanks go to Mrs. Marjatta Saarnivaara and Mr. Arto Tiihonen for reading the text and commenting on it, and Mr. Michael Freeman for the translation.

NOTES

Grateful acknowledgment is made for permission from Sage Publications to reprint sections of this chapter that originally appeared in, Silvennoinen, M. (1994). To childhood heroes. *International Review for the Sociology of Sport*, 29(1), 25–28.

1.   Looking at my scrapbook brought my own ski-jumping experiences to mind with immediate kinetic force. The time, place, state of the snow, and atmosphere returned. Would this compare to what the Finnish psychoanalyst Tor-Björn Hägglund (1998, p. 222–223) terms the "language of the inner spaces." He elaborates in the following:

> A cold hand is squeezing one's throat, there are butterflies in one's stomach, in one's genitals, symbolic words enter one's blood and breathing. As in fairy tales, the language of the inner spaces organises the turmoil of one's inner spaces into images and stories, organises chaos into something meaningful. The language of the inner spaces is not something sentimental or moralising but, instead, conflict and struggling with superior force and one's own inability. (pp. 222–223)

Although this characterization refers to such profound bodily experiences that they can't be grasped in language, except only here and there, it poses a very humbling challenge to the text: "It is what is revealed that constructs the message, not the other way round" (Ricoeur, 2000, p. 105–106).

2.   For the British writer Nick Hornby (2000), football and Arsenal are a continuum from childhood to adulthood. It is a love-hate relationship. It can be neither neutralized nor annihilated; it is a permanent "romance of identity."

3.   The publication in 1992 (in Finnish) of the book *Urheilukirja* (*A Book on Sport*) (Sironen et al. 1992) marked the first significant step in ethnographic narratives in which moving writing held a central position among some Finnish sports sociologists. As far back as 1978 Richard Brown proposed the idea of "poetic sociology"—"an aesthetic view of sociological knowledge where the sociological understanding is yielded by interpretive procedures that focus on meanings that actors give to their own situations" (p. 1–2). He also pointed to "cognitive aesthetics" as a framework that "permits us to move beyond copy theories of truth in both art and in science" (p. 3).

REFERENCES

Benjamin, W. (1982). *Illuminations*. Hannah Arendt (Ed.). Translated by Harry Zohn. London: Fontana / Collins.

Benjamin, W. (1986). *Silmä väkijoukossa: Huomioita eräistä motiiveista Baudelairen tuotannossa* (Über einige Motive bei Baudelaire, 1939, suom. Antti Alanen). Rauma: Odessa.

Bochner, A. P. (2001). *New forms of ethnographic studies.* Delivered as a working paper, University of Jyväskylä, Finland, Jan. 22, 2001.

Brown, R. H. (1978). *A poetic for sociology: Toward a logic of discovery for the human sciences.* Cambridge: Cambridge University Press.

Fiffer, S. S., & Fiffer, S. (1999). (Eds.) *Body.* New York: Avon Books.

Hornby, N. (2000). *Hornankattila* (Fever Pitch, Finnish translation, Jukka Jääskeläinen). Porvoo: WSOY.

Hägglund, T. B. (1998). *Ruumiillisuuden kosketus: Psykoanalyyttisiä esseitä* (The touch of corporeality: Psychoanalytic essays). Jyväskylä, Finland: Gummerus.

Lejeune, P. (1989). On autobiography (From a collection of original texts trans. Katherine Leary). *Theory and history of literature, Vol 52.* Minnesota: University of Minnesota Press.

Ricoeur, P. (1992). *Oneself as another.* Chicago: University of Chicago Press.

Ricoeur, P. (2000). *Tulkinnan teoria: Diskurssi ja merkityksen lisä* (Interpreting theory: Discourse and the surplus of meaning, Finnish translation, Heikki Kujansivu). Helsinki: Tutkijaliitto.

Richardson, L. (2000). Writing: A method of inquiry. In N.K. Denzin & Yvonna S. Lincoln (Eds.), *Handbook of qualitative research* (2nd edition), pp. 923–943. Thousand Oaks, CA: Sage.

Silvennoinen, M. (1992). Puijon mäkimiehet (The ski-jumpers from Puijo). In Esa Sironen, Arto Tiihonen ja Soile Veijola (Eds.), *Urheilukirja* (A book on sport), pp. 145–152. Tampere, Finland: Vastapaino.

Silvennoinen, M. (1994). To chidhood heroes. *International Review for the Sociology of Sport, 29*(1), 25–30.

Silvennoinen, M. (1999). My Body as a metaphor. In Andrew C. Sparkes & M. Silvennoinen (Eds.), *Talking bodies: Men's narratives of the body and sport,* pp. 163–175. Jyväskylä, Finland: University of Jyväskylä, SoPhi.

Silvennoinen, M. (2000). Another way of knowing? *Auto/Biography, 8,* (1&2), 99–104.

Sironen, E., Tiihonen, A., & Veijola, S. (1992). (Eds). *Urheilukirja* (A book on sport). Tampere, Finland: Vastapaino.

PART III

Author Interviews, Notes on Craft

As any of us knows, an empathetic touch can guide and instruct us through a change of character or situation—a teacher who first sparked a desire to learn and ask questions. Developing a new literary style, therefore, has as much to do with "talent" and "disposition," as it does with habits, strategies, and inspiration. To explore a new writerly voice, to seek some distinctive, unique signature, or mark to express one's vision typically follows a change of heart and mind. To garner advice from more practiced others', then, should most certainly leave an impression. In this section two novelists express their vision of fiction and other creative writing forms as ways to represent or portray sport—how people move, their embodied senses. Listen for answers here to two key questions: What connects understanding to writing? Why are evocative writing practices so in synch with the way we move?

CHAPTER 9

An Interview with Jenifer Levin

Joli Sandoz

Joli: *You've written fiction with a variety of characters and settings, ranging from an Israeli family* (Shimoni's Lover) *to an adventurer lost in a mythical island nation* (Snow) *to the coach and athletes at a New England college's Division II swim program* (The Sea of Light). *With all humanity and all the world to choose from, why sport?*

Jenifer: As a human endeavor, sport celebrates the potential of using human power, passion, intelligence and will in both the process of and progress toward transformation. In my first novel, *Water Dancer,* I wrote about sport the way I saw and experienced it—as a door to a world of possibilities, one you can open as far as you like, or dare. The wider you open it, the farther you step into this world and the more you learn about yourself and everything else. I'm interested in writing about people who use sport this way, as a metaphor for the extreme and significant moments and passages in the rest of their lives. Sport as sport actually doesn't engage me—it's this transformational aspect of it that is physically tangible, emotionally and psychologically and intellectually perceived—that's what interests me about the athletic experience. The older I get, the truer this has become. I enjoyed the sheer physical activity of athletics when I was younger, for its own sake; but participation in a sport isn't really satisfying for me now unless it complements and meshes with something else I want to do, something else I'm trying to understand.

Joli: *What sort of events or understandings are these, for you?*

Jenifer: The major, pivotal events—family celebrations, personal tragedies, illness, recovery; really anything transformative and requiring will, stamina, fitness, psychological readiness and patience. These share qualities with serious participation in sport, particularly those sports demanding lots of hours and work, such as competitive swimming or training to run a marathon. Sport has strengthened me not just physically but psychologically for life's inevitable tough moments. The mental and emotional stamina I've needed to survive relationships falling apart, the weird roller coaster of my career as a writer of literary fiction, the agonizing death of my best friend (and other dear friends) from AIDS; adopting my sons in a faraway war-ruined land over a long, lonely and uncertain period of time, then traveling across the world with them and seeing them through all the surgeries and illnesses they have had to endure, and trusting (and helping them to trust) that there is a payoff for all the suffering and patience and seeing it through with humanity and dignity (e.g., endurance)—these are the lessons my participation in sport has given me. And these are the lessons I hope I apply to seeing my way through my work as a writer, as well as through my life as a sentient being. No matter what the trial or the goal, it helps to be fit, to be as prepared as possible, to feel the competence and capacity for doing difficult things—and the self-knowledge!—that hard physical training can give you.

Joli: *How did sport first move into your writing?*

Jenifer: I always wrote, even as a child, and aside from a few painful and dismal years as an adolescent and teen, I was always physically active. Then in my early twenties, while crawling out of the self-destructive psychological and physical patterns of pre-adulthood, I realized that athletic endeavor was an important part of returning me to a full human life. Not only that, but it paralleled other things I wanted to accomplish, aiding and abetting fulfillment of my goals. I started to run, did some weight training, and began swimming again. At the same time, I began writing two seemingly separate series of short stories: one about a swimmer, and one about gay and lesbian life and the experience of coming out in this country. The two themes came together for me in *Water Dancer*. Sport moved into my writing because my life, which was renewed and reclaimed by physical endeavor, was moving in that direction.

Joli: *Editors at the* New York Times, Mademoiselle, Rolling Stone, Ms. *and other publications have published your nonfiction on a variety of topics. What moves you to write fiction as well?*

Jenifer: Good writing tells the truth, no matter what form it takes or what genre it falls into. Nonfiction tries to tell the truth as elegantly as possible using fact, and fiction tries to tell the truth through imagined circumstances and characters. The two forms, nonfiction and fiction, differ quite a bit in terms of craft, though.

There are a number of classical and accepted structures for each, conventions which in my opinion are worth paying attention to, and—more often than not—adhering to. In fiction, there is the question of the dramatic arc, character, timing. In nonfiction, immediate clarity of story and purpose are profoundly important. In both a story must be told with force and grace; the key points of the story must be made boldly, and the key players described in living color. Most importantly, the truth has to be rendered believably—whether it's the human truth told through imaginary circumstance (in fiction), or the fact-based truth of nonfiction. And in both, I think any good writer wants her or his audience to be engaged and entertained. So, for both fiction and nonfiction, some general rules apply: (1) a good story, told clearly and entertainingly; (2) the significant characters fully described, lent human dimension, and rendered indispensable; (3) the key elements of the story highlighted. (Style and timing and craft are essential here). In a very broad, simplified way, I'd say that all forms of good writing accomplish all of the above, be they fiction or nonfiction.

Joli: *Your fiction in general is often praised for its vivid description, and your sport fiction in particular for its "glowing" and "detailed" depictions of physicality and body. For writers, what opportunities and what problems open out from what you called in* Sea of Light *"the truth . . . expressed in the body"?*

Jenifer: As a culture and a species, we are lured continually and falsely away from the physical truth of our existence by a burgeoning economy of slick technology. Sport isn't immune to the encroachment of technology, of course. But part of what makes sport sport (and I'm not talking drag-racing here) is the fact that participants accomplish the major tasks with their very own physical bodies. They may have springier shoes or slicker suits—but inside the shoes and suits are naked human bodies whose arms and legs and fingers and eyes and hearts are doing the work: aiming, throwing, running, swimming, scoring, covering distance.

When you write about the body in action, you bring people back to a recognition of their true selves. Recognition—that "ah-hah!" experience—is what keeps the reader with you. And yes, I think that most of the time our true selves do reside "in" the body . . . but that is not to say that our true selves are synonymous with the body. Rather, a body is a vehicle (and sometimes prison) to the self while that body is alive and kicking. This truth is not necessarily opposed by technology—but technology, when used incorrectly, serves to obscure it. And sport, when played well and with passion, rips away the obscuring veils of daily life, and returns us to a positive realization of our human/animal selves.

Good writing, like any good art, also restores things to full-life size—away from the minimalist confines of the PalmPilot and TV screen. Writers should therefore be brave in the manner of great athletes, unafraid to let it all hang out and GO BIG. People (readers) will love you for it, since people everywhere are sick to death of seeing their reflections rendered smaller and smaller by the increasingly technological world around them. Get outrageous in concept and in execution. Fall on your face, if necessary. Dare—to be fully life-sized and human.

Joli: *In what ways does your own experience shape your writing about athletes and athletics?*

Jenifer: If you're writing about a sport, you owe it to yourself to go try it, even for a significant length of time if necessary. The aspect of putting yourself on the line physically is important here, as is understanding what it's like to be coached, to be a member of a team, and so on. That doesn't mean writers must limit themselves to writing about only what they've actually been through. Imagination goes a long way—but it doesn't go all the way. I first wrote about swimming in *Water Dancer*, for example, because that was my sport. But what I wrote wasn't necessarily about my own experience in swimming; I've never swum a twenty-six mile strait of rough cold water. However, I did have enough swimming under my belt to accurately imagine what that would be like.

Joli: *What other experience or knowledges, in addition to direct engagement, are helpful in writing fiction about sport?*

Jenifer: The most important things for the fiction writer to do, apart from direct engagement, are to live fully, observe wholeheartedly, expose oneself to other forms of art (movies, theater, photography, painting, poetry, etc.) and read, read, read—good books for what they teach one to do and to aspire towards, bad books because they can teach what *not* to do . . . and because sometimes even lousy books contain the outline of good stories.

Joli: *Are there experiential connections between the doing of sport and the act of writing?*

Jenifer: People may sometimes look at the page and think, "Gee, I can't do that. I can run a good mile, but I can't write." There's a tremendous amount of mystification about any art form, really—so much so that people tend to forget the fundamental elements of craft which are so important to any artistic success. When you approach writing as a particular process, though—one that might feel challenging, but a process nonetheless, one ordinary human beings can undertake and succeed in with commitment, flexibility, work, psychological strength and endurance—you will find significant parallels between it and any activity requiring commitment, courage, and sacrifice, including sport. Psychologically, at least, the writing process can feel very much like a solo endurance effort. For me, when I'm writing a novel, there come points where I feel I cannot continue without breaking apart, and peaks at the top of which I feel triumphant—and, as at any finish line, accomplished but extraordinarily alone. Writing can take you into significant pain and solitude, and exactly as in marathon running or any kind of physical pursuit requiring stamina, the only way out is through. Writing's not separate from the body.

Joli: *You've said that you wrote* The Sea of Light *over a span of years, but that most of the writing itself took place in just a few weeks. Could you explain what there is to the writing process for you, in addition to actually putting words on the page?*

Jenifer: The writing process is much, much more than putting words on a page. The time you take mulling things over, letting questions clarify and answers gel in your mind and heart, is just as crucial as the time you take to type on a keyboard when you're working on a story.

Joli: *What practical strategies have you and your writing students found useful for writers beginning to try their hand?*

Jenifer: Write every day, if possible; even if it's just a paragraph about nothing in particular. The act of writing (like practice of anything) makes the act of writing easier, in the end. As I've said before, read as much as you can. Some people respond well to workshops and classes, tending to produce more writing. A word of warning to beginners, though. Don't participate in any workshop or class setting where your ego will be damaged by negative and unhelpful commentary. Remember that, before you write well, often you must write poorly. Successful writing takes place before, during, and after: *before* you sit down to write, because of the tremendous amount of thought and feeling (subconscious and conscious) that you're expending on your story, and because of all the life experience you will bring to bear in understanding it and in telling it; *during* the writing itself, because you will allow yourself to create freely, mistakes, doubts, and all; and *after* the first few drafts are done, because you will then have the experience of editing and amending your work—stepping back to see how it reads, what is missing and so on, and then fixing it. This last is the fun part for me—I call it "putting the icing on."

Joli: *You write about women, men, young, old, working class, wealthy, white, brown, people at times triumphant and at other times stunned by loss. How do you go about conceiving and developing subjectivities/perspectives different from your own?*

Jenifer: It's the job of fiction writers—and, to a certain extent, nonfiction writers as well—to inhabit the perspectives of other people and characters, and to come up with a story that captures readers' attention and beyond, to readers' dreams and subconscious experience. I try to place myself right behind the eyeballs of characters. One way to do that is by asking myself questions from their point of view. For example: What would Bren [a swimming coach in *The Sea of Light*] do in a particular situation? Good, riveting fiction is formed in the nexus between the inevitable actions of a powerful character, and the unstoppable effects of powerful circumstance.

There's an important distinction, I think, between what feeds writing, and the giving writing requires. I think I refer to everything I've ever read and heard and done when I write. Poetry and motion pictures have been my personal major influences (although not exclusively so); these can inspire me as a writer. Being in love sometimes inspires me to write. The satisfaction of completing something else difficult such as a marathon or learning a difficult piece of music—I play classical guitar—or helping my children accomplish something hard but worthy often makes me feel temporarily at peace, and free to write.

Empathy, understanding, the ability to stand right behind the eyeballs of another, and write from that perspective as if it's your own heart you're pouring out . . . that's something else again. That's something you get from being alive, and sensitive to life, and, I think, from being hurt enough that you know what it is to be in pain, to be lonely, to strive with all your might for something that may nevertheless elude you. People can be courageous and yet insensitive. Or they can be sensitive and yet cowardly. A good writer should ideally have a good measure of courage *and* a good measure of sensitivity. That doesn't mean being fearless, or being a terrific person all the time. It just means keeping conscious so that you can see, hear, feel, touch. It means a willingness to keep working hard at cultivating and evolving with whatever you've got, and whatever you've got with others, and then to throw whatever you've got on the table and keep taking a chance with it—you know, keep taking that one more stroke or step. And then when you finish, to let it all go.

Joli: *Given the structured nature of competitive sport, it's all too easy for writers to rely on clichéd plots, emotions and language. What do you do to keep your writing about sport fresh?*

Jenifer: Games, sports, various forms of specialized pursuit, anything requiring expertise and extensive practice toward a specific goal—all of these endeavors provide good structure for any kind of writing because they have inherent points of tension and drama. Whether it's learning to play blackjack, run a marathon, or perform a difficult piece of music, there's a form inseparable from that endeavor that makes it easier to craft a story around it. And in that crafting, the writer faces a choice. She can make the story only about the game . . . or she can write about the amazing permutations of consciousness and the frequent physical changes affecting individuals who play that game. What I mean is that there are levels of writing about sport, just as there are levels of athletic participation. One common perception of athletes in our culture—a perception often acted out by young and/or immature people, especially in relation to team sports—is as tough, insensitive, rather goofy, self-contained (or team-contained) social units who also happen to do difficult physical things. Without meaning to belabor the point, I'd call this approach shallow and careless. Because it's also possible to live, and write about, sport as a series of supreme, multi-textured, multi-layered achievements and experiences.

At the elite level, athletes can become rarefied, singular at times, often quite extraordinary. This is true not just in regards to individual sports like road running, diving, marathon swimming, etc., but also for team sports. Now, I love to watch [men's] pro football. And it seems to me that the actual elite athletes who play pro football are quite different from the standard stereotypical representations of them. Far from being robots, they're often in touch with profound emotions that can't be hidden. What they do takes everything they are, and more; the way they play the game demands that they reveal commitment and passion, ecstasy, grief, and love between men. Again, one thing that's so compelling about sport viewed in depth is that it mimics the moments of extremity and transition in our larger lives: birth, death, and all the peak moments in between. These moments are mythical in dimension, and that's why they stick with us. It's this level of sport that, for me, is worth writing about, worth trying to live—and it's this aspect of sport, and of writing, that remains fresh.

Joli: *Few of your fictional characters are in the sporting mainstream—most are women, and women who are Jewish, Cuban, lesbian, working class, incest survivors, even beginners in sport. Why these subjects?*

Jenifer: My characters seem to me to be just common people. Most people have quirks, and if you explore their truths, they aren't stereotypical. What I'm doing when I write is simply getting into the characters' heads. I think less about them as athletes, and more about how sport will help create or play into the situations they find themselves in as people, at this particular point in their lives.

When I was growing up, during the late sixties and early seventies, women in athletics labored under a dual internal obligation. They loved sport, and at the same time had to fight the implicit accusation that if they were physically competent, they also somehow were not women. As a result, while female athletes burned with tremendous fire inside, not many were able really to let themselves go and be visibly gutsy, exciting, charismatic. They didn't permit themselves to be outwardly passionate, that is, because society in general associated passion connected to physical endeavor with maleness. I didn't read much then that presented women as people who lived and breathed athletics. Today sport, and our public representations of it, have changed tremendously.

We can see that women athletes are very serious about themselves and other sportswomen.

Joli:　*How does intentionality in communicating specific meaning to specific audiences relate to your efforts to craft a particular piece of writing?*

Jenifer:　Whenever I write, I want readers to have an emotional response of "Wow, that really moves me, I feel XYZ." Then I want a sense of recognition, readers seeing their human selves in whatever I'm writing about.

"Message" is a sticky subject. Any writer, of fiction or of nonfiction, is going to be more successful just telling the story. You're communicating because you think X is important for people to know, so tell them about X. There is plenty of message inherent in even the smallest well-told story. And another thing: Steer clear of making everything overly tidy. Truth is messy. People in their real existences are forever contradictory; and it's that, the things about ourselves we cannot reconcile, that make the people and characters we write about the most human—and hence the most fascinating and resonant for the reader. Some writers live in a world of theory, and theory tends to try to make things fit. But in the physical world, the map is not the territory. While theory and actuality can lend a lot to one another, in the end reconciliation and making things dovetail is not as important to successful writing as truth—allowing things and people to be seen as they are.

As far as audience goes, I usually think about just one or two people; some adult from my past, perhaps, or one of my young sons reading what I've written twenty years from now. That's it. With those exceptions, I write because I write. Once it's done, and published, and out there, who knows what anyone else will make of it?

Jenifer Levin has taught writing at the University of Michigan and The Writer's Voice, and leads advanced fiction workshops in New York City. Her novels include two featuring women's swimming, *Water Dancer* and *The Sea of Light*. She also has a short story collection, *Love and Death, and Other Disasters.* Levin's nonfiction has appeared in *Rolling Stone, Ms.,* and *Mademoiselle.* Currently she is working on her fifth novel.

CHAPTER 10

An Interview with Donald Hayes

John Morefield

John: *Your book,* The Dixie Association, *is about a mythical (and mythic) minor baseball league with teams in such places as Selma, Asheville, Milledgeville, Oxford, and Little Rock, where the narrator-hero, an ex-con named Hog Durham, goes to play baseball for the Arkansas Reds, whose manager Lefty Marks has been responsible for Hog's early parole. Lefty's and his team's names are rooted both in baseball tradition and in leftist politics. Most names in the book, other than those of real places, have associations with either southern politics or southern literature. The latter are predominantly allusions to places and characters in the works of William Faulkner. Recognition of these associations is a bonus to the pleasures afforded by the story itself. After reading the novel I was interested in how it came to be written and how—in view of the presumed readership of the this book—your experiences and methods might cast light on the creative process for people who wanted to write about sport, not as fiction, but in ways which had kinship with the fiction writer's approach. Therefore, Donald, could you say whether you think of yourself as first a fiction writer who discovered sport as a subject later on? Or was sport, as baseball, an important part of your experience and makeup before you took up the novelist's path?*

Donald: I was playing baseball long before it occurred to me that I might become a novelist. During the last years I played semi-pro ball, I was trying to write, and it then occurred to me that baseball and a particular baseball team might be the subject matter I should deal with at that time . . . though I'm not sure that this particular answer leads us anywhere . . .

John: *I asked that particular question as a way to get into how (and why) you approached the subject of baseball initially. I try to remember that the readers of this book want to know how fictional techniques offer advantages to writers of sport sociology that traditional quasi-objective or "scientific" social science methods do not offer. To me—and perhaps to you—this seems at first sort of a backward question: I've always wanted to write fiction, which to me is the most important thing there is. If there is a question it is, What will I write about next? But these readers know what they want to write about but are being led by current trends to try what fiction writers do from the beginning—or try to do—which is create a sensorily and emotionally convincing world populated with characters who are the same. So how did your early efforts begin? Did you, for instance, have a mentor or teacher or did you seek consciously to emulate some older writer?*

Donald: The writer who I've been most influenced by, and whose influence I've spent the most time trying to overcome is of course, Faulkner.

John: *Could you mention some specific ways he influenced your development?*

Donald: Faulkner helped me understand the nature of place, and to some extent helped me realize my own place—my connections with family and all of that. I had to struggle to get past Faulkner's influence on my prose. His influence caused me to overwrite—to write bad Faulkner. The best advice I've ever heard about this is the advice John Gardner gave Ray Carver, teacher to pupil: "Read all the Faulkner you can. After you've done that, read all the Hemingway so that you'll get the Faulkner out of your system."

John: *So many of the characters in* The Dixie Association— *J. G. Flemson, Candy Commerce, Woodrow Ratliff, to name only a few—echo characters in Faulkner's novels. Why did you do that?*

Donald: Since *The Dixie Association* is a sports novel, since it is about a game, I wanted to play games even with those influences, so I gave every team in the league a name that has connotations connecting it to either southern politics or southern literature. I did the same thing with the names of the players on each of the teams.

John: *Do you find that the names you give characters can affect the way they behave on the page?*

Donald: I do give my characters names according to my view of how I think they will behave on the page. To some extent, I expect the names to reflect character. That's especially true in *The Dixie Association*. The character comes first, and the name comes second.

John: *I'd like to ask about your protagonist, Hog Durham. He's likeable—sometimes, but to me not all the time; but he is really quite believable. Could you comment on how that character came about?*

Donald: I played baseball for years with a shortstop who had done two stretches in the Oklahoma State Penitentiary. He was a power hitter and a colorful character, but not very bright. At first, I wanted a character based on him to be a character in my novel, but then I realized that I wanted an outsider to be the narrator, and I could think of no one who was more of an outsider than an ex-convict. I wanted the voice to be colorful, colloquial, and intelligent, so what I did was I increased the shortstop's IQ by about fifty points and had him tell the story. I wanted it to be a novel that was at least in part about a character finding a place to belong—about learning how to be part of a community, and about learning how to love someone else. I also, of course, wanted it to be about a baseball season in which a lot happened, but once I decided who the narrator was and what his voice would be like, a lot of other things fell into place.

John: *I'm glad you said that about his "voice," because I wanted to get into that much-discussed but, as I suspect, seldom understood element that is vital to any fiction, to any kind of writing, that lives or moves. But how does one teach or find voice? Is there any one among*

the many good creative writing texts available today that you find
works best or offers exercises useful in finding it?

Donald: I've always found the most useful of the books about
writing was John Gardner's *The Art of Fiction*. It has a number of
useful exercises; it has good discussion of plot and structure and
characterization. I found it to be useful in many ways. I think it's
still by far the best book about writing. I also very much like Ray-
mond Carver's essay about what he learned from John Gardner in
Carver's book *Fires*.

In the case of *The Dixie Association*, I began writing it in the
third person, and about thirty or forty pages into that version of
the novel, a character appeared and made a short talk in the club-
house. I thought what he said was more interesting and had more
energy in it that anything else in the novel up to that point. After
thinking about it for a good time and resisting the impulse, I decided to go back and begin the novel using that voice. It seemed to
me then, as it does now, the right voice for the novel. The question
you were asking is very difficult to answer in any kind of general
way, but I do believe that every novel or story has an ideal voice,
and that it is one of the writer's jobs to find that voice. I don't
know if I can be a whole lot more specific about this.

John: *Maybe my favorite character in the book is one whose voice is*
seldom heard, but who is still a powerful presence, the aging but domi-
nating pitcher Jeremiah Eversole. I especially admire the scene in which
he opens up to Hog about his past, then his story is retold in Hog's
own words. I wonder if you could comment a little on the genesis of
that character and whether you've ever seen a pitcher perform as he does
in the novel, even when, as in one game, he has already lost but refuses
to be humiliated? I thought you conveyed a lot about the inner man
and his struggles by external means.

Donald: My best friend in high school was named Jerry Don
Eversole. He was part Cherokee. He didn't play baseball, but he
physically resembled the character in the novel. The history or
background of the Jeremiah Eversole in the novel is completely
made up. I have seen athletes perform magnificently in times and

places when there seems to be little reason for them even to make the effort, but I've never seen a perfect game. In other words, I've never seen an athlete perform as well as Eversole does in the novel.

John: *Why, incidentally, did you put his story in Hog's mouth instead of letting him speak for himself? Would that have weakened the almost mythic stature he has through most of the book?*

Donald: I thought Hog could tell the story better than Eversole could. Eversole was a man given to silences, and if I allowed him to talk on and on for pages, I would undercut that. Even though he tells his story to Hog in the novel, I thought it wise not to quote him verbatim. I thought it would be more effective to simply have Hog summarize his story in some detail because finally, in that novel, Hog is the storyteller.

John: *Could you discuss the "advantages" that fiction has over other ways of writing when it comes to capturing the "visceral" experiences of sports. In other words, have you tried sport reporting or other non-fiction writing about baseball? Or do you perhaps have any feelings about non-fiction sport writing in relation to sport fiction?*

Donald: One of the great advantages of fiction over nonfiction is that fiction more easily allows the writer to "capture visceral experiences" and to render character in depth. Nonfiction is limited to the literal truth, while fiction can escape those boundaries through imagination. If done well, I believe fiction actually comes much closer to the truth of character and emotion and experience. I've done a little sports reporting, and aside from some colorful anecdotes, I found it limiting. There is some very good nonfiction sport writing; I am a big fan of *Eight Men Out* and *The Boys of Summer*. I'm fond of many other nonfiction books on sport. There are probably more good nonfiction books about sport than there are fiction, but I think that's because not enough good writers have tried writing fiction about sport.

John: *Do you see any similarities between writing and playing a sport?*

Donald: The only connection I can think of between actually participating in sports, or playing ball, and writing, is that to do either of them well requires a great deal of concentration and a great deal of practice. To do either of them, you have to exercise regularly, and you have to work so hard and so frequently at the craft that it becomes something like second nature.

John: *What is your personal discipline, if I might ask?*

Donald: I try to get to work by mid-morning every day. I tend to go to bed late and sleep late, so I try to write from mid-morning to early-to-mid-afternoon, say ten to two. I do that five days a week. I have a full day at the university on Tuesdays and Thursdays, and I can't keep to that schedule on those days, though I try to write at least a sentence or two on those days so that I will keep the habit. The best advice on this I've ever read from another writer was Hemingway's. He wrote five hundred words a day, and he made sure that when the day ended, he left his work knowing what the first sentence was going to be the next day. Very good advice. He never went to his workroom without knowing what the first sentence was going to be. So in a sense, he never faced the blank page.

John: *I think a lot of people have tended to create an aura of mystery or romance about "the creative process." Do you, finally, have anything to say to people who might be insecure about trying to create because they think it involves some mysterious process they can't participate in?*

Donald: I think the creative process has generally been over-romanticized. I think basically you have a good idea for a poem, story, or novel and then you go into your room and work it out for as long as it takes. In that way, good writers aren't so different than any other worker.

Donald Hayes is the author of *The Dixie Association* and *The Hangman's Children*. He is an Associate Professor of English at the University of Arkansas where he is also the director of the program in creative writing.

CONCLUSION

Movement Practices Through Text

Jim Denison

We read qualitative research for many reasons—many good reasons. Perhaps to appreciate the complexity of social life, or to understand people's experiences and how they are bound up in gender, class, race, and power relations. Qualitative research constitutes a personal, yet public journey into the lifeworld of others. As a discipline, or philosophical basis for inquiry, qualitative research offers us promise through the stories and theories we create and share. And qualitative research delivers an open-ended version of the truth, where reasoning and meaning-making operate linguistically not numerically. So we need skilled "qualitative researchers as writers" to communicate effectively these understandings and draw us into their circle of analysis and interpretation. We need qualitative researchers who can touch us emotionally and provide a full-blown rendering of the self. This book has been about preparing such researchers, scholar-artists who can craft language into theory and make us move.

Norman Denzin and Yvonna Lincoln (1994) fancy the term "bricoleur" to describe the qualitative researcher who "understands that research is an interactive process . . . and who also knows that researchers all tell stories" (p. 3). Zygmunt Bauman's (2000) term, "the exiled author," describes the sociological writer who is on the "inside and outside at the same time, and combines intimacy with the critical look of an outsider" (p. 82). Bauman reminds us further that qualitative researchers today must be able to "move with equal ease between several linguistic universes, not one" (p. 83), in order to do as Milan Kundera (1986) says, "crush the wall behind which something that was always there hides" (p. 10). But this investigative directive must not be confused with the journalist's exposé. For uncovering and muckraking is one thing, evoking reality while also analyzing experience is something else entirely.

When I first began to experiment with different modes of qualitative research I wanted to know so much. I wanted to know about people, both myself and others. I wanted to know about life and what it means to be human. I wanted to know how it feels to play, to work, to struggle, and what it is to collapse or to triumph. I wanted to know what it means to fall in love, to fall out of love, to be afraid, or to take a chance. The list, it goes on. Of course, preceding the declaration, "I want to know," must come the admission, "I don't know?" Hence, I have continued to work qualitatively with the "elements" of life for precisely that reason: qualitative research as a way of knowing satisfies the questions I hold about who I am and how I think about the world. Entering the realm of qualitative research, therefore, should never be a methodological decision alone, or to have a brief fling on the "other side." At heart becoming a qualitative researcher is an ontological commitment to a way of sensing who and what we are that acknowledges the complexity and ambiguity of social life as an interactional process.

By way of an example, I wrote a series of three stories (Denison, 1998, 1999, 2000) because of something I didn't know about myself. I didn't know why I was obsessed for seventeen years with breaking four minutes for a mile. Was it because I was seeking a way to make my mark as the youngest child in my family? Was it because of the options and resources available to me at the time? Or was it due to some inner condition I needed to express? I don't know. Even more puzzling to me was why I failed. Maybe it just wasn't meant to be, I thought? Or maybe my VO^2 Max was too low, or my percentage of slow-twitch muscle fibers too high? Or, I asked myself, was my life meant for some other purpose? I don't know.

What I do know, though, is that it was studying, thinking, questioning, and ultimately writing that provided me with some answers. Or, should I say, versions or approximations of the truth. But it wasn't just writing down in any old way what came into my mind about my life as a runner, or what sounded good, or looked pretty on the page that satisfied me. What I appreciate about qualitative research is how new modes of inquiry, or options for knowing arise and present themselves with the times. The new ways of writing promoted through this book—auto-ethnography and ethnographic fiction—are an example of what I'm referring to. Therefore, when I say I appreciate the opportunity to write stories, I mean writing stories as a qualitative researcher.

Ultimately it is the process of sitting alone in front of my computer, thinking, reading, and remembering with words, and meditating on their sound, their rhythm, and their cadence that allows me to know. Writing a story is the best way I can come up with to understand this world, this life; my world, my life. Thus, every day as I write my autoethnographies or ethnographic fictions, mixing theory with memory and imagination, I draw upon a variety of details and images in order to try to show and tell how a life is first lead and then understood. And to be real these details and images must have sound, depth, color, taste, lightness, emotion, and feel. They must also extend outward, touching numerous scattered souls at some level or point they've never known or realized existed. For it is only in this way, the total embodied summoning of all my sensibilities—artistic, intellectual, and critical—into a concentrated, imaginative, aesthetic effort, that I can begin to apprehend what it is I don't know and be satisfied that in the end it all means something. And it's only this way for me that the idea of "research as stories" can come to be.

Nothing, then, should be more crucial or exciting for the qualitative researcher as writer than attempting to capture "accurately," "deeply," and "exactly" what something is or purports to be: a state of mind, an experience, a feeling, a certain kind of relationship. This is what it means to probe and ask insightful "how" and "why" questions. This is what it means to try to get to the bottom of something and understand both its origin and significance. Personaly, I believe the writers in this collection *have* gotten to the bottom of something. Consider Katherine Parrott's chapter (4), her story of love and loss expressed through the beauty and grace of teamwork. Or how Martti Silvennoinen, in his chapter (8), reaches back momentarily to grasp his boyhood. The writers in this book have all taken movement as life, life as movement, and treated it seriously. Not a single contributor was content to present a glib notation of an obvious truth or an obvious discrepancy in the world. Facts or story-points were never put ahead of experience or analysis. The writers in this volume understand that a critical point of view can yield more than a statistic or a quote even. It can be a feeling, an emotion, or a sense of anticipation, too.

In Pirkko Markula's chapter (1), she conveys her battle with thinness and the specter of the perpetually toned and young female form. Without question she has laid the complex and contradictory personal and sociological dimensions of that struggle squarely in our laps. Like all the authors in this book, she has brought us into a fuller relationship with our bodies and how we move. Not only that, her chapter—also like the others'—unfolds before us with sensitivity and grace. In this way, it can be said that the eight qualitative researchers collected here are all passionate storytellers: intellectually so, analytically, emotionally, and creatively.

Movement, one has to conclude after reading this book, is not such an innocent practice. It has extensions and dimensions that are far-reaching politically, socially, and culturally. Sport, physical education, dance, exercise . . . these activities produce institutional and institutionalized selves. The individual as a disembodied decision-making agent is fallacy now. Instead, with Andrew Sparkes's back pain (chapter 2), or Arto Tiihonen's stumbling into manhood (chapter 3), we see how bodies are whole, not split, and how social theory can be demonstrated through specific case studies that show the interrelation between nature, culture, society, and the self. This is cutting-edge scholarship that extends our minds and stretches our spirits. And shouldn't that be why we turn to qualitative research, to hear our hearts beat with brand-new knowledge?

The bricoleur, then, or the exiled-author, or whatever else you want to call today's qualitative researcher is nothing if not a storyteller first (Rorty, 1991). But making a story is natural. The psychologist, Jerome Bruner, believes it's born into every human being, imparting on us a "narrative sense." And in her excellent essay,

"The Storytelling Animal" (1996), Mary Paumier Jones discusses how there does not exist a people without narratives or stories to make sense of themselves. However, telling a story is one thing, it's quite another to be able to reflect on the events and circumstances of a story to provide a critical insight into social life. For it's the reflection a story encites that spells the difference between a predictable melodrama and something else entirely. Something that through various literary devices and scholarly effects apprehends the mystery of life and lights up our world. Would it be an exaggeration to call such a story a masterpiece or a classic? In many ways, I don't think it would be. And in many ways this is what I feel qualitative researchers in this moment—the seventh (Lincoln & Denzin, 2000)—should be aiming to do: combining aesthetic touches with a reflexive and critical understanding of social life that impacts on others and offers a credible account of a cultural, individual, and communal sense of the "real" (Richardson, 2000).

Therefore, as qualitative research expands, touching more disciplines and influencing more faculties, I hope the field will continue to move further and further away from grand over-arching narratives that rely on any sort of narrow or reductionistic methodology. This way, our texts can become "sites for critical conversations about democracy, race, gender, class, nation, freedom, and community" (Lincoln & Denzin, 2000, p. 1048). Something akin to what Bob Rinehart does in his chapter (7), when he helps us imagine and understand adolescent angst, and how such monolithic terms as "at-risk youth" trivialize the trying process of growing-up male in America. Or what David Rowe does (chapter 5), when he takes us so fully into the speech and habits of English working-class culture to reveal how power and oppression present themselves in and through the everyday activities of a soccer fan.

Autoethnography and ethnographic fiction, therefore, as emerging qualitative research practices, should keep us working, wrenching what we can from experience. For who among us doesn't crave the state in which something is being uncovered—that theoretical insight or intuitive flashpoint. Often that's what makes us feel most alive. Which is why autoethnography and ethnographic fiction are such crucial qualitative research and writing genres. Because of all the social science writing forms in use today, I believe that they are best placed to uncover the world with sufficient depth, integrity, and intensity.

I also think that autoethnography and ethnographic fiction are well poised to extend the work of qualitative researchers to a much wider audience. Traditional academic scholarship has often been criticized by the public for being unaccessable, overly theoretical, and jargon-ladden. Interestingly, criticisms have been leveled recently at investigative journalists for exactly the opposite reasons. Letters to the editor in *Harper's* and the *New Yorker*, periodicals often considered to be the pinnacle of American arts and letters and intellectual and creative commentary and analysis, have expressed readers' dissatisfaction with essays and stories that are "speculative," "unqualified," and "specious." One *Harper's* reader, in reacting to a cover story about the underground anarchist movement swelling in the United States, asked, "Was it really wise to send a budding novelist to report on an important social phenomenon?" (Newlin, 2000, p. 6).

This public dissatisfaction with "straight" journalism must be an indication of people's hunger for more critically informed, substantive, and well-grounded stories. Stories that go beyond description and explore the whys and hows of various issues and situations. For in order to develop or explore new terrain, a writer needs to spend time gathering various perspectives and considering multiple points of view while also identifying what has been done before on a given topic. These are standard procedures for the well-trained academic. Journalists, however, tend to be armchair sociologists, who, like armchair quarterbacks bandy about truisms as if they were the first ones to reveal these discoveries. Thus, their work can easily become irrelevant for many readers because it seems to emerge from a vacuum.

As poetic qualitative research approaches advance, and as we become more creative and experimental in our renderings, we must ensure that we maintain certain scholarly standards. But don't read this as a call to establish agreed, universal, preordained criteria, against which any piece of autoethnography or ethnographic fiction should be judged. In today's highly pluralistic research climate where the foundations of knowledge are themselves open to contextualization and indeterminacy, and any constructed perspective of the world is situated and framework dependent, arriving at preordained standards is highly problematic (Garratt & Hodkinson, 1998). However, some autoethnographies and ethnographic fictions are better than others. So what do I mean by better? Partially, I mean that researchers interested in autoethnography and ethnographic fiction must realize that they are placing themselves into a new research tradition where the criteria to succeed will encompass both literary and scholarly standards. On the scholarly side, I agree with Ronald Pelias (1999) who advises us not to forget about reviewing the literature before we sit down to write our evocative tales. I am also wary of Max Van Maanen's (1988) warning that autoethnography and ethnographic fiction, which sometimes put holding the interest of the reader above good analysis, must never be confused for "scoop ethnography" (p. 135).

However, these flaws aren't inherent in autoethnography or ethnographic fiction, just as they aren't inherent in journalism. Therefore, one lesson I hope this book passes on to those interested in autoethnography and ethnographic fiction is that these qualitative approaches don't come with a license to fail to know about, or fail to acknowledge the work of other people, or to disregard how analysis must work in concert with creativity (Sandelowski, 1994). Instead, I hope this book informs readers how to satisfy two tastes at once: one for accessible and captivating prose, another for historically, theoretically grounded research that leaves an impression.

Of course meeting these twin demands won't be easy. But if, as Cornel West (1994) reminds us, we want to avoid living in the twenty-first century at each other's throats, we must attempt to circulate into the mainstream our well-plotted, sacred, existential, trueful tales that challenge readers "to take action in the world, and to reconsider the conditions under which the moral terms of the self and community are constituted" (Lincoln & Denzin, 2000, p. 1054). Only then can we be brought together to better understand everyday life and our place in the world. Imagine for a minute the impact on notions of sexual identity in sport that Toni Bruce's story, "Pass," (chapter 6) could have had if it was published in *Sports Illustrated*? It's certainly as accessible and readable, not to mention interesting as the typical fact piece or celebrity-athlete profile *Sports Illustrated* usually runs. But it's obviously so much more than that, too. And that's my point. And more generally, the point of this book: to succeed as satisfying scholarship autoethnography and ethnographic fiction must go beyond mere "thick description" to show us our world in a way that leads us to ask, Why?—Why do things have to remain the same? And why if we are dissatisfied can't we change our present conditions? This is how autoethnographers and ethnographic fiction writers can transform the wider public debate around many important issues. And what could be a greater measure of success for a qualitative researcher than that?

But why stop there? What's to prevent academics from entering the national consciousness through the screen? Couldn't we author teleplays and screenplays? And what about the novel? To me this seems like a natural extension of autoethnographies and ethnographic fictions: longer, fuller, more sustained plots and stories concerning who we are. All of this might mean that the academy could become a home not just for scholars who contribute to important, yet, let's be honest, obscure refereed journals, but to scholar-artists who want to take their informed and critical understandings of social life to the people.

Naturally, for this to occur the way in which we are recognized and rewarded as academics would need to expand to include the short story, the performance, the essay, the novel, the film. But first, our skills as storytellers need to improve so that we can convince editors, publishers, and producers that as academics we can also express ourselves and our ideas in ways that will attract an audience. The commentaries on writing included in each chapter are meant to serve this very purpose. The points raised by each author, I believe, can help anyone whose interested develop a critical literary sensibility by learning how to interpret culture sensitively and passionately.

As I spelled out with Pirkko in the introduction to this book, it is no longer enough to insert the personal into an ethnographic tale through the simple use of the pronoun "I." Our skills as creative and evocative writers must improve significantly as we embrace the traditions of fiction and nonfiction that effective autoethnography and ethnographic fiction so importantly draw upon. To enter into these literary traditions and succeed as scholar-artists, however, necessitates strategies and lessons. For example, how to "show" and not always "tell." Or how to put dialogue or inflection to good use. And often it's breaking the silence of the first page that stunts the new ethnographic fiction writer the most, but as Bob Rinehart explains, ideas beget stories, and from ideas come opening lines. But it's the author interviews (chapters 9 and 10) that I believe contribute the most salient lessons around writing and the act of creating stories. This is advice and support that comes from the living, out of the mouthes of conversation. And because these "notes on craft" are contextual and dialogical, they can be absorbed wholly as examples of the extent that a commitment to "writing lives" requires. Far more interesting and influential than a series of "how to" chapters, these interviews embody writing as a personal and social act that varies from individual to individual. In this manner, one way or process of writing stories isn't advanced over another. Instead, how one learns to become better at crafting an autoethnography or an ethnographic fiction will depend upon the sensibilites and experiences that individual brings to her or his project. Then the techniques they draw upon to convey and elicit these thoughts can become as C. Wright Mills might have said, "emblematic" of their literary imagination.

In the end, it's only after learning and applying these craft lessons to our already well-informed theoretical understandings of social life and movement that we will be able to meet the twin demands of writing theoretically satisfying and captivating prose. And it is only then that we will avoid being criticized for producing research stories that "read like high school creative writing exercises" (Sanders, 1995, p. 95). The time is now for us to display as qualitative researchers that we have multiple narrative styles at our disposal, and that when called for we can be engaging and accessible in our theorizing. This is what the public desires and also deserves. For part of our mandate as academics should be to serve our communities and contribute more responsibly and openly to the public's needs. People are desperate for new stories to help them live in and understand these postmodern times (Gergen, 1991). Terrorism, globalization, genocide, depression, high school shootings, not to mention such movement and body-related issues as dieting, injury and pain, disability, and sexuality are just some of the topics that our new found sensibilities as critical literary artists could be put to good use. One strong step forward, therefore, into the future, into the seventh moment and beyond, is for us to learn how to use language better to stage and craft experience, and deliver never before seen versions of hope and peace for others to read, re-interpret, and apply to themselves and others. This should lead us to form a true civic social science that elevates the qualitative research story to its rightful place: as a site for rendering and promoting human solidarity.

So to conclude, can we be satisfied with the current developments that have gone into producing the types of qualitative research texts that embody a critical literary style? Or should we be looking ahead into the next moment? From my vantage point there is still so much to be done in the present before addressing the future. That's not to say that we should ignore the future, for that would be pure folly. However, I believe that this book is located squarely in the present, but with a strong commitment to the future. For the future of qualitative research, as I see it, is to help more social scientists understand the present and develop the necessary skills to produce well-crafted, purposeful autoethnographies and ethnographic fictions for the twenty-first century and onward.

The numerous calls being made for performative ethnography, or new fiction and faction-based writing styles must move in sync with those who will initiate and implement these calls. Currently, many academics and graduate students are excited about autoethnography and ethnographic fiction and the potential they hold for generating new insights into their subject matter. But many also remain intimidated by the increased rhetorical demands they present. Our job in the present, therefore, must be to advocate, instruct, and support those who want to shift from writing realist tales to writing in ways that enable them "to be and live differently in relation to themselves and other people" (Andrew Sparkes, personal communication). And I feel that this book is a strong step forwards in that direction. Yes, there will be new terms to come to grips with, and new approaches to consider in order to establish an effective narrative framework, or authorial voice, but we've all done that before. The structure employed in a realist writing project is hardly "natural" either. We had to learn it, and we did. Of course, change takes time, and there are likely to be setbacks and rejections along the way. But this entire book is a testament to change, and by association, the future. For this book couldn't have been conceived let alone published as little as a decade ago. So to become a different type of writer, someone who writes different kinds of tales, I hope this book offers inspiration and guidance. For change doesn't mean abandoning who you thought you were, it only means expanding who you want to be.

REFERENCES

Bauman, Z. (2000). On writing sociology. *Theory, Culture & Society, 17*, 79–90.

Denison, J. (1998). An elephant's trunk. *Sport Literate, 2*(3), 64-83.

Denison, J. (1999). Boxed in. In A. C. Sparkes and M. Silvennoinen (Eds.). *Talking bodies: Men's narratives of the body and sport* (pp. 29–36).Jyväskylä, Finland: SoPhi, University of Jyväskylä Press.

Denison, J. (2000). Tattoo. *Aethlon: The Journal of Sport Literature, 17*, 21–27.

Denzin, N. K. , & Lincoln, Y. (1994). Entering the field of Qualitative research. In N. Denzin & Y. Lincoln (Eds.), *Handbook of qualitative research* (pp. 1–16). Newbury Park, CA: Sage.

Garratt, D., & Hodkinson, P. (1998). Can there be criteria for selecting research criteria?—A hermeneutical analysis of an inescapable dilemma. *Qualitative Inquiry, 4*, 515–539.

Gergen, K. (1991). *The saturated self*. New York: Basic Books.

Jones, M. P. (Winter, 1996). The storytelling animal. *The Georgia Review*, 649–666.

Kundera, M. (1986). *The art of the novel*. London: Faber.

Lincoln, Y., & Denzin, N. (2000). The seventh moment: Out of the past. In N. Denzin & Y. Lincoln (Eds.), *Handbook of qualitative research (2nd edition)* (pp. 1047–1065). Newbury Park, CA: Sage.

Newlin, C. (July, 2000). Anarchy in the U.S.A. (Letter to the editor). *Harper's, 6*–7.

Pelias, R. (1999). *Writing performance: Poeticizing the researcher's body*. Carbondale, IL: Southern Illinois University Press.

Richardson, L. (2000). New writing practices in qualitative research. *Sociology of Sport Journal, 17*, 5–20.

Rorty, R. (1991). *Objectivity, relativism, and truth: Philosophical papers Vol. 1.* Cambridge, England: Cambridge University Press.

Sandelowski, M. (1994). The proof of the pudding: Towards a poetic for qualitative inquiry. In J. Morse (Ed.), *Critical issues in qualitative research methods* (pp. 46–63). London: Sage.

Sanders, C. (1995). Stranger than fiction: Insights and pitfalls in post-modern ethnography. *Studies in Symbolic Interaction, 7,* 89–104.

Van Maanen, M. (1988). *Tales of the field: On writing ethnography.* Chicago: University of Chicago Press.

West, C. (1994). *Race matters.* New York: Vantage.

CONTRIBUTORS

Toni Bruce is a Senior Lecturer in the Department of Sport and Leisure Studies at the University of Waikato in New Zealand. She teaches in the area of sociology of sport and leisure with particular emphasis on the media. Her work has appeared in international journals including *Aethlon, Sociology of Sport Journal, Journal of Sport and Social Issues,* and *The International Review for the Sociology of Sport,* as well as various newspapers. Her current research interests revolve around the intersections of race, gender, and the media in sport.

Jim Denison has recently relocated to England after lecturing in Leisure Studies for seven years at the University of Waikato, New Zealand. He is the author of the forthcoming book *Bannister and Beyond: An Oral History of the Four-Minute Mile* (Breakaway Books). He is a Senior Lecturer at De Montfort Univeristy.

Pirkko Markula is an ethnographer and sport sociologist. A native of Finland, she has lived and worked recently in the United States and New Zealand, and is currently at the University of Exeter in the Department of Exercise and Sport Sciences. Her research interests include how fitness practices and the media shape our understanding of our bodies, and how writing research can be a more self-reflexive process. Her work has appeared in *Qualitative Inquiry, The Journal of Contemporary Ethnography,* and *Sociology of Sport Journal,* among others. In addition, she is a contemporary dancer and choreographer.

John Morefield teaches creative writing and literature at East Tennessee State University, USA. His short fiction has appeared in numerous publications including *Aethlon*, *Columbia*, and *The Florida Quarterly*. He has two novels currently under representation.

Katherine Parrott completed her Master of Leisure Studies degree at Waikato University in 1999, just as she began work as a Sport Development Officer in her home province of Waikato, New Zealand. After two years of focusing on volunteer development in New Zealand sport, she is now realizing a lifetime dream to work and travel around the world, filling a notebook with thoughts and ideas as she goes.

Robert Rinehart is an adjunct professor at California State University, San Bernardino, USA. He published *Player's All: Performances in Contemporary Sport* in 1998; *To the Extreme: Alternative Sport Inside and Out* is forthcoming with co-editor Synthia Sydnor.

David Rowe is Associate Professor in Media and Cultural Studies and Director of the Cultural Industries and Practices Research Centre at The University of Newcastle, Australia. He has published in many international journals, including *Media, Culture & Society, Leisure Studies, Sociology of Sport Journal, International Review for the Sociology of Sport,* and *Social Text.* His books include *Popular Cultures: Rock Music, Sport and the Politics of Pleasure* (1995), *Sport, Culture and the Media: The Unruly Trinity* (1999), and the co-authored *Globalization and Sport: Playing the World* (2001). Professor Rowe is also a frequent media commentator on social and cultural matters.

Joli Sandoz edited two anthologies of women's writing about sport: *A Whole Other Ball Game: Women's Fiction,* and *Poetry on Women's Sport* and, with Joby Winans, *Whatever It Takes,* the first collection of U.S. women's personal essays about sport's meaning (both published by Farrar, Straus and Giroux). Sandoz teaches at The Evergreen State College near Olympia, Washington, USA, and writes on a variety of subjects.

Martti Silvennoinen, docent, born in 1942, works in the Department of Physical Education in the University of Jyväskylä, Finland. As a professor of sports pedagogy he teaches theories of the body and guides qualitative master and doctoral theses. He has written many autobiographical texts about sport and masculinity. He collaborated with Jim Denison, Andrew C. Sparkes and Arto Tiihonen in a study project "Fathers, Sons and Sport."

Andrew C. Sparkes is Professor of Social Theory and Director of the Qualitative Research Unit in the Department of Exercise & Sport Sciences, University of Exeter. His research interests are eclectic and include: interrupted body projects, identity dilemmas, and the narrative reconstruction of self; organizational innovation and change; and the lives and careers of marginalized individuals and groups. These interests are framed by a desire to seek interpretive forms of understanding and an aspiration to represent lived experience using a variety of genres.

Arto Tiihonen has been a co-editor and contributor to several anthologies dealing with body experiences, masculinities, sports culture, and personal writing. His current interests are gender and equality in sports coaching, the evaluation of sports for disabled, and teaching qualitative methods and personal writing. He has recently completed his Ph.D. in sport science, and he is married with two (foster) children. In his youth he was a football (soccer) player and a cross-country skier.

Cultural  Critique

General Editor: Norman K. Denzin

Cultural Critique is a research monograph series drawing from those scholarly traditions in the social sciences and the humanities that are premised on critical, performance-based cultural studies agenda. Preference is given to experimental, risk-taking
manuscripts that are at the intersection of interpretative theory, critical methodology,
culture, media, history, biography, and social structure. Asserting that culture is best
understood as a gendered performance, this international-research monograph series
combines ethnography and critical textual approaches to the study of popular literature, media, myth, advertising, religion, science, cinema, television, and the new
communication and information technologies. This new series creates a space for the
study of those global cultural practices and forms that shape the meanings of self,
identity, race, ethnicity, class, nationality, and gender in the contemporary world.

Preference will be given to authors who engage a variety of critical qualitative,
interpretive methodologies, from semiotics and critical textual analysis to interpretive
and auto-ethnography, personal narrative, and the practices of investigative, civic,
intimate, and immersion journalism. We seek non-conventional, experimental manuscripts. Qualitative methods are material and interpretive practices. They do not stand
outside politics and cultural criticism. Critical methodologies advance the project of
moral criticism. This spirit, critically imagining and pursuing a more democratic
society, has been a guiding feature of cultural studies from the very beginning. Contributors to the Cultural Critique series will forward this project. They will take up
such methodological and moral issues as the local and global, text and context, voice,
writing for the other, and the author presence in the text. Cultural Critique understands that the discourses of a critical, moral methodology are basic to any effort to re-
engage the promise of the social sciences for democracy in the twenty-first century.
Cultural Critique publishes works of ethnopoetry, auto-ethnography, creative nonfiction, performance texts, book reviews, and critical analyses of current media representations and formations. Projected contents (and contributors) will be drawn from
scholarly traditions in the social sciences and humanities, including history, anthropology, sociology, communications, art history, education, American studies, kinesiology,
performance studies, and English. The scope of submissions will be international.

For additional information about this series or for the submission of manuscripts,
please contact:

Dr. Norman K. Denzin
University of Illinois, Institute of Communications Research
228 Gregory Hall, 810 So. Wright Street
Urbana, IL 61801

To order other books in this series, please contact our Customer Service Department:

(800) 770-LANG (within the U.S.)
(212) 647-7706 (outside the U.S.)
(212) 647-7707 FAX

or browse online by series:

WWW.PETERLANGUSA.COM